PITT SERIES IN POLICY AND INSTITUTIONAL STUDIES

# The Presidency and Public Policy Making

GEORGE C. EDWARDS III

STEVEN A. SHULL

NORMAN C. THOMAS

Editors

University of Pittsburgh Press

Published by the University of Pittsburgh Press, Pittsburgh, Pa. 15260
Copyright © 1985, University of Pittsburgh Press
All rights reserved
Feffer and Simons, Inc., London
Manufactured in the United States of America


*Library of Congress Cataloging in Publication Data*
Main entry under title:

The Presidency and public policy making.

  (Pitt series in policy and institutional studies)
  Includes index.
  1. Presidents—United States—Addresses, essays, lectures.
2. Policy sciences—Addresses, essays, lectures.   I. Edwards,
George C.   II. Shull, Steven A.   III. Thomas, Norman C.
IV. Series
JK518.P72   1985          353.03'7          85–40337
ISBN 0–8229–3522–8
ISBN 0–8229–5373–0 (pbk.)

To our wives

Carmella

Janice

Marilyn

# Contents

George C. Edwards III

# Preface:
# Presidential Policy Making

The presidency is perhaps the most important and least understood policy-making institution in the United States. It is difficult to discuss any area of national policy without assigning a prominent role to the White House. This is as it should be. The entertainment value of politics aside, it is because of policy that we are interested in the presidency.

To function effectively as a policy maker, the president must obtain the support or acquiescence of both the public and political elites, options and information on which to base his decisions, and responsive implementation of policies. These requirements involve the president in a set of relationships that form the core of presidential policy making. Around that core is a set of environmental constraints, including the nature of the American political system, the resources of the national government, and the responsibilities of the presidency. In addition, the president's policy choices usually fall within the parameters set by prior commitments that obligate Washington to spend money, defend allies, provide services, or protect rights.

The essays in this book address diverse aspects of presidential policy making. They, of course, do not exhaust the subject, but they do provide fresh insights into the president's role in public policy making. In this preface I have grouped the essays into five sections. The first focuses on the environment of presidential policy making and the constraints it places on the chief executive. The second and third examine relationships with those outside the executive branch that are central to presidential policy making: attempts to lead the public and Congress, respectively. The next section looks at presidential decision making, one of the core questions in policy making. The final section addresses administration or implementation of policies in the executive branch, a topic that has received limited attention in the literature on the presidency. A brief overview of each of the chapters follows.

## The Policy-Making Environment

The first chapter examines the context that shapes the presidential policy-making role. Richard Rose looks at the presidency from a comparative perspective and focuses on some of the principal environmental influences on it. The United States has a unique mix of institutional characteristics, including the separation of powers, judicial review, federalism, and weak parties, that makes the president "an isolated eminence in a system of dispersed powers."

The president, Rose contends, also has fewer resources for leadership than do the leaders of other Western democracies. The national government in the United States takes in a smaller percentage of the gross national product, passes a smaller percentage of the nation's laws, has less responsibility for the economy, and employs a smaller percentage of workers than do the governments of comparable countries. Moreover, the president has less control over the national budget and less influence over legislation than do the leaders of these countries, and our federal government commands a smaller share of total government resources than do other democratic central governments.

If we are to understand presidential policy making, Rose argues, we must come to terms with the environment in which the chief executive functions. This requires that we lower our expectations of what the president can accomplish and concentrate the president's attention on policy areas of high priority such as national security and the economy.

## Leading the Public

As every student of the president quickly learns, the president is rarely in a position to command others to comply with his wishes. Instead, he must rely on persuasion. A principal source of influence for the president is public support for himself and his policies. Public support is a necessary, although not a sufficient, condition for successful policy making. It provides the president leeway and encourages responsiveness on the part of other policy makers. Lack of support can severely constrain the president's policy choices. The relationship between public support for the president and public policy making is also reciprocal. His support rises and falls, at least partially, in response to the outcomes of his policies.

Presidents are not content only to follow public opinion on issues or let their own approval ratings reach some "natural" level. Instead, they are actively engaged in efforts to *lead* public opinion to give them programmatic and personal support. Some attempts to influence public opinion are direct (such as addresses to the nation), and others are more subtle (as when presidents employ symbols and engage in public-relations activities). These are designed to bring the president's message to the public's attention, publicize his actions, and put him and his policies in a favorable light. There is also a dark side to presidential leadership of public opinion. The White House has engaged in efforts to control the information available to the public, sometimes even resorting to lying. It has at times deliberately tried to mislead the public and present a distorted picture of the president and his policies.

All presidents face formidable obstacles to influencing the public, including an inattentive, skeptical, and individualistic audience; their own, often limited, communications skills; the complexity of public policy; the context of their communications; and alternative sources of information, especially the press. Despite these problems, presidents have no alternative to seeking public support. We include three articles on this crucial but poorly understood aspect of presidential policy making. They are empirical analyses of relationships between the president and public opinion and the ways in which those relationships affect presidential policy making and the substance of the president's policy choices.

Benjamin Page and Robert Shapiro analyze the capacity of the president to influence the public's policy preferences. Despite the mythology of the "bully pulpit," their principal finding is that a president's ability to influence the policy preferences of the public is dependent on his popularity. The ability to influence public opinion, in other words, simply cannot be assumed to be a given of the presidential role.

Dan Thomas and Lee Sigelman explore part of the process by which presidents cultivate policy support among the public. Using an experimental design, they show that support for "experimental" policy proposals varies with knowledge of, and support for, the person who has made them. When informed that President Reagan was the source of the proposals, enthusiastic supporters of Reagan evaluated them in favorable terms, but when the source was withheld, these same proposals were unfavorably evaluated by the Reagan supporters. This innovative research shows the impact of cognition, information, and psychological identification on presidential attempts to obtain the public's support for policy.

Finally, Dennis Simon and Charles Ostrom analyze links across presidential decision making, public support for the president, and policy outcomes. They, like Page and Shapiro, find modern presidents in need of popular support but often unable to obtain it, especially once their approval levels have dipped into low numbers. The authors maintain that there is a dynamic, reciprocal relationship between presidential decision making and popular support. Presidential policy making positively influences popular support to the extent that the president's actions enhance the quality of life or are sufficiently dramatic to prompt a "rally" effect. Conversely, because public support affects the president's ability to influence other policy makers, and thus the probability that a policy will succeed, it is a primary determinant of the range and feasibility of the president's policy choices.

Presidential policies aimed at improving the quality of life have a high potential payoff in terms of public support, but they also have a low probability of immediate success. They typically require a long period of time before their effects are felt. A rational political strategy, therefore, dictates that presidents turn to short-term strategies when their popularity slips. The political payoff from short-term strategies, however, is quite temporary and, moreover, if fundamental qualify of life concerns are not adequately met, public support will be permanently eroded. The solution to this dilemma for the president, Simon and Ostrom conclude, is a mixture of long- and short-term strategies designed to protect this most crucial policy resource—public support.

## Leading Congress

If one were to write a job description for the presidency, near the top of the list of presidential responsibilities would be that of working with Congress. Since our system of separation of powers is really one of shared powers, the president can rarely operate independently of Congress. Although the cooperation of Congress is required, it cannot be depended on. Thus, one of the president's most difficult and frustrating tasks is trying to convince Congress to support his policies.

John Burke uses budgetary politics in Ronald Reagan's first three years in office to explore presidential influence in Congress. He identifies five sets of factors, ranging from the distal to the proximate, that affect the president's ability to influence Congress: (1) broad political and economic structures on the national or international levels; (2) formal-legal powers of the president; (3) organizational forms such as the legislative liaison operation in the White House; (4) the immediate political context such as shared party affiliation and policy preferences and public approval of the president; and (5) the president's internal, personal resources that he may exercise as a strategic actor.

Burke argues that the president's personal political skills and his role as a strategic actor, mediated through his ability to exploit his strengths in the external political arena, are the most significant in explaining budgetary politics and outcomes in 1981–1983. The president, moving rapidly with a limited agenda, successfully exploited his public support and the disarray of the Democrats and enjoyed great success in 1981. But such a strategy only works when the requisites for each part are present, complementing and reinforcing each other. When his public approval levels sank and the Democrats were rejuvenated, it was necessary to adapt to the changing environment with a different strategy. Yet Reagan failed to do this. He grew more intractable in the face of opposition and continued to rely on a committed partisan and ideological coalition and on appeals to the public. Burke suggests that the president should have considered adopting an approach similar to that of President Eisenhower: flexible, bipartisan, with the president remaining above the battle, using indirect bargaining in response to changing political conditions and limited appeals to the public.

## Decision Making

One might argue that the essence of the president's job is making decisions—about foreign affairs, economic policy, and literally hundreds of other important matters. This is an enormously difficult and complex task, and it occurs at the confluence of many factors, some proximate and others distal.

One of the most intriguing questions regarding presidential decision making focuses on the relative influence of environmental constraints and personal policy views on policy making. This issue surfaces most prominently in the area of economic policy. Some observers argue that presidents subordinate their economic values, and thus the economic policies they propose, to external concerns for electoral success. Others see economic policy resulting from the interplay of political elites between campaigns.

Stephen Weatherford and Lorraine McDonnell use President Eisenhower's and President Kennedy's management of the economy to show that the president's economic ideology—the president's beliefs and preferences about the allocation of resources between private and social goals, the distribution of income and wealth to individuals and groups, and the stabilization of the economy—is a major determinant of economic policy goals and of the choice of instruments to achieve them. They argue that electoral factors and considerations, which the political business cycle literature claims are the principal determinants of economic policy, are thus only one set of forces at work.

According to Weatherford and McDonnell, Eisenhower's conservative economic ideology led him to pursue long-term economic goals in preference to short-term economic political gains. He believed firmly that market forces should take precedence over governmental action as the primary means of maintaining a healthy economy. In his allocation decisions, Eisenhower resisted the expansion of the public sector. With respect to distributional issues he advocated lower taxes on corporate and personal income as a stimulus to economic growth. He stressed control of inflation and restriction of the gowth of inflationary expectations as the primary instrument of economic stabilization. The major cost to Eisenhower of his conservative economic ideology was loss of control over short-term countercyclical policy.

President Kennedy had a clearly articulated ideology regarding economic policy, one quite different from his predecessor's, and it provided a continuous guide for his proposals. He believed the government should play an active role in stimulating long-term, stable growth and in combating fluctuations in the business cycle. Thus he proposed tax measures to increase both business investment and aggregate demand, traditional countercyclical measures, and reductions in tariffs. Redistribution issues, although important to the president, were of secondary importance in his quest for economic expansion and prosperity. Much in Kennedy's policies threatened the economic status quo and depended on the assent of a suspicious Congress and a skeptical business community. Nevertheless, the president accepted the risks inherent in pursuing his activist policies.

The authors conclude by cautioning against a simple explanation of policy choice based only on the president's economic ideology. Nonetheless, they also caution against an even more simplistic calculus based solely on political gain. If strongly held, they find that the policy beliefs of a president are likely to take precedence over the desire for short-term gains.

Related to the tension between the environment and personal views in presidential decision making is that between situational factors and policy design and organizational factors. Ryan Barilleaux directly addresses this question in his analysis of presidential foreign policy making. He contends that the conventional wisdom employs five criteria for evaluating presidential performance in foreign policy making: (1) policy direction and design; (2) organization and staffing; (3) management and oversight; (4) consensus-building; and (5) achievement. The emphasis of these criteria is on designing effective decision-making processes. The conventional wisdom, Barilleaux argues, underestimates the importance of circumstantial factors in influencing policy outcomes.

To test the relationship between process and outcomes, Barilleaux examines a series of case studies of foreign policy episodes, including crises, noncrisis security issues, and noncrisis, nonsecurity issues. He evaluates each case on each of the five criteria and then compares the successful cases with the failures.

Barilleaux finds that process alone cannot explain the outcomes of the foreign policy episodes he studies. Contextual and situational factors play an important role in determining the success of the president's efforts. Of particular importance, his analysis exposes trade-offs and conflicts between the criteria used to evaluate presidents. Thus, the author argues that we need to strike a balance among conflicting demands and trade-offs in our evaluations of presidential policy making. He also suggests that we broaden our evaluative criteria to include democratic accountability.

One of the most important contributions of Franklin D. Roosevelt to the development of the modern presidency was the institutionalization of staff support for the president in the executive office. His successors have made further contributions to and refinements of organizational support for presidential policy making. The last major staff unit to be institutionalized was the domestic policy office. Margaret Jane Wyszomirski studies the operation of this office using three relational patterns to characterize interaction between the president and other executive officials: (1) principal and agent; (2) master and servant (administrator); and (3) advisee and advisor.

The Nixon Domestic Council and its staff functioned as a presidential agent. The staff, under John Erlichman, possessed substantial policy discretion and de facto ability to direct and oversee the performance of department heads and other line officials. The office was originally assigned an advisory role in the Ford administration, but it was soon cast adrift amid the controversy and infighting surrounding Vice-President Rockefeller's role in the administration. The Carter Domestic Policy Staff performed an advisory role. It was a coordinating support arm for the president. The Reagan Office of Policy Development (OPD) has been a presidential servant performing ministerial functions. The OPD has operated at a distance from the president, whose reliance on a system of seven cabinet councils, the Office of Management and Budget, and an informal legislative strategy group has foreclosed either a substantive policy role or an advisory role for the OPD.

Wyszomirski prefers the advisory role for the domestic policy office. That role gives it considerable but not dominant influence over policy and makes it an important presidential resource. The role of agent, although most influential, incurs substantial political and administrative costs for the president. The role of servant or administrator gives the staff minimal influence on policy and limits the domestic policy office to internal coordination. As the author points out, whatever role the domestic policy office plays in an administration depends upon a number of factors, including the relationship between the president and the White House domestic policy assistant; presidential preferences and practices regarding the dependability and utility of his cabinet and other line officers; the character and quality of the skills of the domestic policy assistant and of the domestic policy staff; and the existence and performance of competing or overlapping agencies, particularly within the Executive Office.

The case of the domestic policy office illustrates the problems and prospects of other presidential staff agencies. Staff units are an important presidential resource, but presidents may use them in a wide variety of ways, each with its own costs and benefits.

So how do presidents decide how to decide? Paul Anderson argues that although scholars have devoted much attention to the questions of how presidents have organized the White House and how they should organize it, observers have paid much less attention to the question of why presidents adopt the particular organizations they do. Typically, he argues, we explain White

House organization in terms of both the president's personality and style and the need to satisfy the decision-making objectives of high quality information and advice.

Yet presidents employ a variety of advisory systems during their tenures and seek advice in different ways at any given time, while their personalities, personal styles, and decision-making needs remain relatively stable. Anderson argues that we need to broaden our explanations of White House organization to include a variety of other presidential goals and interests. The presidency is an organization, and organizational theory can provide useful insights that complement those of the personality and decision-making approaches to White House organization.

Focusing on foreign policy making, Anderson finds that the president has interests in policy, politics, and management in addition to decision making. He is not just a decision maker, but a political leader and chief executive as well. There are also institutional imperatives and political constraints on the president. Thus, the solution to the president's problem of deciding how to decide will reflect his diverse set of goals and interests and the structure of the policy-making environment.

## Administration

Ever since the Great Depression the American public has turned to the White House for policies designed to stabilize the economy and achieve prosperity. Yet the president finds himself with more responsibility than authority to manage the economy. Perhaps the only instrument of macroeconomic policy available to the president for use on his own authority is voluntary wage and price guidelines.

James Anderson focuses on these policies in the Johnson and Carter administrations. He uses three management problems as the framework for comparisons: (1) substantive standards; (2) administrative arrangements; and (3) techniques for obtaining compliance. The Carter standards were more elaborate, substantively informed, clearly defined, and visible than Johnson's, and they were administered with greater fairness and concern for due process. The Johnson administration, on the other hand, manifested greater willingness to use the power of the presidency to secure compliance through appeals, arm-twisting, and threats. This gave the Johnson wage-price guidelines more coerciveness, and presumably greater effectiveness, than Carter's. This suggests that administrative formality and procedural sensitivity are less important than the tangible and intangible techniques used to secure compliance as determinants of the effectiveness of the guidelines.

Ronald Reagan's Executive Order 12291 is the latest and most ambitious in a series of regulatory review requirements employed by recent presidents to gain more control over administrative rulemaking. Under its terms, executive agencies are required to prepare analyses of proposed regulations and to submit these analyses to the Office of Management and Budget for review. In turn, OMB, as the agent of the president, enjoys substantial powers to delay, alter, and block agency initiatives.

President Reagan has claimed that "Executive Order 12291 for the first time provides effective and coordinated management for the regulatory process." In their analysis of E.O. 12291, Bill West and Joseph Cooper argue that this is an exaggeration, for review has been far from comprehensive. They show, however, that E.O. 12291 has proved to be an effective means for identifying and for modifying or preventing those agency rules most troublesome to the administration and its key constituents. Moreover, the extent and potency of review could be increased simply by augmenting OMB's relatively meager staff. Beyond its current effects, therefore, the Reagan order may be significant as a fairly early development in the evolution of a much stronger and more institutionalized administrative presidency. Indeed, West and Cooper feel that this may well be the case, given the fundamental changes that have occurred in the nature of bureaucratic politics and the pressures they have generated for presidential adaptation.

The premise behind this book and the logic of the essays in it is that policy making provides a perspective by which to examine and bring together links between policy-making institutions, their bases of support and legitimacy, their connections to other policy-making institutions, and their own internal organization. In short, the policy-making perspective means that institutions need to be studied comparatively and interdependently. If we are to increase our understanding of how the presidency actually functions and how its incumbents vary, we shall need to move beyond airy speculation or noncomparative analyses of presidential organization. For the policy-making perspective requires us to know as much of public opinion or Congress or decision and organization theories or of the executive in other governments as of the presidency itself. The essays in this book reflect the need both to compare and to develop analytic interdependence. They are important steps to thinking and continuously rethinking the presidential policy role.

# The Presidency and Public Policy Making

Richard Rose

# The Job at the Top: The Presidency in Comparative Perspective

The presidency of the United States is a unique institution, but the difficulties it faces are in no sense unique. The problem of giving direction to government is as old as government. The survival of the institutions of governance laid down in the 1780s is prima facie evidence of the success of the American experience. In the twentieth century, France, Germany, and Italy have each tried and rejected a variety of constitutions and forms of leadership, some democratic and some nondemocratic. Only the British prime ministership can claim an age equal to that of the presidency. But Americans are normally not inclined to believe that what is oldest is best.

Cross-national comparison starts from the identification of a common problem, namely, the functional need to give direction to government. Comparing the way in which this is done in the United States and Britain, Germany, and other European countries creates an awareness of both differences and similarities in the way in which modern democracies respond to a common problem. Reviewing the experience of other countries does not promise a quick technological fix, for a particular institution cannot be transplanted from one national context to another and necessarily flourish in the same way. Yet the Founding Fathers sought to learn from the mistakes of their European cousins, recognizing that this experience was greater than their own. The 1949 German *Grundgesetz* (Basic Law) reflected a conscious attempt to check the excesses of Hitler's Reich by drawing lessons from other nations, not least the United States. Comparison is valuable, for it makes one understand the variety of ways of giving direction from the top.

## Institutional Similarities and Differences

Government is a set of institutions; the first task of comparison is to gain an understanding of the differences in institutional mechanisms for giving direc-

3

tion to government. Differences extend far beyond the office of the individual at the top. In Europe as in America, the job of giving direction to government is more than a one-person job; it is the keystone of the arch of government. Just as one cannot understand how the White House works without understanding Congress, so one cannot understand a prime minister's role without understanding that of parliament. In Rockman's (1983) phrase, to study the subject requires an examination of the one (the single most important officeholder), the few (those with whom the leader must deal face to face to exercise influence), and the many (involved in bureaucratic and electoral interdependencies).

The American president's role as political leader is roughly comparable to the job of a prime minister in a parliamentary system of government. Although the two offices are concerned with the same task, giving direction to government, the resources and means at hand are very different. A prime minister has a few ex officio powers, but most powers are vested in the few, the cabinet, or the many, parliament, as the representative of the national electorate. The prime minister is both leader and servant of government. The pyramid of power does not lead to a single individual at an Oval Office desk, but to a cabinet table, around which sit the chief figures in the majority party or parties in parliament.

Comparing the basic features of the American presidency and of the political leaders of the four largest nations in Europe—Britain, France, Germany, and Italy—emphasizes that there is little that is unique about specific attributes of a top office (table 1). The French president is popularly elected, as is the American, and elected independently of the legislature. Neither the American president nor the Italian head of government requires (or can be confident of having) a legislature in which his own party holds a majority. The German *Bundeskanzler* has always belonged to the largest party in parliament, but is subject to the constraints of a coalition partner, and of the Bundersrat, a second chamber composed of delegates of the *länder,* the states making up the Federal Republic.

All political leaders risk losing office because of electoral defeat, but prime ministers are vulnerable to removal between elections by losing the confidence of the majority party or coalition in parliament. The average duration in office of the White House incumbent is virtually the same as that of a British prime minister (4 years as against 4.8 years); it is substantially longer than that of an Italian prime minister, but less than a German chancellor or a French president. Viewed from Washington, the differences observable within Europe may seem less than their collective similarities, but they are differences nonetheless.

France is unique in having a prime minister as well as a president. The president is undoubtedly the chief political officer in the Fifth Republic, being able to appoint or dismiss the prime minister (Massot, 1979). The independent election of a president for seven years without accountability to a parliament elected for a maximum of five years enhances the president's authority. In the

TABLE 1
Institutional Characteristics of Leaders in the United States and Major European Nations

| | United States | Britain | France (5th Republic) | Germany | Italy |
|---|---|---|---|---|---|
| Title | President | Prime Minister | le Président | Bundeskanzler | Il presidente del Consiglio dei Ministri |
| How chosen | Popular election | Election, or by parties in Parliament | Popular election | Election, or by parties in Parliament | Party coalition |
| Term of office | 4 years | Indeterminate; up to 5 years | 7 years | Up to 4 years | Duration of coalition |
| Relation to Parl/Congress | Independent | Integral | Independent | Integral | Integral |
| Majority party in legislature | May/may not be the same | Must be the same | Usually same | The same | Christian Democrats dominate coalition |
| Second chamber important | Yes: Senate | No | No | Yes: Bundesrat | No |
| Removal | Election defeat | Election defeat or loss of party confidence | Election defeat | Election defeat or constructive vote of no confidence | Coalition collapse |
| Number postwar leaders | 8 | 9 | 4 | 6 | 17 |
| Duration in office average leader[a] | 5 years | 4.8 years | 7.5 years | 6.3 years | 2.4 years |

Sources: Britain—Rose, 1980, 1980a; France—Massot, 1979; Germany— Mayntz, 1980; von Beyme, 1983; Italy—Pallotta, 1976; Cassese, 1980.

a. Calculated on the assumption of leader completing current term of office, except for Italy, which is taken December 1984.

first quarter-century of the Fifth Republic, the president has normally had the formal support or sympathy of the majority in parliament; President Mitterand claimed 56 percent of the seats in the national assembly in 1981 with 38 percent of the votes (Quermonne, 1981). Moreover, a French president gives direction to a state that is intrinsically *dirigiste,* mobilizing senior civil servants and friendly politicians to run major departments without hindrance from parliament or the prime minister. As one former prime minister, Jacques Chirac, explained, the prime minister conducts the orchestra but the president writes the music. The Fifth Republic has functioned more like a parliamentary system with a majority party supporting the president than like the presidency in America. As Frears (1984) notes, the president can govern without "the mechanisms of restraints on executive power called checks and balances." This centralization of authority makes France extreme among parliamentary systems, and very different from a nominally similar system, the American presidency.

The American presidency remains unique in its mix of characteristics. Unlike prime ministers in parliamentary systems, the American president must work with a separately elected Congress. Formal separation is enhanced by the absence of an American party system with the discipline characteristic of European parties. The division of powers in federalism is not unique to the United States, nor is the system of judicial review. But combined with the separation of powers between the executive and Congress, the net effect is to give the president an isolated eminence in a system of dispersed powers, whereas a prime minister is integrated in a system of collective power.

Parliamentary systems differ fundamentally from the American system because a prime minister is accountable to parliament, whereas the president is not accountable to Congress. The mechanism of party can effectively vest control of parliament and cabinet in a single person (the prime minister as leader of the governing party) or a single group (the prime minister, the party leader in parliament, and an extraparliamentary party secretary), or in a cabinet coalition that effectively brings together leaders of different parties or factions within a party. When a cabinet unites the leader of the party in parliament and of the executive branch, then the distinction between the two branches of government is effectively abolished. The political linkage of the two branches concentrates power in cabinet.

Differences in party systems create differences between parliamentary systems of government, affecting the extent to which authority is centralized and a cabinet is stable. Where one party holds the majority of seats in parliament, then a prime minister who is also party leader enjoys maximum authority. However, this is normally the case in only four of the sixteen systems of Western government (table 2). All four of these systems, Australia, New Zealand, Canada, and Britain, use the first-past-the-post electoral system for electing members of parliament. This system of *dis*proportional representation usually manufactures a majority of seats in parliament for a party that wins less than 50 percent of the popular vote. In Germany and Austria one party normally has a virtual majority in parliament, enjoying great strength vis-à-vis its smaller coalition partner. Norpoth (1982) aptly describes Germany as having "coalition government at the brink of majority rule." In France the president has usually enjoyed support by a national assembly in which party lines are less clear-cut than in Britain.

In the majority of European countries, political divisions within society and proportional representation in elections result in either coalition government (Colliard, 1978, pp. 114 ff.), with several parties sitting in cabinet, or a minority government that depends on the votes of several parties in parliament to sustain a majority. This is invariably the case in Denmark, Finland, the Netherlands,

TABLE 2
The Variability of Majority Party Dominance

|  | One-party majority in parliament, 1945–83 | |
| --- | --- | --- |
|  | Years | % |
| *Single-party control of parliament (4)* | | |
| Australia (Liberal-Country or Labour) | 39 | 100 |
| New Zealand (National or Labour) | 39 | 100 |
| Britain (Conservative or Labour) | 38.5 | 99 |
| Canada (Liberals or Progressive Conservatives) | 29 | 74 |
| *One party dominant in cabinet (3)* | | |
| Austria (Socialist or People's Party) | 20 | 51 |
| France (Gaullists or Socialists)[a] | 8 | 32 |
| Germany (Christian Democrats or Socialists) | 4 | 12 |
| *Mixed systems: One party dominant or coalition (4)* | | |
| United States (Democrats or split)[a] | 20 | 51 |
| Ireland (Fianna Fail or coalition) | 19 | 49 |
| Norway (Labour or coalition) | 16 | 41 |
| Sweden (Socialist or coalition) | 5 | 13 |
| *Coalition cabinet the rule (6)* | | |
| Italy | 5 | 13 |
| Belgium | 4 | 10 |
| Denmark | 0 | 0 |
| Finland | 0 | 0 |
| Netherlands | 0 | 0 |
| Switzerland | 0 | 0 |

*Source:* Calculated from Mackie and Rose (1982), updated by the author. In France and Germany the period is shortened by constitutional change.
a. Years same party holds presidency and majority in the national assembly/congress.

and Switzerland, and single-party majorities are so distant in time in Italy and Belgium that they do not characterize either country today. Three countries have a mixed system: the alternatives are a coalition government (of bourgeois parties in Norway and Sweden, of Fine Gael and Labour in Ireland) or government by a dominant party (Socialists in Norway or Sweden; Fianna Fail in Ireland). In the array of seventeen nations examined in table 2, the United States is in the middle; half the time since 1945 Congress and the White House have been in the hands of the same party, the Democrats, and half the time control of Congress and the White House has been divided between Democrats and Republicans.

One important implication of the prevalence of coalition government is that a prime minister is usually *not* installed in office by the choice of the national electorate. The only time that this can be said to occur is when a politician leads his party into an election campaign and emerges with sufficient seats in parliament to become prime minister without any coalition bargaining. But this is not normally the case (cf. Herman and Pope, 1973). A complex set of negotiations is normal, with a great variety of institutional mechanisms employed (Browne and Dreijmanis, 1982). A prime minister with a parliamentary majority may retire or resign under pressure midway through the life of a parliament, leaving the choice of his successor to his party rather than the electorate. Of the nine changes in prime minister in postwar Britain, five occurred as a result of an election, and four by changing the governing party's leadership during a parliament. In European coalition systems, a change in coalition partners is twice as likely to occur during the life of a parliament as afer an election. In Italy, for example, there have been ten general elections since 1946, but thirty-nine different governments, an average of four changes of government for each general election (Marradi, 1982).

A second important implication is that a prime minister is likely to be more immediately vulnerable to ejection from office than is an American or French president with a fixed term of office. The separation of powers protects the American president from the loss of confidence in Congress, as well as protecting Congress from having the president discipline it by the threat of dissolution. A president must be a wheeler-dealer in relations with Congress. But the penalty for failing to make a deal is frustration, not loss of office. By contrast, a prime minister must be a political juggler, at all times maintaining the confidence of two or more parties. Dropping the confidence of one party can be worse than a setback; it can lead to the collapse of the coalition and the prime minister's ejection from office. This is particularly true of those prime ministers, about one-third of the total, who do *not* represent the largest party in parliament (Colliard, 1978, p. 130).

The collapse of a coalition may lead to a parliamentary crisis requiring months of negotiation to resolve, with a caretaker administration meanwhile giving only passive direction to government. In Italy, chronic coalition crises have produced a literature of criticism with titles such as *Surviving Without Governing* (di Palma, 1977); *La crisi italiana* (Graziano and Tarrow, 1979); and *Esiste un governo in Italia?* (Cassese, 1980b). Whereas an American president requires a panoply of secret service men to guard him against losing office by an assassin's bullet, a prime minister can claim no such protection against political defenestration. From Scandinavia to Italy, many politicians would regard a fixed four-year term of office as a positive benefit; none would recommend exporting instability.

The third important implication is that constitutional engineering does *not* determine the direction of government, as is illustrated by differences between a majority government in Britain and Germany and coalitions in Denmark and Italy. It is party, not parliament, that determines whether a cabinet is a stable or an unstable coalition. Americans who admire the parliamentary system of government could not achieve this simply by constitutional amendments making the president accountable and dismissable by Congress or giving the president the power to dissolve Congress. Because parliamentary government is a system, its characteristics—particularly the character of the party or parties in charge—depend upon the electoral system, the parties and voters, as well as upon rules about legislative-executive relations. Because the choice of members of parliament is in the hands of the voters, no constitutional rule can determine whether voters collectively sustain a stable single-party government or whether their choices produce a coalition. In Europe, complaints about the weakness of parties and lack of discipline are at least as frequent as complaints in Washington about presidential weakness and executive fragmentation.

In view of the substantial differences between being prime minister of a single-party government as against a coalition government, the pages that follow will normally refer to a European country with a cabinet and prime minister having a majority or dominant party in parliament (e.g., Britain and Germany). This will focus on the greatest contrasts between democratic systems of government on opposite sides of the Atlantic. It is important to bear in mind that many systems in Europe are hybrids, having a cabinet and parliament that are interdependent but government by a coalition as precarious as an American president's coalition in Congress.

## Resources for Leadership

When attention is turned to the resources that a government can direct, European governments appear much more similar, and different from the United States. The head of a European government, whether of a single party or a fissiparous coalition, is responsible for directing a much larger share of national resources than is the president of the United States (Rose, 1984a). The differences have two principal causes. The first is that the mixed economy welfare states of Europe command a larger portion of their national resources than does the United States, which has not adopted a full set of welfare state programs or taken a large number of basic industries into government owner- ship. Secondly, as a federal system, the United States centralizes far fewer resources in national government than do unitary systems in which the central government may be responsible for health and education and collect nearly all the taxes of a country. The goods and services directly delivered by the executive branch, such as defense, pensions, debt interest payments, and producer subsidies, are few.

The simplest measure of the total amount of resources mobilized by govern- ment is the proportion of the Gross Domestic Product claimed by taxes. By this familiar criterion, the United States ranks far below average (cf. table 3). Nine of thirteen European countries collect more government revenue centrally than all levels of government—federal, state, and local—collect in the United States. The median European country, France, claims 41.2 percent of the national product in taxes, one-third more than the United States at 30.7 percent. When population or military might is the measure, American government appears big, but when tax effort is the measure, it is relatively small.

Because the United States has a federal system of government, Washington collects a lower proportion of the national product in tax revenue than does the

TABLE 3
The Proportion of the Gross Domestic Product
Claimed by Government as Tax Revenue

|  | Central | Regional & Local | All Levels |
| --- | --- | --- | --- |
| Sweden | 34.4% | 15.5% | 49.9% |
| Norway | 37.4 | 10.0 | 47.4 |
| Netherlands | 45.7 | 0.5 | 46.2 |
| Denmark | 32.0 | 13.1 | 45.1 |
| Belgium | 40.4 | 2.1 | 42.5 |
| Austria | 32.8 | 8.7 | 41.5 |
| France | n.a. | n.a. | 41.2 |
| Ireland | 36.0 | 1.5 | 37.5 |
| Germany | 25.3 | 11.9 | 37.2 |
| Britain | 32.3 | 3.6 | 35.9 |
| Finland | 25.2 | 9.3 | 34.5 |
| United States | 21.5 | 9.2 | 30.7 |
| Switzerland | 18.1 | 12.6 | 30.7 |
| Italy | 29.8 | 0.3 | 30.1 |

Source: Calculated from 1980 data reprinted in OECD (1981, tables 1, 11). Public expenditure as a share of the Gross Domestic Product is slightly higher because of reliance upon borrowing to finance some spending.

central government of any European country except confederal and atypical Switzerland. The federal government in Washington collects 21.5 percent of the national product in tax revenue, compared to the median figure of 33.3 percent in Britain. In the Netherlands, notwithstanding chronic problems of coalition formation, the Dutch government can boast of having more than twice as much of the national product to disburse than does the president's budget. The president's limited budgetary role—to make proposals to Congress, which then determines appropriations and taxes—further diminishes the importance of that office by comparison with a prime minister heading a cabinet making taxing and spending recommendations that parliament will pass with scarcely a single amendment.

Public employment is a second major resource of government. Insofar as a leader requires followers, then public employees are reliable followers, being bureaucrats paid by the state to follow rules laid down from above. But these conditions give strength to national political leaders only insofar as public employees are numerous and under the direction of central government, not state and local authorities. In a modern welfare state, public employment is also significant in revealing which institutions of government are responsible for delivering such major services of government as education and health care, two of the most important and the most labor-intensive welfare programs of contemporary governments.

When the scale of total public employment is examined, the collective resources of government in the United States again appear relatively small. Whereas 18.8 percent of all workers are employees of government in the United States, in major European countries the proportion is from a quarter greater to double, reaching to 38.2 percent in Sweden (table 4). Moreover, differences

TABLE 4
The Extent of Centralization of Public Employment
(as % of total employment)

|  |  |  |  |  | Totals | |
| --- | --- | --- | --- | --- | --- | --- |
|  | All Public | Ministries | Nationalized Industries | Other[a] | Central | Regional & Local |
| Sweden | 38.2% | 7.3% | 8.8% | 1.5% | 17.6% | 20.6% |
| France | 32.6 | 13.3 | 8.1 | 4.4 | 25.8 | 6.7 |
| Britain | 31.4 | 4.2 | 8.0 | 7.0 | 19.3 | 12.1 |
| Germany | 25.8 | 3.4 | 9.3 | 2.6 | 15.2 | 10.6 |
| Italy | 24.4 | 9.0 | 7.3 | 4.9 | 21.2 | 3.2 |
| United States | 18.3 | 4.0 | 1.3 | 0.1 | 5.4 | 12.9 |

*Source:* Calculated from data in Richard Rose et al., *Public Employment in Western Nations* (Cambridge University Press, 1985).
    a. Principally health services.

between the United States and European nations have been increasing through the decades (Rose, 1985). The only programs where American levels of mobilizing employees are similar to or higher than European averages are military defense and education.

When public employees are analyzed by the level and type of institution, the position of the federal government, and therefore of the president, appears smaller still.

Central government institutions—ministries, nationalized industries, and other agencies such as health services—account for only 5 percent of total employment in the United States, as against 15 to 25 percent in Europe. The United States has a larger proportion of public employees in state and local government than most European countries, but because it has fewer public employees, this total is not large.

The president of the United States heads an executive branch of government that has fewer employees in proportion to the labor force (4.0 percent) than governments in Europe. Whatever views a president has about a given program, the people down the line delivering the program cannot easily be given directions, for they work for politicians elected by very different constituencies. The political links between congressmen and state and local jurisdictions add a further constraint to the exercise of presidential influence upon programs delivered by other levels of government. By contrast, in France and Italy even school teachers are employees of the central government, and financial controls can be exploited to influence nationalized industries, hospitals, and even doctors.

The difference in the personnel at the call of the president and a European cabinet is qualitative as well as quantitative. A disproportionate number of federal employees in America are in the military, working in a chain of command headed by the president as commander-in-chief. National security is a principal concern of the president, and he has unique military resources at hand. By contrast, in a European government, school teachers or unionized employees of nationalized industries are likely to dominate employment by national government, groups of workers who are much more likely to be recalcitrant, and, however important their services to citizens, of far less immediate significance to a country's prime minister.

The third resource of government—laws—is also much more in the hands of a cabinet in Europe than in the hands of the president in Washington. Because a parliamentary system requires that the government have the confidence of the legislature, it can effectively control the actions of parliament on major legislation. The great bulk of legislation introduced each year is prepared and presented by members of the cabinet, and the great bulk of measures proposed by ministers is approved by parliament. The control of the year's legislative output occurs in coalition as much as in single-party cabinets (table 5).

The American president has far less influence upon legislation than does a prime minister. In Washington, only one-tenth of the acts of Congress will be measures sponsored by the president. Moreover, a significant number of acts will be passed against the wishes of the White House. In a parliamentary system, even statutes not originating in the government are normally enacted with the tacit approval of the government. Whereas a president will be unable to get Congress to enact half the bills that he puts forward to Congress, a prime minister can be confident that nearly all the measures proposed by his government will be enacted by parliament. From 1954 to 1975, the White House on average secured congressional approval for 43 percent of its proposals; in Britain the proportion of government bills approved was 97 percent (cf. Wayne, 1978, table 5.2; Rose, 1985a, table 3.12).

An American president's influence upon legislation is also constrained by two other institutions not normally significant in Europe. The first is the Supreme Court's power of judicial review, which not only affects the implementation of laws enacted by Congress, but also inhibits actions by the president in his executive capacity. Secondly, the American federal system vests law-making powers in fifty state legislatures, a degree of fragmentation unknown even in federal systems of Europe. State legislatures enact on average nearly six hundred laws a year, and these acts can differ significantly from each other and from acts of Congress (see Council of State Governments, 1982, pp. 86–89, 206 ff.).

Two conclusions follow from this review of the resources available to the president as against prime ministers: (1) governments in Europe command a far

TABLE 5
The Proportion of Laws Sponsored by Government Annually

|  | All Acts | Government-sponsored | |
| --- | --- | --- | --- |
|  | No. | No. | % |
| Netherlands | 271 | 270 | 99.6 |
| Denmark | 177 | 178 | 99.4 |
| Switzerland | 29 | 27 | 93.0 |
| Belgium | 163 | 150 | 92.0 |
| Austria | 170 | 143 | 84.0 |
| Britain | 72 | 58 | 82.0 |
| Germany | 111 | 90 | 81.0 |
| France | 93 | 67 | 72.0 |
| Italy | 588 | 103 | 18.0 |
| United States | 452 | 47 | 10.0 |

Sources: Principally calculated from Inter-Parliamentary Union, *Parliaments of the World*, 1976, table 49. U.S. figures, annual average, 1970–75, calculated from Wayne, 1978, table 5.2.

larger share of society's resources—whether measured by money, manpower, or laws—than does government in the United States; (2) central government commands a far larger share of total government resources in Europe than does the federal government in Washington. Bigness, normally treated as a virtue by Americans, is not an unalloyed advantage when it comes to government; the big benefits of European governments have big costs (see Rose, 1984, chap. 4). But it is a reminder to Americans who express anxieties about the size of government in the United States today that, "You ain't seen nothing yet."

## Sizing Up the Presidency

In Europe, "more is better" describes the contemporary approach to government. Institutionally, the parliamentary system concentrates government in the hands of a collective cabinet with the resources of an expert civil service. Programmatically, every government in Western Europe except the Swiss is committed to a far higher level of welfare state provision than is the United States and mobilizes a larger share of society's resources.

Americans appear to have as their motto, "more from less government." Programs make less collective provision for the welfare of citizens, especially at the federal level. Institutionally, the leadership of the federal government is not so much centralized as it is isolated in the hands of the president. In Richard Neustadt's (1960) vision of the presidency, the man in the Oval Office is isolated in action just like the Western sheriff in *High Noon*. The European concept of political leadership is collective, whether the scene is a cabinet room, a battlefield, or a mass demonstration.

The differences between government in Europe and America are such that comparison underlines contrasts, not similarities. Yet a recognition of differences can be instructive, expanding our concept of what is doable, that is, what actions are possible for a government to undertake, whether or not they are deemed desirable. The performance of big governments in postwar Europe should give pause to Americans who assume that government is a priori ineffective or incompetent. The means and ends of government in Scandinavia may well be unacceptable to a majority of American voters. But the unheroic institutions of Scandinavian public policy demonstrate the capacity of government to act effectively on a scale well beyond that deemed possible in Washington.

In every society, institutions of governance derive their effect not only from the intentions of their designers, but also from the character of the society of which they are a part. Any attempt to import European ideas to Washington must recognize that America is not a land in a political void as was Germany in 1945, but a country with well-developed, deeply rooted institutions of government. Moreover, the variety of the American system is often an object of admiration for Europeans who dislike a form of centralization in which too many roads seem to lead to Rome, to Paris, or to London.

The most reasonable assumption about American government in the foreseeable future is that it will continue to be exceptional. Major constitutional changes are *not* widely and strongly supported. In the past century only two constitutional amendments have altered the federal government in an important way; each, the direct election of senators, 1913, and votes for women, 1920, was enacted more than sixty years ago. Moreover, these amendments did not alter the fundamental separation and division of powers that make American government exceptional in its pluralism. Whatever critics of American government (or presidents themselves) may think, there appears to be no widespread popular demand for centralizing authority in the White House. Toward the end of the Carter administration, the Gallup poll asked a nationwide sample whether they thought the president, Congress, or both should have major responsibility for economic policy, foreign policy, and energy policy. In each case, the median respondent wanted both institutions to share responsibility (Wayne, 1982, p. 19).

The importance of checks upon government—even to the extent of checks without balance—is fundamental to the American system and in fundamental contrast to the idea of the parliamentary system. Americans prefer the system as it is, maintaining checks upon the executive. A 1980 poll found that 51 percent endorsed the view that "when a president and a Congress are of opposite political parties, it gives balance to our government," as against 36 percent believing "we need a president and Congress to be of the same political party to enact laws efficiently and quickly" (Lipset and Schneider, 1983, p. 38). If Americans wish to strengthen the ties between president and Congress, then the remedy is at hand, without a constitutional amendment. It is to vote a straight party ticket rather than engage in the increasing practice of ticket-splitting.

*Sizing up the presidency means cutting the president's ambition down to size.* Activist prescriptons for the president can change; but they do not increase the capacity of the president to alter what is not amenable to change. High expectations are not a prescription for presidential success; they are likely to lead to failure, confusing the crucial distinction between what is mutable and what must be taken as immutable within a four-year term of office.

The fight against inflation should begin by controlling our expectations of what the president can do. One way to fight the rhetoric of unreasonable expectations is to focus upon what the president cannot do by comparison with prime ministers of the mixed economy welfare states of Europe. First, a president cannot count on the legislature endorsing government bills and budgets, as can the head of government in a parliamentary system, for Congress and the presidency are not organically linked. The second difference is that the president cannot count on cabinet and subcabinet appointees to be his agents, rather than agents of their department, of congressional committees, of iron triangles, or issue networks (see Heclo, 1978). By contrast, a prime minister can rely upon party discipline and doctrines of collective cabinet responsibility to ensure sufficient cooperation to give direction to government (Rose, 1980). A prime minister's cabinet is the team that registers his success or failure just as does a football manager's team. However, a president cannot rely on the executive branch to follow his instructions; he is like a tennis or golf star, a player who must score on his own.

When the programs of mixed economy welfare states are compared with those in the United States, a president's responsibilities are further diminished in size. A president does *not* raise up to 40 percent of the national product in federal taxes or give direction to 20 percent of the nation's labor force, for government in the United States does much less than a typical European state. It does not take responsibility for basic national industries, and those programs that tend to grow fastest are not those under the president's control (see Rose, 1984a, pp. 213 ff.). In the past three decades, education, the responsibility of thousands of school districts in fifty states, has grown greatly in its claims on the nation's resources. By contrast, military defense, uniquely the responsibility of the president, has registered a relative decline in its claims on resources. Income-maintenance payments for social security are uncontrollable statutory commitments; the Social Security Administration is bound to keep mailing out checks to everyone entitled to a pension until Congress alters the law. Another rapidly growing spending program, payment of interest on the debt, is similarly an uncontrollable obligation.

American government today is far bigger than it was in the era of Franklin Roosevelt's New Deal. But growth has not been concentrated in programs immediately under the command of the White House. It has occurred principally in services delivered by state and local government and in cash-transfer programs laid down by act of Congress. Collectively, many different subgovernments have the capacity to deliver a great host of programs without presidential direction.

The president's program responsibilities are very different from those of a prime minister. All modern states have a small number of things that, by definition, they must do, such as protecting national security through diplomacy and military defense, raising taxes and issuing money, and maintaining law and order. There are a larger number of things that they choose to do, such as mobilizing economic resources in industry, trade, and agriculture, and providing welfare services in health, education, and income-maintenance (see Rose, 1976). But all these programs cannot be the responsibility of one individual. In a parliamentary system, a large number of program responsibilities can be centralized in a cabinet. In the American system, they are not centralized in the White House; they are dispersed, or not done at all.

What is it, then, that makes the president's contribution to government important? The most distinctive feature of the president's program responsibilities is national security. So great is the role of the United States in the world today that international affairs and American national security are interdependent. Prime ministers of smaller European democracies are only spectators in international affairs, and the prime ministers of France, Germany, and Britain are no longer so important as they once were. The president of the United States is virtually unique in the importance of his international responsibilities. Whereas a British prime minister can get by with only one full-time diplomat at 10 Downing Street, the president has dozens of national security advisors and a National Security Council to coordinate advice. National security responsibilities make the president not only central in American foreign policy, but also a great force globally.

The second distinctive program responsibility of the president is inchoate: responsibility for the economy. It is inchoate because presidents disagree about how much influence the government ought to have upon the economy, and there is not yet a set of institutionalized White House mechanisms for discharging economic responsibilities (Porter, 1981). What happens in Washington today has a substantial impact upon the American economy and also upon an open international economy in which America is a major force. Yet within the United States, total government outlays as a proportion of the national product have increased by only 5.4 percent from 1960 to 1980. By comparison with other Western countries, government in the United States has become relatively smaller. In 1960 public spending as a proportion of GNP was only 0.7 percent below the OECD average; it is now 6.1 percent below that average (OECD, 1982, table 6.4).

The greatest change affecting the presidency since 1960 is not that government has gotten bigger but that *the world has gotten smaller*. The world has become smaller in the sense that national policies and politics can no longer be kept separate from international (or transnational) policies and politics (LeLoup and Shull, 1979). The increasing openness of national economies to world trade has brought great economic gains, but at the cost of greater national vulnerability. President Kennedy could enter the American presidency as the unchallenged leader of the free world, whether conceived in military might and alliances or in terms of economic hegemony. As long as America's power vis-à-vis other nations was great, it could simultaneously lead and be independent of other nations. But this privileged position was undermined by multiple shocks: dollar devaluation in 1971, the OPEC oil price rises of 1973 and 1978, and changes in the structure of what is no longer a bipolar balance of power. The institutionalization of an annual seven-nation world summit in 1975, in which the president is only one among seven leaders, symbolizes White House recognition of the interdependence of America and other nations (see Putnam and Bayne, 1984).

Decades of free trade and of expansion of European and non-European economies have created an international economy in which America is deeply implicated as the world's leading industrial nation with the world's leading currency. The interdependence of nations in the open international economy is asymmetrical; having the dollar as the national currency is different from being a government based on francs or kronor. Yet every nation is alike in one sense: each is vulnerable to unintended or unwanted consequences of actions taken by other nations.

The making of economic policy ought to be the first priority of the White House today, for this is the point at which America's interdependence has been growing rapidly and where the president's capacity to influence events is less developed. Moreover, it is here that the United States is most vulnerable, not to threats from military opponents, but to competition from its friends and allies. Whereas an intercontinental missile war can be fought from a fortress distant from all other nations, a peacetime economy can no longer be run successfully in isolation from the rest of the world.

In an open international economy, divisions between domestic and international policy become increasingly artificial. A president cannot pursue an active and effective international policy without simultaneously being in touch with the national economy, though hardly commanding or managing it. In a cabinet system a prime minister can rely upon close cooperation with a foreign minister and a treasury minister and upon legislative endorsement of their actions. Here the uniqueness of the presidency is at a disadvantage.

In order to compete successfully with other Western nations, the president today must strengthen his capacity for handling the economy. This may require the identification of a senior presidential appointee to be the lead spokesperson for the administration on economic affairs generally; the creation of an Economic Affairs Council, analogous to the National Security Council, to coordinate views among appointees concerned with diverse economic matters; the development of a small White House staff to meet the president's immediate interest in engaging and disengaging with particular economic problems; and the creation of procedures to manage the overlapping interests of the National Security Council and an Economic Policy Council (cf. Rose, 1985b; see also Destler, 1981; Porter, 1983).

To strengthen institutions for selective intervention in economic policy is the opposite of introducing cabinet government to Washington. It will widen the distance between the exceptional issues to which the president attends and the concerns of most agencies headed by presidential appointees. Any move to devote more attention to one issue must recognize that less time will be available for other matters. The presidency in the 1980s must adopt a stoic attitude toward most domestic issues, aiming to do more by doing less. Resources of time, people, and the president's scarcest commodity, political capital, should be concentrated on those few centrally important concerns of governance that are uniquely the responsibility of the president. The choice is not between policy making by subgovernments as against policy making by a central governmental authority: both are inevitable.

The president's problem is how to call in issues of major concern while maintaining buffers against involvement in secondary concerns. To say that the president "only" has to worry about peace and prosperity is to elevate, not denigrate, his tasks. The man at the top cannot worry about all the activities of government. By accepting disengagement from many lesser responsibilities, the president can enhance his capacity by concentrating upon what the White House can best influence.

# REFERENCES

Browne, Eric C., and John Dreijmanis, eds. 1982. *Government Coalitions in Western Democracies*. New York: Longman.

Cassese, Sabino. 1980a. Is there a government in Italy? Politics and administration at the top." In *Presidents and Prime Ministers*, ed. R. Rose and E. Suleiman, pp. 171–202. Washington, D.C.: American Enterprise Institute.

———. 1980b. *Esiste un governo in Italia?* Rome: Officina Edizioni.

Colliard, Jean-Claude. 1978. *Les régimes parlementaires contemporains*. Paris: Presses de la Fondation Nationale des Sciences Politiques.

Council of State Governments. 1982. *The Book of the States, 1982–83*. Vol. 24. Lexington, Ky.: Council of State Governments.

Destler, I. M. 1981. National Security II: The rise of the assistant (1961–1981). In *The Illusion of Presidential Government*, ed. H. Heclo and L. Salomon, pp. 263–85. Boulder, Colo.: Westview.

Di Palma, Giuseppe. 1977. *Surviving Without Governing: Italian Parties in Parliament*. Berkeley: University of California Press.

Frears, John. 1984. France in the Mitterand presidency. In *Policies and Politics in Europe*, ed. F. Ridley. London: Croom Helm.

Graziano, Luigi, and Sidney Tarrow, eds. 1979. *La crisi italiana*. Turin: Einaudi.

Heclo, Hugh. 1978. "Issue networks and the executive establishment." In *The New American Political System*, ed. A. S. King, pp. 87–124. Washington, D.C.: American Enterprise Institute.

Herman, V. and J. Pope. 1973. Minority governments in western democracies. *British Journal of Political Science* 3: 191–212.

Inter-Parliamentary Union. 1976. *Parliaments of the World*. London: Macmillan.

Leloup, Lance T., and Steven A. Shull. 1979. Congress versus the executive: The "two presidencies" reconsidered. *Social Science Quarterly* 59: 704–19.

Lipset, S. M., and William Schneider. 1983. *The Confidence Gap*. New York: Free Press.

Mackie, T. T., and Richard Rose. 1982. *The International Almanac of Electoral History*. 2d. ed. London: Macmillan.

Marradi, Alberto. 1982. Italy: From centrism to crisis of the center-left coalitions. In *Government Coalitions in Western Democracies*, ed. E. C. Browne and J. Dreijmanis, pp. 33–70. New York: Longman.

Massot, Jean. 1979. *Le chef du gouvernement en France*. Paris: La Documentation Française.

Mayntz, Renate. 1980. Executive leadership in Germany: Dispersion of power of Kanzlerdemokratie? In *Presidents and Prime Ministers*, ed. R. Rose and E. Suleiman, pp. 139–70. Washington, D.C.: American Enterprise Institute.

Neustadt, Richard E. 1960. *Presidential Power*. New York: Wiley.

Norpoth, Helmut. 1982. The German Federal Republic: Coalition government at the brink of majority rule. In *Government Coalitions in Western Democracies*, ed. E. C. Browne and J. Dreijmanis, pp. 7–32. New York: Longman.

OECD. 1981. *Long-Term Trends in Tax Revenues of OECD Member Countries, 1965–1980*. Paris: OECD.

OECD. 1982. *Historical Statistics, 1960–1980*. Paris: OECD.

Pallotta, Gino. 1976. *Dizionario politico e parlamentare*. Rome: Newton Compton Editori.

Porter, Roger B. 1981. The president and economic policy. In *The Illusion of Presidential Government*, ed. H. Heclo and L. Salomon, pp. 203–27. Boulder, Colo.: Westview.

————. 1983. Economic advice to the president: From Eisenhower to Reagan. *Political Science Quarterly* 98: 403–26.

Putnam, Robert, and Nicholas Bayne. 1984. *Hanging Together: The Seven-Power Summits*. London: Heinemann.

Quermonne, Jean-Louis. 1981. Un gouvernement presidentiel ou un gouvernement partisan? *Pouvoirs: Revue Française d'Etudes Constitutionnelles et Politiques* 20:67–86.

Rockman, Bert A. 1983. Presidential and executive studies: The one, the few, and the many. Paper presented at the annual meeting of the American Political Science Association, Chicago.

Rose, Richard. 1976. On the priorities of government. *European Journal of Political Research* 4: 247–89.

————. 1980. Government against sub-governments: A European perspective on Washington. In *Presidents and Prime Ministers*, ed. R. Rose and E. Suleiman, pp. 234–47. Washington, D.C.: American Enterprise Institute.

————. 1980a. British government: The job at the top. In *Presidents and Prime Ministers*, ed. R. Rose and E. Suleiman, pp. 1–49. Washington, D.C.: American Enterprise Institute.

————. 1984a. *Understanding the Big Government*. London and Beverly Hills: Sage Publications.

————. 1984b. *The Capacity of the President: A Comparative Analysis*. Glasgow: University of Strathclyde, Studies in Public Policy No. 130.

————. 1985a. *Politics in England: Persistence and Change*. 4th ed. Boston: Little, Brown.

————. 1985b. Can the president manage the American economy? *Journal of Public Policy* 5: in press.

————, ed. 1985. *Public Employment in Western Nations*. Cambridge: Cambridge University Press.

Rose, Richard, and Dennis Kavanagh. 1976. The monarchy in contemporary political culture. *Comparative Politics* 8: 548–76.

Von Beyme, Klaus. 1983. *The Political System of the Federal Republic of Germany.* Aldershot, Hants.: Gower.

Wayne, Stephen J. 1978. *The Legislative Presidency.* New York: Harper and Row.

———. 1982. Expectations of the president. In *The President and the Public,* ed. Doris Graber, pp. 17–38. Philadelphia: Institute for the Study of Human Issues.

Benjamin I. Page and Robert Y. Shapiro

# Presidential Leadership Through Public Opinion

*[The president's] is the only voice in the national affairs. Let him once win the admiration and confidence of the country, and no other single force can withstand him. . . . If he rightly interpret the national thought and boldly insist upon it, he is irresistible.—* Woodrow Wilson

*The President can and does and probably should shape popular attitudes, and not just respond to them passively.*—Elmer E. Cornwell, Jr.

It is often claimed that in the struggle to influence policy the president of the United States has a special advantage: he can bypass Congress and appeal directly to the general public, which in turn puts pressure on its representatives to agree with the president's proposals. Thus the president is said to exert policy leadership through public opinion.

This claim has gained plausibility with the accumulating evidence that policy making actually is affected by public opinion (Page and Shapiro, 1983a; Shapiro, 1982; Monroe, 1983, 1979; Weissberg, 1976). If public opinion matters, a presidential strategy of indirect influence might succeed. Moreover, we know that most presidents since Theodore Roosevelt and Woodrow Wilson have advocated such leadership and have made serious efforts to influence public opinion (see Cornwell, 1965; Grossman and Kumar, 1981; Tulis, 1982). In recent years a large staff devoted to communication has grown up in the White House, producing a barrage of press releases, presidential press conferences, and televised addresses to the nation.

The only missing piece in this picture is a demonstration that presidents can in fact influence Americans' opinions about policy. The empirical evidence is surprisingly scanty (e.g., Rosen, 1973; Sigelman, 1980; Edwards, 1983). It is easy enough to find examples in which policy preferences seem to have changed after presidential efforts at persuasion, but harder to know how typical such cases are or whether the congruent movement of rhetoric and opinion may be coincidental. Systematic research has been hampered by lack of identical survey questions asked before and after presidents' persuasive efforts: quite mistaken conclusions about opinion change can be drawn by comparing responses to questions that differ slightly (see Roshco, 1978). Existing compilations of cases are open to suspicion of conscious or unconscious selection to prove a point and suffer from a number of other methodological defects.[1]

In short, research has not shown to what extent or under what circumstances presidents can actually affect the public's policy preferences. By using an unusual data set in our possession we have been able to make some progress toward answering these questions.

## Data and Research Design

In the course of our ongoing research project concerning connections between public opinion and public policy, based on national opinion surveys conducted by various organizations between 1935 and 1980, we have gathered a great deal of data about Americans' policy preferences. In particular, we have collected the marginal frequencies of responses to several hundred policy preference questions that were asked in identical form at more than one point in time. We have previously described the nature and extent of opinion changes as revealed by some of these data (Page and Shapiro, 1982) and the extent to which public policy has moved in accordance with public opinion changes (Page and Shapiro, 1983a; Shapiro, 1982).

These opinion data also permit us to make a simple quasi-experimental test of the impact of presidents and others upon public opinion. We can identify a set of instances in which opinion questions were repeated at reasonably close time intervals, disregarding for the moment whether or not changes in opinion occurred or in what direction. Taking such pairs of opinion measurements (at times "T1" and "T2") as our cases or units of analysis, we can then content analyze the mass media for policy-relevant statements between each T1 and T2 and attempt to predict the amount and direction of opinion change (if any) by the amount and the directional thrust of statements and actions by presidents, their administrations, the opposition party, and other sources.

In this essay we report the results of a first effort at such an analysis. We examined the *New York Times* for material relating to fifty-six pairs of repeated survey questions asked by the Harris (n=41) and Gallup (n=15) organizations. These cases are not in any precise sense a random sample, but they have the great virtue of being selected quite independently of any concern about presidents; they should thus allow an unbiased test of propositions about opinion leadership. The cases are reasonably diverse, drawn from five different decades beginning with the 1930s, although there is some concentration in the early 1970s. They perhaps overrepresent recent policy questions concerning energy and inflation, but they cover a wide variety of foreign and domestic issues including defense, foreign aid, Vietnam, welfare, income taxes, political campaigning, civil rights and civil liberties, and education.

About half the cases involve significant (6 percentage points or more) changes in public opinion, and half do not. The average length of the interval between T1 and T2 is about four and a half months. For a fuller description of our data and methods, (see Page and Shapiro (1983b).

We began our study of media with the *New York Times* primarily because of the existence of easily available microfilms dating back to the 1930s, but we also expect that much of the national and international reportage in the *Times* finds its way, in diluted form, through other newspapers, magazines, television news, and word of mouth to the general public. That is, the *Times* may not be a bad indicator of the general thrust of news that reaches the citizenry. (We are now testing this assumption, particularly with respect to TV news; see Page and Shapiro, 1984). Moreover, the *Times*—with its complete coverage, frequently including full texts of speeches—offers an exceptionally good way to learn about the original sources for, and the quality of, information transmitted to the public by other means.

For each case our students and research assistants coded all relevant page one stories during the T1–T2 interval, noting the major *source* of each story (the president, his administration and fellow partisans, members of the opposing party, interest groups, experts, editorial commentary, foreign actors, objective conditions or events); each story's *salience,* in terms of length and position; the *direction* of impact it would be expected to have upon policy preferences (for or against the particular policy) given an intelligent, attentive audience with average American beliefs and values; and some judgments concerning the *quality* of the information conveyed, including its logic, factuality, and degree of truth or falsehood.

The crux of the media coding is ascertaining the directional thrust of stories: that is, what impact they would be expected to have on average American citizens. Such a task requires considerable care in training and supervising coders; we were also careful to mask the public opinion data (providing only dates and exact question wordings, but no information about public responses) so that coders were not biased by knowledge of whether or how policy preferences actually changed. Our work so far indicates that it is possible to code nearly all relevant stories with reasonable reliability on a five-point directional scale, consisting of categories "clearly pro," "probably pro," "uncertain or neutral," "probably con," and "clearly con," in relation to the main policy alternative outlined in an opinion question.

The five numerical values representing points on the pro-con scale (running from $+2$ to $-2$, with 0 for neutral) can then be summed and averaged over time, both for media contnt as a whole and for stories based on particular sources, to provide measures of total and average directional thrust during the period. These sums and averages of pro-con codes for presidential and other sources between T1 and T2 constitute the main independent variables with which we use regression analysis to estimate the impact of each political actor or information source (or of all taken together) upon the magnitude and direction of changes in the public's policy preferences.

## Findings: Popular and Unpopular Presidents

As we have reported elsewhere (Page and Shapiro, 1983b), when we analyzed all fifty-six cases in this manner we were surprised to find little or no effects upon public opinion by any particular actors (including presidents) or even by all media content taken together. No matter whether we looked at sums or averages of pro-con codes, at only the most relevant stories, or at coders' subjective predictions of what changes would occur, we found nothing; nor did analysis of some cases in which we coded editorial page or pre-T1 media content reveal much. In none of these cases, nor when we entered all eight independent variables (eight sums, eight averages) simultaneously in multiple regressions, did we find any coefficients that would be significantly different from zero in a sample. Seldom have we encountered such an overwhelming series of negative findings. It appeared that neither presidents nor their administrations nor any other source as reported in the *Times* had any significant impact upon public opinion.

We should note that the apparent failure of presidential persuasion did not result from lack of presidential effort. Our coders found numerous reports of presidents' actions and proposals and speeches that made clear the president's policy preferences. For all fifty-six cases, including some of rather minor importance and low visibility, we found an average (mean) of 3.6 relevant stories coded as primarily presidential in source. These were supplemented by many more stories from other administration sources—an average of 12.7 of them—which generally followed the president's line, during the same periods of approximately four and a half months per case.

Presidents were trying, then; why wasn't the public listening or responding? We thought of a possible reason. At the time of some of our cases, particularly a number of Harris cases from the early 1970s, presidents were quite unpopular: Nixon had been undone by Watergate; Ford suffered from his Nixon pardon and from the OPEC oil boycott, price rises, and the ensuing recession; Carter was blamed for economic troubles at home and crises abroad. Perhaps this unpopularity, this lack of political standing or public prestige, undercut their credibility and their powers of persuasion, obscuring the positive impacts of more popular presidents.

Fortunately, in order to permit some analysis of source credibility, we had noted for each case the popularity of the president at the time of the first (T1) opinion measurement for that case, using Gallup data on the percentage of Americans approving the president's handling of his job at that time. Inspection of these data showed that we were indeed dealing with some unpopular presidents. The median presidential popularity for all our cases was an anemic 48 percent approving. In fact, in seventeen of our cases, nearly one-third of the total, fewer than 35 percent of the American public approved of the president's handling of his job! Little wonder that the public did not respond to these presidents' efforts at opinion leadership.

In order to test the credibility hypothesis we partitioned the set of cases roughly in half according to whether presidents were at least minimally "popular" (approval rating of 50 percent or more) or "unpopular" (below 50 percent), and performed the same kind of analysis on each subset of cases as we did for the entire data set.

Some plausible findings appeared. When presidents were popular, the data indicated, they did indeed affect public opinion—and so did certain other actors. On the other hand, when presidents were unpopular, they had no effect at all or perhaps even a negative impact, actually dissuading the public from their policies (see Sigelman and Sigelman, 1981). There was a hint of positive influence by the opposition party and by interest groups, but in general, for the cases in which presidents were unpopular, we could find no systmatic effects of any media-reported stories from any sources upon public opinion. Adjusted $R^2$'s fell to zero and no individual coefficients would (if we were dealing with a sample) have been significant. This suggests that societal institutions generally may have had low credibility at these times, or at least that absent a popular president, no other actors could take his place as opinion leader (see Page and Shapiro, 1983b).

In order to sharpen these findings further we examined a slightly smaller (n=21) subset of cases in which presidents were still more popular, with approval ratings of 57 percent or above. The results are given in table 1. Taking the multiple regression reported in the first column first, it is clear that for these popular president cases the net directional thrust of various sources reported in the media (measured by the *sum* of pro-con codes for T1–T2 stories from each source) does a very good job of accounting for the extent and direction of opinion change. The multiple correlation coefficient (R) of .86 is quite high, as is the proportion of variance accounted for ($R^2$). Even after adjustment for the small number of cases, these variables account for more than half the variation in opinion change, which is particularly impressive when one remembers that some of the measured opinion change is random due to unavoidable sampling error in the original opinion surveys. In other words, there is reason to be

TABLE 1

The Impact of Media Content from Various Sources
upon Americans' Policy Preferences
(popular president cases only)

| Source of P. 1 News Stories | Measure of Media Content | | |
|---|---|---|---|
| | Sum of Pro-Con Codes | Average of Pro-Con Codes | |
| President | 1.81[a] | 5.47 | 4.74[a] |
| | (0.73) | (2.86) | (1.95) |
| Administration | −0.29 | 4.33 | |
| | (0.24) | (4.18) | |
| Opposition party | −1.09 | −2.15 | |
| | (0.89) | (2.54) | |
| Interest groups | −1.28[b] | −4.75 | |
| | (0.33) | (2.76) | |
| Editorial | 7.65[b] | 2.63 | |
| | (2.32) | (5.72) | |
| Experts | 0.00 | −1.21 | |
| | (0.59) | (3.07) | |
| Foreign sources | 0.29 | −1.44 | |
| | (0.68) | (4.52) | |
| Events | −2.50 | −8.53 | |
| | (4.59) | (5.86) | |
| (constant) | −2.18 | −4.79[a] | −3.80 |
| | (1.19) | (2.11) | (1.80) |
| R | 0.86 | 0.72 | 0.49 |
| R² | 0.74 | 0.51 | 0.24 |
| Adj. R² | 0.57 | 0.19 | 0.20 |

Note: Based upon twenty-one cases in which presidents had approval ratings of 57 percent or higher. Entries are unstandardized (b) coefficients from multiple regressions of percentage point changes in policy preferences with the media content variables. Standard errors are given in parentheses.

   a. Significant at $p < .05$ if these cases constituted a sample.
   b. Significant at $p < .01$.

satisfied that the media content variables as we conceptualized and measured them do well at accounting for public opinion changes in this set of cases where the president is popular.

Furthermore, this analysis indicates that popular presidents have a rather substantial effect on public opinion. The presidential coefficient of 1.81 means that a net balance of a single definitely favorable statement or action (coded $+2$ on our five-point pro-con scale) can produce about 3.6 percentage points ($+2$ times the 1.81 coefficient) of favorable opinion change as compared with neutral or nonexistent presidential action.

This should not be taken to imply that presidents could indefinitely multiply their speeches and thereby multiply their influence, because presidential time and energy is limited and, anyhow, saturation might set in. In actuality there was more than one presidential story in only half of our fifty-six cases, and more than four presidential stories in only about one-quarter ($^{15}/_{56}$) of them. Moreover, presidents are seldom entirely unambiguous in policy advocacy, and some of their statements and actions tend to dilute or undercut the effect of others; the net balance or sum of pro-con codes was less than a wholehearted 2.0 (in absolute value) in well over half our cases. Still, the 1.81 coefficient signifies a substantial effect, on the average, of news stories emanating from the president.

Furthermore, the analysis of pro-con sums in table 1 indicates that when presidents' rhetoric is taken into account, other voices in their administrations have no significant independent impact at all. They may amplify a popular president's message, but if they go off in a different direction they are without effect. Likewise, the opposition party tends to get nowhere. If anything, it may have a slightly negative impact. Among American politicians, then, a popular president ordinarily stands alone as the preeminent leader of public opinion.

Outside the ranks of public officials, too, popular presidents face few rivals. Interest groups actually appear to have a substantially negative effect on the public; public opinion tends to move in the opposite direction from what such groups seek. This finding is somewhat puzzling unless it reflects desperate and counterproductive efforts by groups to go public when they are already losing battles in lower-visibility political arenas. Experts and scholarly studies appear to have no direct effect at all on the public; presumably their impact (if any) is transmitted through politicians or other public persons. Similarly, objective conditions and events seem to change the policy preferences of the public only as those events are interpreted by public figures, presumably because the policy implications of events seldom speak for themselves.

Among all the nonpresidential sources of stories we studied, only one besides the president shows a strong positive effect: the source we labeled "editorial," which refers to page one *New York Times* stories which expressed interpretation or commentary relevant to one of our policy questions. According to our estimate, one such front page editorial or commentary would on the average produce some 15 percentage points of opinion change if it were definitely favorable toward a policy. This would be media power with a vengeance. We should note, however, the very skewed distribution of this variable: there were no such stories at all in the vast majority of cases, but a very occasional front page editorial judgment tended to coincide with large opinion changes, yielding this high estimate. We are inclined to believe that there is a genuine effect of media and/or elite judgments and interpretations of events, but we cannot be sure of the magnitude of the effect. Tentatively, then, only the media themselves (or some elite consensus they may reflect) appear to rival the president's capacity for opinion leadership.

The remaining columns of table 1 indicate that our variables based on *average* pro-con thrust of various sources are less successful in accounting for opinion change. That is, not surprisingly, repetition matters: half a dozen favorable stories (added up in the sum variables) have more effect than one story of the same directional thrust, whereas the average pro-con variables treat these two situations as equivalent. The adjusted $R^2$ for this equation is small and none of the eight individual coefficients would be significant. Still, it is interesting to note that the estimates of the coefficients are similar in sign and relative magnitude to those we just discussed: popular presidents seem to have a substantial effect on public opinion; the rest of the administration adds little (relative to the standard error of estimate); opposition party effects are nil or negative; interest groups tend to have a negative effect; and once again experts and foreign sources wash out. In this case events appear to have a slight negative (i.e., contrary to expected) effect, and the editorial impact mostly vanishes because a single editorial no longer looks so powerful compared with averages for other sources based on larger numbers of stories. But none of these results would be statistically significant in a sample.

The third column of table 1 is based on a misspecified equation that includes only the presidential independent variable. In order to estimate presidential effects correctly, one should simultaneously control for other relevant factors. We have included the third column mainly to indicate the very healthy zero-order correlation ($r=.49$) between the average pro-con thrust of presidential stories and opinion change. Moreover, it supports the inference from the second column that presidential stories in a T1–T2 period with an average content coded 1, or "probably pro," tend to cause about 5 percentage points of favorable opinion change. Again, a substantial effect.

Finally, we also analyzed separately all the cases in which presidents were even more popular, with approval ratings of 60 percent or higher. This set of cases is too small ($n=14$) for us to be very confident about the results—the adjusted $R^2$'s dropped to .31, .21, and .18. But the estimate of presidential effects was higher than in the prior analysis: a coefficient of 2.45 rather than

1.81 for the presidential pro-con sum variable, indicating that a net balance of one definitely favorable speech or action could produce nearly five points of opinion change. Taken together, then, our findings indicate that popular presidents can indeed lead public opinion, and the more popular they are, the more effectively they can do so.[2]

## Successes and Failures

It may be useful to consider some concrete examples involving popular and unpopular presidents. Of course our findings are based on statistical tendencies; we cannot be sure about the causal relationships involved in any one instance. But we can at least describe some of the cases in which presidents' efforts and public opinion did or did not move in the same direction, referring to these somewhat loosely as cases of presidential success and failure, respectively.

At the beginning of 1941, President Franklin D. Roosevelt's popularity stood at a high level, with 71 percent of Americans approving his handling of his job as president. For some time he had been warning of the dangers to the United States of a German victory over Britain and urging the need for U.S. assistance; by the first week of January 1941, 60 percent of the Americans interviewed by Gallup thought it was more important for the United States "to help England win even at the risk of getting into the war" than to keep out of war ourselves.

During the next two months Roosevelt and his administration kept up a steady stream of talk and action favoring aid to Britain. Roosevelt discussed aid in general terms in his State of the Union message (reported 7 January 1941), and then introduced into Congress a lend-lease bill that would give him broad discretionary authority to aid the Allies (10 January 1941). He orchestrated administration testimony and statements in favor of the bill by Secretary of State Hull (16 January 1941), O.P.M. Director Knudson (19 January 1941), Treasury Secretary Morgenthau (29 January 1941), and War Secretary Stimson (30 January 1941). After the administration accepted some limiting amendments and the House passed the bill (9 February 1941), Roosevelt denied that there would be any controversy over further destroyers for Britain and applied administration pressure for quick Senate passage. Roosevelt himself opposed any further restrictions in the bill (26 February 1941), and in a speech delivered at the Academy Awards ceremony called lend-lease a big factor in the defense of the Western Hemisphere (28 February 1941). After a bitter filibuster the Senate passed the Lend-Lease Bill (9 March 1941), and the president signed it into law (12 March 1941), starting aid immediately. When the Gallup organization repeated its survey question during that same second week of March, it found 67 percent of Americans choosing to help England even at the risk of getting into the war, a rise of 7 percentage points.

A 7 percentage point change in policy preferences over a two-month period is unusually large; such changes generally occur only very slowly if at all (see Page and Shapiro, 1982). This must be counted a great success for Roosevelt. Yet from another perspective the modest absolute size of the change also suggests that there are rather severe limits to any president's powers of opinion leadership. Here, after all, was a very popular president (more popular than any we have had in recent decades) who made lend-lease his first priority and for many weeks devoted most of his own and his administration's energies to it; who had important bipartisan support for his position, especially from Wendell Wilkie; who could rely on public appeals from Winston Churchill and on the discouraging facts of the war to bolster his case; and who ultimately gained overwhelming approval of his program from Congress. Yet even after all that persuasive activity and after the accomplished fact of legislation, only an additional 7 percent of Americans supported aid to Britain.

Another apparent success is Harry S. Truman's advocacy toward the end of World War II of a unified command for the U.S. armed forces. A Gallup poll in mid-December 1945 showed that a little over 60 percent of Americans who held opinions favored unification, which had been proposed by the War Department and backed by Eisenhower and other generals. (This 60 percent level of support actually represented a substantial drop from two months earlier, apparently because of strong navy opposition to the plan.) In late December, Truman, who had a 63 percent approval rating, called upon Congress to legislate unification (20 December 1945); he eventually quieted navy opposition by engineering a compromise in which the army and navy would be coordinated but "independent" within the new department (27 January 1946), and he prepared a public speech backing unification (6 April 1946). In mid-April Gallup found a little over 67 percent public approval for unification, a 7 percent gain. Truman apparently recouped some of the losses of the previous autumn.

A final example of possible success: in early to mid-August 1945, Gallup found only about 17 percent of Americans approving of "removing all price ceilings now." President Truman, however, then enjoying a honeymoon approval rating of 82 percent, urged the various price, wage, and production agencies to "restore a free economy" and delegated powers for them to do so (19 August 1945). Accordingly, the War Production Board cut back controls on passenger auto output (25 August 1945), and the Office of Price Administration proposed a slight price rise for autos (26 August 1945), though it continued control of rents (28 August 1945) and of prices generally. Truman's mild endorsement of a "free economy" and the actions he urged on his administrators (as well as the impending end of the war itself) may have contributed to the 5 percentage point rise, to 22 percent, in public approval of removing price ceilings that was revealed by a new Gallup poll conducted early in October 1945.

These apparent successes by popular presidents, while not overwhelming in magnitude, do certainly contrast with some failures experienced by unpopular presidents.

At the end of 1974, for example, after the OPEC oil boycott and price rises, only 19 percent of Americans told Harris interviewers that they agreed "we had better find ways to get along with the Arabs, even if that means supporting Israel less." President Ford, whose approval rating then stood at a weak 37 percent, gave no public hint of reducing support for Israel: he deplored the Arab blacklist as repugnant to the United States (27 February 1975); he had Defense Secretary Schlesinger declare his confidence that the United States could still successfully support Israel in a Middle East war (24 January 1975); and he had Secretary of State Kissinger and others emphasize development of new fuel sources and conservation rather than accommodation with Arab countries. Still, when the Harris question was repeated in March 1975, more than 29 percent of Americans agreed with the pro-Arab statement, a gain of 10 percentage points. The increasingly apparent logic of U.S. dependence on Arab oil wealth appears to have overwhelmed contrary sentiments expressed by the president and by AFL-CIO leaders and others.

Similarly, toward the end of September 1973 nearly 65 percent of Americans told Harris interviewers that they favored setting "a priority of use for the public of available supplies of oil, gas, and electricity" in order to help alleviate shortages. President Nixon, whose popularity then stood at a feeble 33 percent approval and was dropping toward its post-Watergate low, proceeded to press for a whole series of conservation and allocation measures. He urged a retail price rise for gasoline (25 September 1973), which the Cost of Living Council allowed; he exhorted householders to save heat by turning down thermostats (10 October 1973); and the White House adopted a supply management plan for winter heating oil. Then, after the late-October OPEC oil cutoff, Nixon asked Congress for crisis action to relax environmental controls, lower speed limits, and the like (8 November 1973)—all amounting to setting priorities on the use of energy. The administration floated trial balloons about taxes on or rationing of gasoline (10 and 12 November, 1973). Throughout the next several months Nixon and his officials repeatedly urged "tough strong action" (25 November 1973), including oil allocations, emergency powers, and a standby gasoline rationing plan. Nixon asked for voluntary reductions in energy consumption (20 January 1974), and in his State of the Union message pledged to ease the energy crisis (30 January 1974). A month later he denied that the energy crisis was past and predicted that shortages might remain (26 February 1974).

Still, despite this onslaught of presidential rhetoric and action, when Harris interviewers repeated the question at the beginning of April there was no rise at all in the proportion of Americans that favored setting energy use priorities. In fact, there was a drop of 2 percentage points to just under 63 percent. Despite administration denials that the crisis was over (e.g., by energy "czar" Simon), the end of the OPEC embargo in mid-March may have taken some of the steam out of proposals for controls. In any case, the unpopular Nixon did not succeed in mobilizing additional public support.

## Conclusion

Our evidence indicates that Cornwell and others are right. Presidents, at least *popular* presidents, can indeed bring about changes in the policy preferences of the American public and thereby exert pressure on other decision makers. The strategy of indirectly influencing policy through public opinion can bear fruit. This strategy is available only to popular presidents, however; unpopular presidents have no effect at all or maybe even a negative impact on public opinion.

The evidence presented here is neither exhaustive nor conclusive. In the future we plan to study more cases in order to be more certain about the magnitude of presidential effects and to explore further the circumstances under which opinion leadership is or is not successful: whether, for example, leadership works best on domestic or foreign issues; on issues of high or low salience; in periods of higher or lower levels of mass education and media coverage. Answers to these questions will help illuminate the boundaries of presidential influence (e.g., by indicating whether the "two presidencies" thesis applies to opinion leadership) and the nature of historical trends.

We have also begun to study the content of television and other media and investigate the quality—the truth, logic, factuality—of information conveyed by presidents and others. There remains work to do on the question of causality. Time asymmetries alone cannot rule out the possibility that in some cases presidents do not influence the public but rather anticipate changes in opinion and act accordingly or respond (more quickly than the public) to the same outside factors that affect the citizenry. Thus the findings may to some degree reflect reciprocal relationships or spuriousness, although we would judge this problem to be limited.

Clearly the phenomenon of presidential opinion leadership has important implications for democratic politics. Although a full understanding must a-wait research on unanswered questions, we can offer some tentative observations now.

We believe that opinion leadership is not inherently incompatible with democracy. Rational citizens do not and cannot inform themselves fully about complex policy questions; division of labor is as necessary in politics as in other activities. Skillful presidents, sharing the public's basic values, are in an excellent position to act as agents for the people, learning what citizens cannot know and communicating the implications: inspiring, mobilizing, and inform-ing people about which policies will best advance the citizens' interests. We would add a modern gloss to Woodrow Wilson's concept of "interpreting" public opinion. As Downs (1957) tells us, information costs pose a serious barrier to democracy and political equality; but a president can provide correct information and correct inferences, helping people to know what policies they would favor if they were fully informed and perhaps helping to overcome the influence of interest groups and other possibly antidemocratic forces.

There can, of course, be a darker side to opinion leadership: the demagoguery that was so feared by Madison and Hamilton and other Founders (see Tulis, 1982). We see demagoguery as the manipulation of opinion, the providing of misleading or incorrect information that turns citizens against their own interests. In foreign affairs, especially, presidents have been known to deceive the public, as in the case of the Tonkin Gulf incident that was used as a pretext to escalate the Vietnam war and in a number of other cases, perhaps including the recent invasion of Grenada (Wise, 1973; Goulden, 1969; Taylor, 1983). Power in the hands of one man can be used for evil as well as good. Not all our modern presidents have been Roosevelts or Wilsons. It is not surprising, therefore, that observers' views of presidents' power to influence opinion, like views about other presidential powers, tend to vary with the observers' own political attitudes and to shift over time with historical circumstances and with the orientations and qualities of those occupying the office of president (see Page and Petracca, 1983, pp. 1–2, 383–88).

Despite the possibility of demagoguery our findings should perhaps offer some comfort to the apprehensive. Opinion leadership is not quick or easy; the public is not very malleable and there is time for counterargument and deliberation. Intensive efforts over several months by highly popular presidents appear to bring about changes in opinion poll results of only some 5 or 10 percentage points, hardly a tidal wave. On few issues can presidents afford to invest even that much effort. And popular presidents, the only ones who enjoy any success, may (as evidenced by their very popularity) tend especially well to embody the basic values of the American public. It may not be too much to hope, therefore, that efforts at opinion leadership tend to succeed mainly when they have facts on their side and are in harmony with the basic values of the people.

## NOTES

For help with data analysis and the design and carrying out of media coding procedures we are grateful to Glenn Dempsey, John S. Treantafelles, John Kendzior, Theodore Rueter, and the students of P.S. 233 (Chicago) and P.S. V3711 (Columbia). For gathering the opinion data we thank John M. Gillroy and a talented staff. Support was provided by the Columbia University Council for Research in the Social Sciences and the National Science Foundation Grant SES-7912969. We thank Gordon Bennet,

George Edwards, John Kessel, W. Philips Davison, David Prindle, Mark Petracca, and Terry Sullivan for their comments and suggestions.

1. The leading compilation is one provided by Louis Harris to Senator J. W. Fulbright for use in Senate hearings concerning television coverage of the president and congress (U.S. Senate, 91st Cong., 2nd Session, 1970, pp. 14–21). Harris's data on opinion "before and after" presidential speeches have been widely reprinted, for example by Weissberg (1976, p. 235) and Edwards (1983, p. 43), but our own investigation of original Harris news releases indicates that this compilation is not helpful. Of Harris's fourteen cases, five are concerned with presidential performance, not specific policy, so they are not relevant to the issue at hand. Three more involve one-shot survey questions asked only after presidential speeches, which cannot tell anything about opinion change. The six remaining cases all have serious flaws or limitations:

*The 1963 Test Ban Treaty.* The compilation's percentages are based on different groupings of response categories at the two time points. Question wordings are not reported and may not be identical.

*Resumption of bombing North Vietnam in 1966.* The two survey questions differ dramatically in wording. *Before* the president's speech: "Despite the pause in bombings of North Vietnam and the ceasefire, suppose the communists refuse to sit down and talk peace. Would you then favor or oppose all-out U.S. bombings of every part of North Vietnam?" *After:* "Do you think President Johnson was right or wrong to resume bombings of North Vietnam after the recent pause?"

*Withdrawing some American troops from Vietnam in 1969.* According to the releases of 19 May and 7 July, the questions have different wordings and the responses are grouped differently.

*Sending troops into Cambodia in 1970.* The questions are strikingly different. The *before* question offers a lengthy disquisition on Cambodian politics and then asks "Should we send American troops into Cambodia . . . ," or send advisors and conduct bombings, or stay out. The *after* question asks ". . . do you think President Nixon was right in ordering the military operation into Cambodia. . . ?"

*The 1963 tax cut.* The 2 December press release indicates, perhaps mistakenly, that *both* surveys were conducted after Kennedy's August speech. No question wordings are reported.

*Gun control in 1968.* Increased support for gun control may well have had less to do with President Johnson's speech than with Robert Kennedy's assassination. No question wording is given in the second (17 June) release.

2. It is possible, of course, that since *recent* presidents have been less popular, the popularity effect we have inferred might be spurious—attributable to some unspecified historical trend which simply happened to coincide with low levels of presidential support. To test for this possibility we examined the influence of popular presidents only during the most recent time period. We still found a sizeable presidential effect.

# REFERENCES

Cornwell, Elmer E., Jr. 1965. *Presidential Leadership of Public Opinion.* Bloomington: University of Indiana Press.

Downs, Anthony. 1957. *An Economic Theory of Democracy.* New York: Harper.

Edwards, George C., III. 1983. *The Public Presidency.* New York: St. Martin's.

Goulden, Joseph C. 1969. *Truth Is the First Casualty.* Chicago: Rand McNally.

Grossman, Michael Baruch, and Martha Joynt Kumar. 1981. *Portraying the President: The White House and the News Media.* Baltimore: Johns Hopkins University Press.

Monroe, Alan. 1979. Consistency between public preferences and national policy decisions. *American Politics Quarterly* 7: 3–19.

———. 1983. American party platforms and public opinion. *American Journal of Political Science* 27:27–42.

Page, Benjamin I., and Mark P. Petracca. 1983. *The American Presidency.* New York: McGraw-Hill.

Page, Benjamin I., and Robert Y. Shapiro. 1982. Changes in Americans' policy preferences, 1935–1979. *Public Opinion Quarterly* 46:24–42.

———. 1983a. Effects of public opinion on policy. *American Political Science Review* 77:175–90.

———. 1983b. The mass media and changes in Americans' policy preferences: A preliminary analysis. Paper presented at the annual meeting of the Midwest Political Science Association, 20–23 April, Chicago.

———. 1984. Television news and changes in Americans' policy preferences. Paper presented at the annual meeting of the Midwest Political Science Association, 11–14 April, Chicago.

Rosen, Corey M. 1973. A test of presidential leadership of public opinion: The split-ballot technique. *Polity* 6:282–90.

Roshco, Bernard. 1978. The polls: Polling on Panama—Si; Don't Know; Hell, No! *Public Opinion Quarterly* 42:551–62.

Shapiro, Robert Y. 1982. The dynamics of public opinion and public policy. Ph.D. diss., University of Chicago.

Sigelman, Lee. 1980. Gauging the public response to presidential leadership. *Presidential Studies Quarterly* 10:427–33.

Sigelman, Lee, and Carol K. Sigelman. 1981. Presidential leadership of public opinion: From 'benevolent leader' to 'kiss of death'?" *Experimental Study of Politics* 7:1–22.

Taylor, Stuart, Jr. 1983. In wake of invasion, much official misinformation by U.S. comes to light. *New York Times,* sec. I (November 6):8.

Tulis, Jeffrey Kent. 1982. Political rhetoric and presidential leadership. Ph.D. University of Chicago.

U.S. Congress. Senate. 1970. *Public Service Time for the Legislative Branch. Hearings Before the Communications Subcommittee of the Committee on Commerce.* 91st Cong., 2d sess. Washington, D.C.: U.S. Government Printing Office.

Weissberg, Robert. 1976. *Public Opinion and Popular Government.* Englewood Cliffs, N.J.: Prentice Hall.

Wise, David. 1973. *The Politics of Lying.* New York: Vintage.

Dan Thomas and Lee Sigelman

# Presidential Identification and Policy Leadership: Experimental Evidence on the Reagan Case

That the power to persuade is central to presidential leadership is virtually axiomatic among observers of the presidency. In *Presidential Power* Richard Neustadt (1960) states flatly that "power is persuasion," and persuasion inevitably involves the public. There is a considerable measure of complementarity at work here: if the public can be persuaded that a president's position on policy problems is sound, the resulting public support can become a powerful bargaining chip as the policy-making process unfolds in more confined institutional settings. When affirmed by public opinion, the presidential agenda assumes the character of a mandate too powerful to be easily ignored by Congress, the bureaucracy, or any other set of interests (Edwards, 1980, 1983).

How are we to understand a president's success (or failure) in cultivating "policy followership"? If presidential positions on key policy issues are popular with the public, how can we know whether such popularity actually results from presidential persuasion rather than sheer coincidence or a shared but unorchestrated vision? Together, these questions provide the point of departure for the present study. Our purpose is to explore, by experimental means, the phenomenon of presidential policy influence, focusing on one of the several explanations that theoretical speculation has brought to bear.

More specifically, we investigate the possibility that public support for the president's policy initiatives is the end product of the psychological process of identification at work at the interplay between the leader and those who are led. Identification in this sense is a psychoanalytically inspired term, employed originally by Freud in his psychodynamic conception of group behavior. Though it has been defined in a vast variety of ways by authors both inside and outside the psychoanalytic mainstream, we prefer to abide by the definition proposed by Freud himself. According to Freud (1922, p. 63), identification is "the endeavor to mold a person's own ego after the fashion of one that has been

37

taken as a model." Identification was at the fore of Freud's psychodynamic account of leader-follower relations. The leader was assumed to represent a common "ego-ideal" with whom group members shared an identification as well as an ideology. Accordingly, it is not difficult to discern the persuasive significance of identification: after all, what loyal group member would openly disavow the dictates of one who, whether consciously or not, serves as his internalized ego-ideal? This is not to say, however, that identification has been emphasized solely within psychoanalytic theory. Social psychologists Hollander and Julian (1969, p. 394), for example, have concluded that "for any leader, the factors of favorability and effectiveness depend upon the perceptions of followers. Their identification with him implies significant psychological ties which may affect materially his ability to be influential."

In the only research thus far to explore the policy implications of public identification with the president, Thomas and Baas (1982) used presidential identification to predict citizens' subjective support for and behavioral compliance with major provisions of Jimmy Carter's energy program.[1] Their findings bore out the psychodynamic proposition: not only were Carter-identifiers significantly more enthusiastic about the president's energy policies, they displayed behavioral support as well in a host of home- and automobile-related energy conservation efforts. Furthermore, when checked against the effects of several competing explanations, including party identification, ideology, support for the institution of the presidency, support for the political system as a whole, and self-interest, psychological identification with Carter remained virtually unchallenged as an independent source of pro-Carter policy attitudes and energy-conservation actions consistent with those attitudes.

The present study seeks to determine whether the same patterns of relationship prevail for a different president and for different domains of public policy. Unlike the Thomas-Bass analysis, which focused exclusively on energy policy, the present study examined the effects of presidential identification on policy leadership across three different types of policy issues. Moreover, the research reported here is cast in an experimental framework that affords an opportunity to address a troublesome issue of "causality" confronted but not conquered in the Thomas-Bass study. Their evidence of a correlation between presidential identification and pro-Carter positions on energy can be interpreted in two ways. Thomas and Baas argued that one's policy stance is a function of the extent to which one already identified with Carter. However, their data do not rule out a reversal of this causal reasoning, to the effect that Carter earned his status as an ego-ideal by virtue of his policy leadership, as demonstrated, particularly on the domestic front, in the field of energy. From this perspective, all the Thomas-Baas data really demonstrate is the presence of a sizeable "similarity-attraction" effect: like subjects in interpersonal attraction experiments, respondents may have simply been stating favorable opinions of a president whose own opinions, as manifest in his energy policies, they admired.

## Data and Methods

*Split-Ballot Format and Policy Response Measures*

In order to resolve this interpretive problem, we decided to focus our analysis on policy issues about which there was little, if any, public information and on which President Reagan had taken no known public stand as of September 1981. Accordingly, the policy issues (all phrased as policy "proposals") we selected were such that prior opinionation, either strongly pro or con, was not very likely.[2] These proposals, all presented to half of our respondents, were worded as follows.

1. A Family Assistance Act has been proposed. This plan would guarantee $2,800 per year to each low-income family of four, with amounts increasing if the family had some income of its own. What's your position?

2. An amendment to the Family Protection Act of 1981 has been proposed. According to the proposed amendment, any relative would be entitled to set aside $2,500 per year as tax exempt income if earmarked for a child's education. What's your view on the amendment?

3. It has also been proposed that the United States cut back on levels of its military assistance to countries in Western Europe. Would you support or oppose such a move?

Accompanying each proposal was a rating scale, ranging from $-4$ (strongly oppose) to $+4$ (strongly support), on which each respondent was asked to indicate approval or disapproval of the policy in question. For the remaining half of the respondents, the same proposals were prefaced with wording attributing the idea to President Reagan, for example, "President Reagan has recently proposed a Family Assistance Act . . ." Substantively, the policy content of the proposals was identical in the unattributed and attributed conditions. Respondents who completed the second form of the questionnaire thus reacted to the very same policy stimuli except for the addition of one crucial cue: the "fact" that the president was the source of the proposal.

*Respondents*

The sample for this study comprised 178 undergraduate students at the University of Kentucky and 82 undergraduates at the University of Northern Iowa. These students were drawn from freshman- and sophomore-level political science classes at the two schools during September 1981. The two sets of participants were quite similar demographically and politically. The median age of the Kentucky students was nineteen, with 78 percent being freshmen or sophomores, while the counterpart figures in the Iowa sample were eighteen and 85 percent. In both states, the median positions on liberal-conservative and Democratic-Republican scales (which ran from 1 to 9) were 5, exactly at the midpoint. Preliminary analyses with each sample separately showed no substantial difference between the two sets of respondents. Accordingly, the two subsamples were merged into one large sample for the analyses reported below.

## Presidential Identification

To assess the degree to which respondents were identified with President Reagan, we employed a modified "Q technique" procedure (Stephenson, 1953; Brown, 1980). Participants "described" each of three objects (President Reagan, self, and ideal-self) by rank-ordering a set of forty personality-descriptive traits drawn from a larger inventory (Anderson, 1968). These rankings, which ranged along a continuum from +4 ("most like" the object described) to −4 ("least like"), were then correlated for each person separately to generate two indices of presidential identification. The first index is the correlation between each person's description of self and Reagan; the second is the intra-individual correlation of Reagan with respondent ideal-self ("how I would like to be in an ideal sense").

Although highly intercorrelated (r=.81), the two measures do differ in theoretical respects. The most obvious and important distinction is that the first index ($M = .40, SD = .31$) views identification in terms of perceived similarity between the respondent's self and President Reagan, while the second ($M = .53, SD = .28$) sees identification as the degree of fit between a respondent's own ego-ideal and the president. Because of the latter's "predictive" advantage over the former and because we feel that the latter is more consistent with Freud's (1922) original formulation, we focus in the report that follows on the Reagan/ideal-self index.

## Attribute X Treatment Interaction Design

At the issue is the effect on policy evaluations of the continuous variable, presidential identification, under two conditions of a randomly administered "treatment." More specifically, the impact of presidential identification on support for Reagan's policy proposals is contingent on a respondent's "knowledge" (given by the attribution "treatment") that such proposals are or are not the president's. The effect we anticipate would be revealed by the discovery of significantly different patterns of relationship between policy evaluation and presidential identification for the two treatment groups.

## Findings

Let us first examine the mean ratings given the three policy proposals by respondents in each condition. For illustrative purposes, we have dichotomized respondents on the presidential identification measure, dividing at the median, so as to generate a series of four-celled tables that are combined in table 1.

The first thing to note about these scores is that the grand means, with one

TABLE 1
Summary of Policy Evaluations, by Attribution Condition
and Presidential Identification

| Identification | Assist | | | Protect | | | Military | | |
|---|---|---|---|---|---|---|---|---|---|
| | No Attribution | Reagan Attribution | | No Attribution | Reagan Attribution | | No Attribution | Reagan Attribution | |
| Low | 0.28 (61) | 0.37 (71) | 0.33 (132) | 2.33 (61) | 2.32 (71) | 2.33 (132) | 0.66 (61) | 0.80 (71) | 0.73 (132) |
| High | −0.61 (70) | 0.24 (58) | −0.23 (128) | 2.00 (70) | 2.36 (58) | 2.16 (128) | −0.46 (69) | 1.10 (58) | 0.25 (127) |
| | −0.20 (131) | 0.31 (129) | 0.05 (260) | 2.15 (131) | 2.34 (129) | 2.25 (260) | 0.06 (130) | 0.94 (129) | 0.50 (259) |

exception, are not very large. Only on the Family Protection Act item is the overall mean ($M = 2.25$) larger than 1; "average" opinionation on the other two items hovers close to zero ($M = .05$ for the guaranteed income and .50 for reduced military aid). This means that overall our respondents were neither very favorably nor very unfavorably disposed to any of the proposals. Of greater interest, though, is the dispersion of scores; it should probably come as no great surprise that there was less consensus about the guaranteed income and military aid proposals than about the Family Protection Act. The latter after all, is a proposal to tax-shelter income set aside for a child's education; it would be surprising if such a proposal engendered much opposition on the part of tuition-conscious college students.

Policy evaluations are affected by attribution to the president on the two items whose variances sustain meaningful statistical tests. The significance for the guaranteed income proposal showed that the means for the unattributed and attributed conditions were significantly different ($p = .048$); this was also the case ($p < .002$) for the military aid proposal. Responsible for these differences is the fact that the ratings of both proposals were more favorable with the president's name attached than without. More specifically, attribution to Reagan offset hostility toward the guaranteed income plan, but the net effect was to neutralize negative sentiment rather than to mobilize positive support for the proposal. Similarly, support for the military spending proposal did not rise to an impressively enthusiastic level as a result of Reagan's endorsement; again, attribution made what were otherwise neutral or indifferent opinions modestly supportive of the proposed plan. Although a significant attribution effect did not materialize for the widely favored Family Protection proposal, the tendency was in the very same direction: attributed to Reagan, the measure was viewed more enthusiastically than when unattributed.

But more critical to our concerns is the policy response behavior of the two identification groups *across the attribution conditions*. Examining table 1 in this light, we can observe very little evidence, if any, of "movement in the support column" for low-Reagan-identifiers. But, for high-Reagan-identifiers, we witness a rather pronounced "elevation" in policy support due to attribution. In other words, presidential sponsorship of a given policy measure is not likely to have uniform effects in shaping favorable public sentiment on the issue (Sigelman and Sigelman, 1981). For those who were indifferent (or hostile) toward Reagan, presidential endorsement appears to have had little bearing on support for a particular policy proposal. For avowed Reaganites, in contrast, presidential endorsement assumes virtually charismatic proportions, converting what on their own merits would appear to be either lackluster initiatives or outright policy blunders into persuasive, or even appealing, public policy options.

In figure 1, we treat attribution as a control variable and display the Pearson correlations between presidential identification (in its original interval-scale form rather than dichotomized, as above) and the three policy measures individually and collapsed into one additive composite. Figure 1 thus allows us to examine more clearly the impact on policy response of presidential identification across attribution groups. What matters, for our purposes, is whether the relationships differ for respondents in the two "treatment" conditions. The appropriate tests, then, are to be found in the significance of the difference between each pair of correlations. As is indicated, the predicted differences did materialize: regardless of the particular issue at stake, the relationship between presidential identification and policy approval is significantly different for respondents in the two conditions. And, as expected, the correlations are stronger and more positive for respondents in the Reagan Attribution group than for those in the unattributed "control" condition.

In other respects, figure 1 displays a somewhat perplexing asymmetry in the pattern of relationship between presidential identification and policy support. *In absolute terms,* none of the coefficients in the Reagan Attribution condition is significantly greater than zero, while *all* the coefficients in the No Attribution condition are significantly (p < .05) and *negatively* so in magnitude. For the moment we shall postpone comment on what such asymmetry might signify in an interpretive sense.[3] At this point, however, it is important to emphasize that the *inverse* correlation of presidential identification and policy support is found only when no source is specified for the policies in question. Accordingly, we should not overinterpret these associations alone; nor should we allow them to

FIGURE 1

Correlations between Policy Support Ratings and Presidential
Identification, by Attribution Condition

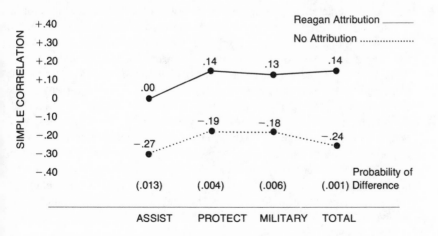

obscure the much more important finding that our "treatment" group, by comparison, is significantly more sensitive to the influence effects of identification with the president.

In figure 1, as we have noted, attribution is treated as a control rather than as a treatment variable. But in prior research (see note 2) as well as in our earlier analysis (table 1), attribution alone emerges as a significant factor affecting ratings of policy issues. A more complete analysis, then, would be to examine the *interactive effects* on policy response of *both* identification and the attribution. To test for this interaction, we inserted attribution, presidential identification, and their multiplicative product in a multiple regression analysis of each policy variable. The recommended procedure tests for the significance of the interaction effect by inserting the interaction term as the final step after variance attributable to the linear main effects has been explained (Pedhazur, 1982).

Summarized in table 2, along with the correlations between relevant pairs of variables, are the results of these regression analyses. The most noteworthy feature of these findings is the support they provide for our governing proposition: across all the policy measures, the interaction term is a highly significant predictor of policy response. Moreover, as revealed by the relative magnitude of the various regression coefficients, the impact of the interaction term is consistently more powerful than is either of the noninteractive terms. Thus, attribution alone can account for varying levels of policy support on two of three issues. But controlling for identification, both in the linear and multiplicative sense, causes the attributional effect to vanish altogether on two items and to emerge only on the Family Protection proposal, precisely where it was absent in the analysis summarized in table 1. Identification itself continues to be a formidable predictor of policy response: all the regression coefficients gauging their contribution are significant at ($p < .01$).

The most important information conveyed by table 2 concerns the contribution of the interaction term in explaining policy responses. In this connection, it is instructive to examine, along with the bottom row of regression coefficients, the two additional sets of figures displayed in the middle portion of the table: the total explained variance for each analysis and the Uniqueness Index, which reports the explained variance solely attributable to the interaction term. The explained variation of policy ratings is not particularly large for any of the issues, with values ranging from a low of 3 percent to a high of 6.4 percent. (This excludes the summed composite policy rating, for which nearly 12 percent of the total variance is explained by these predictors in concert.) More important, however, are the uniqueness values attributable to the interaction term. The percentage of explained variance uniquely attributable to the interaction term ranges from slightly more than 30 percent to fully 90 percent on the individual items and accounts for more than half the explained variance in the composite index.

TABLE 2
Regression Analyses Summary

| Predictors | Assist | Protect | Military | Total |
|---|---|---|---|---|
| **I. Three-Predictor ATI Model** | | | | |
| A. Attribution[a] | −.137[c] | −.251* | −.094 | −.249** |
| | (.13)[d] | (.05) | (.20) | (.22) |
| B. Identification | −.290*** | −.203** | −.199** | −.370** |
| | (−.15) | (−.03) | (−.03) | (−.12) |
| A x B Interaction | .323*** | .378*** | .353*** | .567*** |
| (INTERACT)[b] | (.10) | (.10) | (.21) | (.23) |
| R² | .056 | .030 | .064 | .119 |
| Uniqueness Index (UI)[e] | .020 | .027 | .024 | .061 |
| **II. Five-Predictor Model** | | | | |
| (adding party identification | | | | |
| and liberalism-conservatism) | | | | |
| A. Attribution | −.134 | −.215* | −.144 | −.260** |
| B. Identification | −.182*** | −.167** | −.190*** | −.291*** |
| C. INTERACT | .355*** | .337*** | .416*** | .601*** |
| D. Party identification | −.196*** | −.067 | −.009 | −.141** |
| | (−.27) | (−.06) | (−.02) | (−.19) |
| E. Liberalism-conservatism | −.184*** | −.001 | −.074 | −.142** |
| | (−.27) | (−.03) | (−.06) | (−.20) |
| R² | .150 | .029 | .075 | .173 |

a. Attribution: 0 =unattributed; 1 =attributed to Reagan.

b. INTERACT =Identification Score X Attribution (with former a continuous variable and latter dummy coded as above).

c. Main entries are standardized regression coefficients (betas).

d. Shown in parentheses are the simple (Pearson) correlations for each predictor/ criterion pair.

e. UI is the explained variance uniquely attributable to INTERACT, calculated as the net change in R² when INTERACT is added to the regression equation *after* other predictions.

*p<.05
**p<.01
***p<.001

In explaining citizen evaluations of public policy, previous studies have devoted considerable attention to the effects of party identification and liberalism-conservatism (see, e.g., Page and Brody, 1972; Aldrich et al., 1982). Each is seen as a cognitive filter capable of affecting a person's regard for policy stimuli for which personal stakes, interest, and information are low. To weigh the contribution of these political variables vis-à-vis the psychodynamic considerations built into the identification model, we added party identification and liberalism-conservatism as predictors in a final series of multiple regression analyses; the results from these analyses are reported in the lower part of table 2. (The party identification and liberalism-conservatism measures are both 9-point self-rating scales scored in the GOP/conservative direction.) Although party identification and liberalism-conservatism are each correlated significantly with ratings of the guaranteed income proposal, neither outperforms or diminishes the contribution of presidential identification to variation on this or any other of the policy response measures. Thus there is little if any evidence to suggest that the relationships uncovered above can be attributed to the "third factor" effects of either party affiliation or political conviction.

In its entirety, then, the evidence examined here vindicates the view, advanced initially by Thomas and Baas (1982), that presidential identification constitutes an avenue of opinion leadership. A president's prospects for policy leadership are elevated to the extent that he serves as an object of popular identification while backing policies perceived to have his stamp of approval.

## Concluding Discussion

These findings support the idea that policy leadership by the president can be partially understood as a by-product of the process by which members of the public come to identify psychologically with the nation's most visible political leader. Our findings are therefore consonant with those of Thomas and Baas (1982) on public reactions toward President Carter's energy program. Focused on a different president and on different policies, the present study replicates and extends the conclusions reached in the earlier research. It also strengthens them. As a result of the experimental approach taken here, we are more confident in dismissing an alternative to the psychodynamic account of followership implied by the notion of presidential identification. As noted earlier, results from the Thomas-Baas survey could have been interpreted in similarity-attraction terms. That is, people who were sympathetic toward Carter's work in energy could have identified with him in consequence—an interpretation that reverses the causal flow of our argument. Our findings, however, severely diminish the credibility of the similarity-attraction alternative. In the first place, we investigated areas of policy on which, with one exception, President Reagan had taken no clear nor widely perceived position. This alone militates against the similarity-attraction interpretation. Moreover, Reagan's admirers were not, as an aggregate, sympathetic to the policy proposals that bore his name in our research instrument. On the contrary, as the data for respondents in the unattributed condition clearly show, those particularly fond of Ronald Reagan could not have been so in consequence of a match between "his" views and "theirs" on the experimental policy questions. It therefore seems safe to surmise that the directional "flow" is from presidential identification to policy opinion and not vice versa.

We are at pains to account for the degree to which identification with Reagan operated so asymmetrically on policy opinions, pro and con. Our findings suggest that President Reagan's powers of persuasion are especially formidable on the "con" side and not nearly so formidable on the "pro" side of issues. We found compelling circumstantial evidence to this effect in the behavior of respondents who, while highly identified with Reagan, were reacting to policy statements unaware of their origin. The degree to which such persons responded negatively to the proposals remains somewhat mysterious as does the muted policy support of highly identified respondents in the Reagan attribution condition. Our analysis indicates that ideology cannot account for these tendencies. Why, then, should identification with the president be operative at all? After all, we are referring to respondents who had no "knowledge" of the proposals' proponents(s). A resolution of this matter must, quite obviously, await further research. In this light, however, a promising direction for additional investigation is perhaps to be found in the notion of leadership (and followership) "style." Could it be that the Reagan style is preeminently oppositional in tone? Is it conceivable that Reagan's own political ascendency was rooted in such a frustrated sense of antagonism on the part of his supporters that virtually *any* federal program except increased defense spending evoked suspicion or hostility? Earlier, Sears (1978) and Lowery and Sigelman (1981) pointed to a "mad as hell and not going to take it anymore" quality in the charismatic tax-revolt leadership of Howard Jarvis. Might not a similar dynamic be operative in the followership of President Reagan? Clearly, these are formidable questions—and they comprise only a few of the issues raised by the present research. Though difficult, we regard them as important enough to warrant serious consideration.

In closing, it bears mention that political science has long paid lip service to the idea that presidents are objects of deep-seated and intensely emotional feelings on the part of ordinary citizens. As partial testimony to the depth of such sentiment, several studies undertaken in the wake of John Kennedy's assassination delivered the same assessment of public reactions: beneath the shock lay feelings of profound personal distress (see, e.g., Greenberg and Parker, 1965; Wolfenstein and Kliman, 1965). In surveying these accounts, Greenstein (1968), in fact, used the phrase "disproportionate grief" to capture the sense of loss felt by so many of those willing to share their reactions. To Greenstein, the intensity of this grief made sense only as a signal of the extent to which the fallen president served as a popular object of psychological identification prior to his death. Although this possibility received some backing in studies of other presidents (see, e.g., de Grazia, 1945; Easton and Hess, 1960), the idea that a president might draw upon such attachments to serve political ends has scarcely been considered. Such an idea deserves serious consideration, as should be clear from the foregoing. That such an idea is amenable to empirical analysis, possibly along lines followed here, should be just as clear.


## NOTES

Appreciation is expressed to Fred Ribich for his help in the collection of the Iowa data in this study and to George C. Edwards III for his helpful comments on an earlier draft of this paper.

1. Operationally, identification with the president was assessed by Thomas and Baas in the same fashion as here, i.e., as the correlation between respondents' "Q-sort" descriptions of their "ideal-self" and President Carter.

2. Actually, President Reagan *had* gone on record as favoring the tax exemption provision central to the second policy proposal prior to our survey. However, this position was not very widely advertised; nor was it framed in the context of an amendment to the "Family Protection Act of 1891." For earlier split-ballot studies of presidential opinion leadership, see Rosen (1973) and Sigelman and Sigelman (1981).

3. Conceivably, the unfavorable evaluation accorded the proposals by the Reagan-identified in the No Attribution condition could be explained by the "liberal" content of the proposals. Such a case would appear to be on its strongest footing in connection with the guaranteed income proposal. Favorable ratings of this proposal—both in this study and in a previous one (Sigelman and Sigelman, 1981)—correlate inversely with conservatism, thus raising the possibility that the ideological content of this item accounts for its antagonistic reception by Reaganites. Reactions to the other two policy items are less easily explained in these terms, since overall ratings of both are uncorrelated with ideology. The content of the military aid item could nevertheless be interpreted in "dovish" terms and so could pose a conflict for those of Reagan's constituents concerned about the Soviet threat and supportive of bolstered military commitments to counter it. The family protection proposal, though, represents a policy position actually endorsed by Reagan. Yet, as indicated, ratings of this item are unrelated to conservative self-identification. Moreover, it is more generally true that liberalism-conservatism is simply inadequate as a counterexplanation for this curious pattern of results.


## REFERENCES

Aldrich, John H.; Richard N. Niemi; George Rabinowitz; and David W. Rohde. 1982. The measurement of public opinion about public policy: A report on some new issue question formats. *American Journal of Political Science* 26:391–414.

Anderson, Norman. 1968. Likeableness ratings of 555 personality-trait words. *Journal of Personality and Social Psychology* 9:272–79.

Brown, Steven R. 1980. *Political Subjectivity: Applications of Q Methodology in Political Science*. New Haven: Yale University Press.

De Grazia, Sebastian. 1945. A note on the psychological position of the Chief Executive. *Psychiatry* 8:262–72.

Easton, David, and Robert Haas. 1960. The child's changing image of the president. *Public Opinion Quarterly* 22: 632–44.

Edwards, George C., III. 1980. *Presidential Influence in Congress*. San Francisco: W. H. Freeman.

———. 1983. *The Public Presidency*. New York: St. Martin's.

Freud, Sigmund. 1922. *Group Psychology and the Analysis of the Ego*. London and Vienna: International Psychoanalytic Press.

Greenberg, B., and E. Parker, eds. 1965. *The Kennedy Assassination and the American Public*. Palo Alto: Stanford University Press.

Greenstein, Fred. 1968. Private disorder and the public order: A proposal for collaboration between psychoanalysts and political scientists. *Psychoanalytic Quarterly* 32:261–81.

Hollander, Edwin P., and James W. Julian. 1969. Contemporary trends in the analysis of leadership processes. *Psychological Bulletin* 71:387–97.

Lowery, David, and Lee Sigelman. 1981. Understanding the tax revolt: Eight explanations. *American Political Science Review* 75:963–74.

Neustadt, Richard. 1960. *Presidential Power*. New York: Wiley.

Page, B., and R. Brody. 1972. Policy voting and the electoral process: The Vietnam War issue. *American Political Science Review* 66:979–95.

Pedhazur, Elazar J. 1982. *Multiple Regression in Behavioral Research: Explanation and Prediction*. 2d. ed. New York: Holt, Rinehart and Winston.

Rosen, Corey M. 1973. A test of presidential leadership of public opinion: The split ballot technique. *Public Opinion Quarterly* 6:282–90.

Sears, David O. 1978. The Jarvis Amendment: Self-interest or symbolic politics? Department of Psychology, University of California, Los Angeles.

Sigelman, Lee, and Carol Sigelman. 1981. Presidential leadership of public opinion: From "belevolent leader" to "kiss of death"? *Experimental Study of Politics* 7:1–22.

Stephenson, William. 1953. *The Study of Behavior: Q Technique and Its Methodology*. Chicago: University of Chicago Press.

Thomas, Dan B., and Larry R. Baas. 1982. Presidential identification and mass-public compliance with official policy: The case of the Carter energy program. *Policy Studies Journal* 10:448–64.

Wolfenstein, M., and G. Kliman, eds. 1965. *Children and the Death of a President*. New York: Doubleday.

Dennis M. Simon and Charles W. Ostrom, Jr.

# The President and Public Support: A Strategic Perspective

In 1981, as Ronald Reagan was being inaugurated as the fortieth president of the United States, there was widespread speculation that the presidency was squarely in the middle of a crisis. In Light's (1982) terminology, the institution was in a "no win" predicament. The primary reason for this state of affairs is related to the president's resource base or power situation. According to Light, the "cycle of declining resources" which confronts all occupants of the Oval Office means that a president's influence over government policy making will erode over the course of his term in office. As his resources decline, the image of the president is transformed from imperial to impotent.

One manifestation of this decline in resources can be seen by examining the president's popular support. The initial time path of Ronald Reagan's popularity resembled that of previous presidents who were consumed by the so-called crisis. His initial approval rate of 51 percent was the lowest starting level in the history of the Gallup Poll.[1] Although his popularity rose during the early part of 1981, it dropped below 50 percent earlier in the term than any other previous president's. During Reagan's second year in office, his popular support eroded further, ending the year at 41 percent. In January 1983, it sank to 35 percent. Not only is this the earliest that any president fell below the 40 percent level, but many pundits argued that such ratings were symptomatic of another "no win" administration. From that point, however, the president's support increased steadily so that by January 1984, it was 57 percent—an impressive twenty-two point rise over the course of the third year. Excepting Eisenhower, this is the highest level of support enjoyed by any president at the beginning of the fourth year in office. Furthermore, it represents the first time in the history of the Gallup poll that a president has fallen below 40 percent and risen to sustain a level above 50 percent.

In a political sense, the time path of Reagan's public support is close to optimal. It provided him with the capital needed to pass the fundamental items on his agenda—the tax and budget cuts of 1981. He also managed to recover lost support and replenish his resources just as the 1984 election campaign began. Since this pattern stands in marked contrast to the experience of recent presidents, Reagan's first three years in office raise a number of important questions. Is the path a historical accident? Is it possible for a president to manage support so that it is high at politically opportune times? Does the Reagan recovery signal an end to the crisis?

We will address these questions by focusing first on the general relationship between the president and public support. This segment of the analysis is designed to consider several issues pertaining to the dynamics of public support and the crisis of the modern presidency. Second, the discussion will consider the general prospects for escaping the dilemmas of presidential government. Finally, we will return to the case of Reagan and offer an explanation for his "recovery" of public support.

## Research on the Modern Presidency

In recent years there has arisen a substantial new literature on the American presidency. This research includes empirical analyses of popular support for presidents (e.g., Hibbs, 1982a, 1982b; MacKuen, 1983), program initiation in the executive branch (e.g., Light, 1982), and the determinants of the president's legislative success (e.g., Edwards, 1980). Additionally, increasing attention has been directed to questions of how presidents can cope with the constraints imposed on the office. The results are several works which examine presidential leadership of public opinion (e.g., Edwards, 1983), approaches to bureaucratic control (e.g., Nathan, 1983), and strategies for handling the seemingly contradictory roles of the office (e.g., Greenstein, 1982). Finally, the new literature also consists of evaluative and normative analyses of the problems and failures experienced by modern or postwar presidents (e.g., Hodgson, 1980; Cronin, 1980).

Although some tangential connections have been drawn among these studies, research on the presidency has, for the most part, proceeded independently within the substantive categories of public opinion, legislative relations, policy making, and normative assessment. As such, there have been few attempts to combine these substantive concerns into a single research agenda or design. The absence of such connections need not be the case, and for this reason it serves as the rationale for this discussion. To elaborate, the topics that constitute the foci of recent research, as we shall argue, share one important commonality—a relationship to presidential decision making. For example, program initiation and legislative outcomes can be characterized as results that are related, either directly or indirectly, to the choices made by presidents; similarly, the commonly acknowledged constraints on the office as well as public opinion represent factors that can be expected to impinge on the choices made by presidents. Despite such connections, systematic and empirically testable explanations of presidential decision making continue to be a neglected concern in the research agenda on the presidency.

One purpose of this essay is to sketch such an agenda. The analysis that we present is an outgrowth of our prior research on public support for American presidents and our current work on presidential decision making (Ostrom and Simon, 1984, 1983). As such, this paper serves as both a conclusion and a preface. Our public opinion research essentially supports and expands the conventional wisdom (Kernell, 1978) which asserts that evaluations of presidential performance are determined by the quality of economic, social, and international outcomes experienced by the public. Accordingly, this discussion attempts to draw some conclusions about presidential decision making on the basis of this "outcomes-to-approval" relationship. One conclusion pertains to the determinants of presidential choices. If, as some prior research suggests, public support is valued by the president, then we can expect it will influence presidential decision making. Our initial investigations of this proposition demonstrate that public support exerts a significant impact on the use of force in the international arena (Ostrom and Job, 1982) and the exercise of the veto (Rohde and Simon, 1983). Such results suggest an "approval-to-outcomes" connection in the sense that presidential efforts to influence outcomes will depend on the level of public support. Thus, the possibility of a reciprocal relationship between outcomes and approval arises.

This essay has four objectives. The first is to present a coherent scheme for studying the relationships among presidential decision making, public support for the president, and the character of policy outcomes. Second, the discussion is designed to develop the proposition that there is a dynamic, reciprocal relationship between presidential decision making and public support for the president. Our third objective is to examine the consequences of this reciprocal relationship. The discussion will suggest that this relationship can generate "vicious circles" of declining public support and presidential influence that affect both the character of public policy and the ability of the president to survive politically. As a result, the analysis also provides a basis for evaluating claims regarding the inevitable plight and failures of modern presidents. Finally, we also present evidence from the Reagan administration to show that the so-called dilemmas of presidential government can be overcome and that the vicious circle of eroding support and influence can be broken.

## The Growing Prominence of Public Support

The relationship between public support and the power of the president is both substantial and intriguing. In *Presidential Power,* a widely acclaimed analysis published in 1960, Richard Neustadt observed that the power of a president is largely determined by his ability to persuade. This power, he argued, cannot be equated with the image of unlimited authority conveyed in textbook descriptions of the office. It is not constant during the tenure of a single president or for different presidents. Rather, the power to persuade depends upon the president's ability to acquire and exploit three resources: constitutional and statutory prerogatives, a favorable reputation among Washington decision makers, and public support.

Although public support was only one of three, approximately coequal determinants of presidential power in Neustadt's original characterization, the political landscape has changed in the years since his study was originally published. Since that time the prominence of public support has been enhanced for several reasons. First, the president's prerogatives—the authority to act unilaterally—have been narrowed by a reassertive Congress (e.g., Sundquist, 1981). Second, the value of the political party, both as an organization useful to the president and as a "tie that binds" decision makers to presidential goals, has declined, further depleting the president's resources. Finally, because the public has grown increasingly distrustful of government and politicians (Abramson, 1983; Miller, 1974), political experience seems to have become more of a liability than an asset in election campaigns. As the election of both Jimmy Carter and Ronald Reagan suggest, the image of an "outsider" to Washington and the rhetoric of antigovernment appear to be the more electorally profitable strategies. Yet such strategies also make it more difficult to cultivate a favorable reputation among those in Washington who will ultimately be the targets of the president's persuasive efforts. In sum, presidents now enter office with fewer prerogatives, derive less value from the political party, and are confronted by an increasingly skeptical Washington establishment. As a consequence, the president is forced to rely on popular support, and this, in turn, has enhanced its prominence as a determinant of presidential power.

The growing relationship between presidential power and public opinion is not solely due to the structural changes in American government since the original publication of Neustadt's work. The behavior of modern presidents is now subjected to closer scrutiny as well. It is continuously monitored, analyzed, and broadcast to a public that has come to rely on television as the major source of information about politics and government. In effect, the president serves as the focal point of television news coverage. While television transmits information, polling organizations measure public reaction to this information, particularly via the presidential approval question. The approval or performance rating of the president has itself become a regular feature in newspaper headlines and network news broadcasts.[2] Together, television and public opinion polling have narrowed the gulf between the president and the public.

## The Value of Public Support

Although it is clear that the president's public standing has grown more newsworthy during the past thirty years, the significance of these performance evaluations remains subject to debate. For example, in his analysis of the modern presidency, Pious (1979, p. 16) argues that factors such as the president's public standing exert, at best, a marginal impact on presidential power. Further, there are those who regard such performance evaluations with outright skepticism. Roll and Cantril (1972, p. 129) have argued that "popularity ratings represent little more than an artifact of the polling technique created in response to journalistic interest, and they certainly are not meaningful for guidance at the presidential level." Essentially, such observations assert that aside from the journalistic curiosity that the polls stimulate, public evaluations of presidential performance have little political consequence. This implies that the potential significance of public support is tied to its value as a determinant of political outcomes and behaviors. If public support is unimportant in explaining outcomes, then, as Roll and Cantril suggest, presidents could be advised to ignore the polls and scholars encouraged to direct their attention elsewhere. However, such is not the case.

A variety of empirical research shows that public support exerts an impact on the following outcomes: (1) congressional elections (e.g., Tufte, 1978); (2) presidential elections (e.g., Abramson, Aldrich, and Rohde, 1982); (3) roll-call support among members of Congress (e.g., Edwards, 1980); (4) presidential victories on congressional roll calls (e.g., Simon, 1981); (5) citizen assessments of congressional performance (e.g., Parker, 1977); (6) citizen confidence in the institution of the presidency (e.g., Dennis, 1975); and (7) citizen trust in government (e.g., Miller, Brudney, and Joftis, 1975). Although assessments of a president's performance are not the sole determinants of such attitudes or behaviors, it is clear that evaluations of the president's performance are valuable and thus instrumental to successful presidential decision making. This suggests that the pattern of public support over time will exercise a noteworthy influence on the fortunes of an administration.

## Trends in Popular Support

The enhanced status of presidential popularity has been marked by a strong downward trend in monthly support. Table 1 shows that there are substantial differences in the mean levels of public support for each president from 1953 to 1980. Whereas both Eisenhower and Kennedy enjoyed popularity levels in excess of 65 percent, subsequent presidents have not fared as well. In fact, when one looks at the overall picture, there is a marked downward trend in average approval from term to term during the 1953–1980 period. Table 1 also suggests that there have been two major eras in public support for the president. From 1953 to 1963 the average level of popular support was 66.5 percent and the standard deviation was very small. During this eleven-year period, popularity dipped below 50 percent only once. From 1964 to 1980 the picture is much different. The average level of public support was barely 50 percent. Thus, presidents since Kennedy have inherited the problems of their predecessors and faced new problems that developed with a reduced amount of their most apparent resource—public support.

There is also a marked popularity trend within each presidential term. Table 2 displays the mean annual approval scores for presidents Eisenhower through Carter. The pattern of decline over the course of each term is unmistakeable. The data show that with the exception of the Eisenhower terms, approval regularly declines during the first three years in office. While the fourth year may be accompanied by a slight upturn in approval, the prestige lost over the first three years is never recovered. In only one instance, the Eisenhower first term, is the mean level of public support in year 4 greater than year 1.

Note as well that the decline to low levels of support has grown more precipitous over time. To identify these low levels, we have divided the president's approval ratings into three popularity zones (see note to table 2). Table 2 also presents the number of months that each president occupied each of these zones. Between 1953 and 1963, approval never dropped into zone 3. In fact, there are only eight months during this period in which approval was lower than 55 percent. Beginning with Johnson's full term, however, every president has fallen into zone 3 at some time during their administration. Most significantly, the table shows that the drop into zone 3 is not a momentary phenomenon. President Carter, for example, spent over half of his four-year term with an approval rating less than 45 percent.

TABLE 1
Levels of Presidential Approval, 1953–1980

|  | Mean Approval | St. Dev. Approval | High | Low |
|---|---|---|---|---|
| Eisenhower | 65.2% | 7.0 | 79% | 49% |
| Kennedy | 70.3 | 7.2 | 83 | 57 |
| Johnson | 55.6 | 13.4 | 80 | 35 |
| Nixon | 50.8 | 12.1 | 68 | 24 |
| Ford | 47.5 | 6.5 | 71 | 37 |
| Carter | 46.3 | 12.4 | 75 | 21 |
| 1953–1963 | 66.5% | 7.4 | 83% | 49% |
| 1964–1980 | 50.7 | 12.4 | 80 | 21 |
| 1953–1980 | 56.3 | 12.7 | 83 | 21 |

TABLE 2
Within-Term Levels of Presidential Approval

| President | Year | | | | Time in Zone | | |
|---|---|---|---|---|---|---|---|
| | 1 | 2 | 3 | 4 | 1 | 2 | 3 |
| Eisenhower (1) | 69.3% | 65.4% | 71.3% | 73.3% | 100% | 0% | 0% |
| Eisenhower (2) | 65.0 | 54.6 | 63.3 | 61.1 | 83 | 17 | 0 |
| Kennedy | 76.0 | 71.6 | 63.5 | — | 100 | 0 | 0 |
| Johnson | 66.4 | 51.2 | 44.0 | 41.5 | 31 | 34 | 35 |
| Nixon (1) | 61.4 | 56.9 | 49.9 | 56.4 | 60 | 40 | 0 |
| Nixon (2) | 41.8 | 25.9 | — | — | 16 | 5 | 79 |
| Ford | — | 53.9 | 43.1 | 48.9 | 7 | 69 | 24 |
| Carter | 62.4 | 45.5 | 38.1 | 39.5 | 27 | 19 | 54 |

Note: In defining the three zones, the 50 percent approval level is emphasized because it represents the point at which the president either gains or loses "majority support" in the public. Thus, we have stipulated that the president is in zone 1 whenever his popularity is over 55 percent, in zone 2 whenever his popularity is between 45 percent and 55 percent, and in zone 3 whenever his popularity is below 45 percent. Although arbitrary, these categories do provide a meaningful categorization of the president's power situation. A president whose popularity is greater than 55 percent is clearly a "majority" president. Similarly, an approval level below 45 percent is symptomatic of a "minority" president. Finally, a president whose popularity hovers around 50 percent is on the verge of becoming a "minority" president. Furthermore, it is an open question as to whether his support will decline to even lower levels.

These low levels of support appear to imprison the president as well. Table 3 provides a comparison of month-to-month changes in approval for 1953–1980. An examination of the diagonal entries suggests that there is a great deal of stability. When a president is in zone 1 at time T, the probability of remaining there at time T+1 is .92; for zone 2, this probability is .72; and for zone 3, this probability is .89. Of particular interest is the fact that, once in zone 2, the president has an equal, though small, probability of moving to either zone 1 or zone 3. However, once a president enters zone 3, there is very little chance of escaping. Thus, not only is there a between- and within-term trend in public support, but once a president enters a lower zone, there is a very small chance of moving back into a higher zone. This presidential track record clearly supports Greenstein's (1982, p. 3) observation that "the American Presidency has become conspicuously problematic, devouring its incumbents with appalling regularity." Given these trends and the accompanying conclusions about a 'throwaway" or "no win" presidency, it is important to determine whether the decline in support is inevitable and whether, once in popularity zone 3, the president is trapped.

## The Determinants of Popular Support

To address the issues of inevitability and impossibility, it is necessary to answer three questions: (1) What *standards* are employed to evaluate presidential performance? (2) What is the *relative importance* of these standards? (3) What specific *outcomes and conditions* are associated with these standards?

Although the recent literature that offers comprehensive explanations of popular support (e.g., Kernell, 1978; Hibbs, 1982a, 1982b; MacKuen, 1983) has addressed these concerns, the generality of the answers must be questioned because the research has had a difficult time with the Eisenhower administration. Either the models cannot explain his consistently high level of popularity (e.g., Kernell, 1978) or his terms in office have been omitted from the analysis (e.g., Hibbs, 1982a, 1982b; MacKuen, 1983). The strategy of omission presents a number of problems. First, Eisenhower was the last president to serve two complete terms and emerge with his public standing intact. Second, he faced a war, a scandal, and a significant economic downturn without suffering the staggering declines in popularity that have beset subsequent presidents. In short, he was the quintessential popularity manager. Just as surely as we must account for the future, we must be able to explain the past.

The first question focuses on the standards or dimensions of presidential evaluation. Two basic types of standards are discussed in the literature. First, there is general agreement that the public holds the president responsible for

TABLE 3
Month-to-month Comparison in Popularity Zones, 1953–1980

|         |        | Month T + 1 | | |
|---------|--------|--------|--------|--------|
|         |        | Zone 1 | Zone 2 | Zone 3 |
|         | Zone 1 | 181    | 15     | 0      |
|         |        | (.92)  | (.08)  | (.0)   |
| Month T | Zone 2 | 10     | 52     | 10     |
|         |        | (.14)  | (.72)  | (.14)  |
|         | Zone 3 | 1      | 6      | 55     |
|         |        | (.02)  | (.09)  | (.89)  |

*Note:* The results in the table are based upon a crosstabulation between approval zones in month T and month T+1. The figures in parentheses represent the resulting probabilities of remaining or moving out of a particular zone. For example, the Zone 1–Zone 1 cell shows that the probability of being in Zone 1 in month T+1 given that the president was in Zone 1 during month T is .92 (181, the cell frequency, divided by 196, the sum of the row 1 frequencies in the table).

maintaining a reasonable quality of life (Kernell, 1978; Hibbs, 1982a, 1982b). The president, from this point of view, must strive to maintain peace, prosperity, and domestic tranquility. Deviations from these desirable states are viewed as the result of presidential incompetence. Second, both MacKuen (1983) and Brody (1983) suggest that there is an emotional and symbolic component to presidential evaluations as well. From this perspective, the president must act in a dramatic fashion to arouse the public and thereby retain their esteem. This implies that the public judges the president "by his ability to evoke the proper symbolic responses when he acts." Because the dramatic feature of "events on the public stage have a substantial impact on popularity" (MacKuen, 1983, p. 185), each president must engage in "high politics" and cultivate the image of an astute manager of crises and events.

The second question pertains to the relative importance of the evaluative standards over time. The key issue is whether the public evaluates each president according to the same standards. The consensus is that to some extent they do. The research provides this answer in the sense that the models use the same sets of factors to account for the rise and fall in presidential approval. However, existing models also include term-specific factors to account for "constant" differences between administrations. For some reason, there is a different equilibrium level for each president. In addition, some empirical work has estimated different coefficients for each president (Kernell, 1978; Mac-Kuen, 1983).

One possible explanation for the term-to-term differences can be identified by considering the changes in the structure of public priorities over time. To explore this possibility, we have relied on the responses to the following Gallup question: "What do you think is the most important problem facing the country today?" On seventy-nine occasions between 1953 and 1980, this item was administered to national samples. These responses can be employed to measure the relative salience or importance that the public attaches to quality of life concerns such as war, general foreign affairs, social, economic, and other domestic problems. To accomplish this task, we have grouped all relevant responses to the most important problem question into four general categories—the economy, foreign affairs, social unrest, and Vietnam—and calculated the proportion of the public citing each problem in a given poll.

Table 4 presents the average value of each of these proportions for each popularity zone. Perhaps the most interesting finding is that the president is most likely to be in zone 1 when foreign policy is the most important public concern. This category is defined to include those problems in which the themes of preserving peace and harmonious international relations are domi-nant. The most frequently cited examples are the threat of war or nuclear war, relations with the Soviet Union and China, and resisting communist expansion, as well as more specific concerns relating to Berlin and Cuba. The association

TABLE 4
Most Important Problem by Popularity Zone

| Problem | Zone 1 | Zone 2 | Zone 3 |
|---|---|---|---|
| The economy | 20% | 42% | 45% |
| Foreign affairs | 39 | 10 | 5 |
| Social unrest | 16 | 19 | 14 |
| Vietnam war | 7 | 18 | 14 |

of foreign policy and zone 1 stems from the consensual nature of these issues. That is, they resemble valence issues (Stokes, 1966; Page, 1978) in the sense that underlying preferences are nonideological and focus upon conditions that are positively valued by the public. Most importantly, because the idea of an external threat is voiced, a we/they point-of-view prevails and reinforces the consensus. There is a marked contrast in popularity levels when issues of dissensus top the list of public concerns. When such controversial problems as inflation, unemployment, war, or social unrest are dominant, a president will not remain in zone 1. Insofar as these issues are concerned, there is very little difference between zones 2 and 3. Thus, the increased importance of controversial issues appear to be partly responsible for the declines in support documented in table 2.

The third question focuses upon the specific determinants of public support. Despite much disagreement about measurement and the precise specification of the "approval equation," the literature emphasizes that the public standing of the president is experiential and not determined by some mechanistic set of predispositions among the public. The conventional wisdom arising from this research concludes that the following factors can be expected to exert an impact on public support: the economy (inflation, unemployment), war (casualties, troops deployed), and international crises or "rally points." In addition, recent efforts (Ostrom and Simon, 1984; MacKuen, 1983; Brody, 1983) have broadened this conventional wisdom by demonstrating that the president is held accountable for a more extensive set of outcomes (e.g., legislative performance, actions toward the Soviets) and that there exist general classes of approval-enhancing events (e.g., diplomatic initiatives, personal misfortune) and disapproval-enhancing events (e.g., scandals, protest demonstrations, political violence).

Table 5 presents a comparison of the key determinants of public support and the three presidential popularity zones. These data clearly show that each zone is associated with a different configuration of outcomes. On one hand, zone 1 is marked by an aggressive stance toward the Soviet Union and by relatively low levels of inflation, troops in Vietnam, war casualties, and scandal-months. On the other hand, zone 3 is distinguished by a more cooperative tone toward the

TABLE 5
Determinants of Public Support by Popularity Zone
(average monthly values)

| Variable | Zone 1 | Zone 2 | Zone 3 |
|---|---|---|---|
| The economy[a] | | | |
| Unemployment | 5.1% | 5.8% | 4.7% |
| Inflation | 2.5% | 5.3% | 8.2% |
| Vietnam War | | | |
| U.S. troops (in 1000s) | 57 | 149 | 129 |
| U.S. killed (in 1000s) | 7.5 | 18.2 | 26.0 |
| Actions/Rhetoric toward USSR[b] | −7.0 | 1.5 | 1.8 |
| Scandal (months)[c] | .05 | .15 | .26 |
| Events (per month)[d] | | | |
| Foreign | .13 | .11 | .15 |
| Domestic | .06 | .07 | .11 |
| Overall | .19 | 18 | .26 |

a. The economic data was gathered from editions of Business Conditions Digest (Series 43 and 320c for unemployment and inflation). The reader will note that unemployment is not strongly related to popularity zone.

b. The measure of U.S. rhetoric and action toward the Soviet Union is based upon an updated version of dyadic conflict data from COPDAB (Azar, 1978) and the weighting scheme developed by Azar and Havener (1976). These data were then used to calculate a monthly measure of U.S. action. As constructed, negative (positive) values denote aggressive (cooperative) actions with the magnitude conveyed by the absolute value of the measure.

c. Scandals include: Sherman Adams (2/58–12/58); Walter Jenkins (10/64); Watergate (3/73–8/74); Bert Lance (7/77–1/78); Peter Bourne (8/78); Billy Carter (7/80).

d. The events data represent an expanded version of the events listed in table 1 of MacKuen (1983). Although the selection of appropriate events and the assessment of their impact on public support remains a subject of debate (e.g., Edwards, 1983), MacKuen's list is the most comprehensive published to date. We examined this list and selected those events that directly involved the president. That is, we identified those events that would not have occurred without an intentional action on the part of the president. To this list we added similar events for the Eisenhower and Kennedy years.

Soviets and by relatively high levels of inflation, casualties, and scandal-months. Thus, rather distinct quality of life profiles accompany movement from zone 1 to zone 3. An examination of the set of presidential rally-type events reveals that there is only a moderate relationship between the frequency of the events and the popularity zones.

The results presented in tables 4 and 5 suggest that the decline in the time path of public support both between and within terms is not governed by some repeatable and unalterable dynamic. Instead, it has an experiential base comprised of both outcomes and public concerns. Thus, the results lead to the general conclusion that the impact of any performance dimension on popular support is *jointly dependent* upon the *quality* of an outcome and the *perceived salience* of the dimension to which the outcome pertains. This implies that, in principle, entrapment in zone 3 is not an inevitable result of modern presidential government.

Additionally, these results lead to a plausible explanation for the difference between the support levels in the 1953–1963 and 1964–1980 periods. Table 6 illustrates that the extraordinarily high levels of support enjoyed by Eisenhower and Kennedy can be attributed to four factors. The first is the dominance of consensual foreign policy issues from 1953 to 1963. The attention of the public during this period focused on problems involving the Soviet Union and the Cold War. This configuration of public concerns was highly beneficial to Eisenhower and Kennedy for it not only diverted attention from divisive domestic problems (an average value of 28.2 percent), but it also enhanced the visibility and value of presidential actions in the international arena. In the 1964–1980 period, public attention shifted from foreign policy to a more divisive set of concerns. In rather rapid succession, the public endured a prolonged and indecisive war, a scandal of unprecedented magnitude, and a period of substantial economic problems. The overlap of war, scandal, and economic distress essentially dissolved the favorable context in which Eisenhower and Kennedy operated.

Second, the actions and rhetoric that the Eisenhower and Kennedy adminis-

TABLE 6
Two Eras of Public Spport: A Comparison

| Measure | 1953–1963 | 1964–1980 |
| --- | --- | --- |
| Public concern with consensual foreign policy issues | 50.3% | 10.4% |
| Public concern with divisive foreign and domestic issues | 28.2% | 82.1% |
| U.S. actions/rhetoric toward the USSR | −9.0 | 0.1 |
| Ratio of approval-enhancing to disapproval-enhancing events[a] | 1.67 | 0.67 |
| Level of external political efficacy | 59.3% | 38.6% |

a. The events ratio was calculated by dividing the number of approval-enhancing events (crises, diplomatic initiatives, personal misfortune) by the number of disapproval-enhancing events (e.g., domestic protest and violence, scandals, controversial policy decisions). These general types of events are discussed more fully in Ostrom and Simon (1984).

trations directed toward the Soviet Union were, particularly when compared to the 1964–1980 period, primarily conflictual in nature. This aggressive stance reinforced the prevailing structure of public concerns and increased public support for both presidents (Ostrom and Simon, 1984). Third, both presidents were the beneficiaries of the rally effect generated by approval-enhancing events. Crises, diplomatic activities, and personal events were relatively more frequent during this period and, as the "events ratio" displayed in table 6 shows, the net impact of events was positive in nature.

Finally, the period from 1953 to 1963 is distinguished by relatively high levels of external political efficacy.[3] As several studies (e.g., Miller, 1974; Abramson, 1983) of the 1964–1980 period have shown, the dissatisfaction generated by Vietnam, Watergate, and a stagnant economy was generalized and led to erosion of such long-term attitudes as political efficacy and trust in government. As a result, the presidents who served during this period were evaluated by a constituency that was substantially more cynical and less naive than the public faced by Eisenhower and Kennedy.

The comparison of these periods shows that the erosion of support experienced by Johnson, Nixon, Ford, and Carter was a product of the interaction between the generally unsatisfactory outcomes experienced by the public and the structure of public concerns. Similarly, the Eisenhower and Kennedy popularity levels are not, as some analysts suggest, anomalies but a result of a relatively efficacious public primarily concerned with foreign policy issues, presidential behavior that reinforced these priorities, and the frequent occurrence of approval-enhancing events. The comparison of these eras suggests then that presidents can formulate strategies for avoiding or escaping from zone 3.

## Presidential Decision Making

For the president seeking to avoid a decline or to move out of zone 3, there are essentially three available courses of action. First, he can try to alter the standards used to judge his performance. This approach is likely to be difficult because the bases of evaluations have remained fairly constant throughout the past thirty years. An examination of responses to Gallup's most important problem item reveals that the issues of peace, prosperity, and domestic tranquility have dominated the public agenda during the 1953–1980 period. Indeed, as we have argued elsewhere (Ostrom and Simon, 1984), these three major problems constitute a set of fundamental demands upon which presidential performance is judged. Therefore, as a management strategy this approach is not likely to be successful.

Second, the results in table 4 have important implications for managing popular support: a president can try to change the salience of the evaluative dimensions. This is potentially effective because the relationship between public support and a given performance dimension is relative. For example, the impact of the economy on public support will depend not only on the quality of economic outcomes but also upon the perceived importance of competing problems such as international or domestic stability (Ostrom and Simon, 1984). The fact that public concern focused on consensual issues throughout the 1950s explains why the recession of 1958 cost Eisenhower significantly fewer approval points than the penalty imposed on Nixon during the early 1970s when public priorities were more concentrated on the economy. Similarly, the value of the relatively prosperous economy of 1965–1967 to President Johnson was negated as public attention increasingly focused on the Vietnam war. Perhaps the most overt use of this strategy occurred when Nixon directed the public's concern away from the Vietnam war to social problems. Although he was not totally successful, the war exacted a smaller toll on Nixon's public standing and allowed him to escape the fate experienced by Johnson (Ostrom and Simon, 1984). Even though altering the salience of performance standards is possible, it involves diverting attention and convincing the public that other problems are more pressing. Unless the new problem is consensual in nature or can be solved in short order, the shift will have, at best, a minimal impact on public support.

The final, and most accessible, strategy option available to the president is to take actions that will bring about an acceptable quality of life by influencing outcomes or focusing attention on the political stage. There are two considerations that will have an impact on the president's choice of strategy in this context. First, he will be concerned with the *probability of success*. Given the persistence of the problems associated with quality of life concerns, it seems clear that innovative, comprehensive, and coordinated government action will be required. According to Pious (1979, pp. 150–55), for example, innovation may assume one of two forms. It may substantially expand the scope of government authority, creating new agencies, missions, and operating procedures. Innovation may also operate in the opposite direction by retracting government authority through retrenchment and program dissolution. Both forms of innovation share the commonality of significantly altering the status quo. A comprehensive policy is oriented toward the long run, addresses all dimensions of a problem, and employs a variety of mechanisms in an effort to achieve an enduring solution. Finally, a coordinated policy is one that overcomes the jurisdictional rivalries inherent in the congressional committee system and the administrative conflicts in the executive branch. From the president's perspective, the problem of producing innovative, comprehensive, and coordinated policy clearly depends upon his ability to influence those individuals who share decision making authority in various substantive domains. As research on presidential policy making reveals (e.g., Light, 1982; Fishel, 1979), this task requires substantial capital and is complex, both technically and politically. Thus, there is no guarantee of success.

The probability of success associated with acting on the political stage is substantially greater. All a president needs to do is to find an appropriate stage; he can amplify a crisis, deliver a televised speech, or take a trip. The probability of success is enhanced because the president is able to act unilaterally. There are few constraints on the rhetorical and symbolic levers at his disposal. In this way, a president, through his command role, can take actions that may only be tangentially related to quality of life concerns and be evaluated positively. All that is required is an independent presidential action and the publicity that it generates. As such, success is very likely.

The second consideration is the *nature of the benefits* to be derived from a given strategy. If a president is able to bring about the intended changes in the quality of life, the political benefits are likely to be substantial. If an improved quality of life persists, the benefits will endure. Furthermore, this positive impact will be enhanced over time because of the retrospective character of citizen evaluations (e.g., Hibbs, 1982a). A president's popular support is affected by both past and current conditions.

Actions on the stage of high politics are likely to generate more immediate though transitory benefits. Because such behavior has a consistent, albeit short-lived, impact on presidential popularity, it becomes an attractive alternative for a president looking to enhance his standing with the public.

Therefore, attempts to manage public support can take one of two forms: attempt to influence outcomes and the quality of life or engage in some form of political drama. The probability of success and the benefits vary considerably. The presidential decision calculus involves choosing between two strategies. One strategy, directly attacking the quality of life problem, has a lower probability of success and a higher potential pay-off. The other strategy, acting on the political stage, has a higher probability of success and a lower potential pay-off. It would appear that, from an expected value point of view, the benefits that follow from a quality of life strategy will offset the lower probability of success and make it the obvious presidential choice. However, this characterization of a presidential management calculus overlooks one very important factor—the significance of public support.

As Neustadt (1960, pp. 92–93) notes, any chance of influencing the policy making process and coordinating government action lies in maintaining a high level of public support. "A President's prestige . . . may not decide the outcome in a given case but can affect the likelihoods in every case and therefore is strategically important to his power. If he cares about his prospects for effectiveness in government, he need be no less mindful of the one than the other." Declining approval, therefore, translates into a declining probability of success for subsequent presidential efforts to influence government action. As such, the public standing of the president will exert an impact on which policy choices are made (Light, 1982). This, in turn, implies that presidential support and presidential policy making are *reciprocally* related. On one hand, presidential policy making will influence public support to the extent that the choices of the president (1) influence the outcomes for which the president is held responsible or (2) are dramatic enough to trigger the "rally" effect. On the other hand, because public support determines the president's ability to influence other actors and thus the probability that a given initiative will be successful, public support will determine both the range and feasibility of the choices available to the president. All in all, this reciprocal relationship creates a decidedly political context for presidential government.

We have shown (Ostrom and Simon, 1983) that this reciprocal relationship can generate a vicious circle that undermines successful policy making. For example, the relative influence of Congress and the president on the content of public policy will vary as approval moves from zone 1 to zone 3. It is likely, therefore, that policy making will grow more incremental and uncoordinated as approval declines. This, in turn, reduces the prospect that durable solutions for existing problems will be constructed and implemented. Consequently, popular support will continue to decline. This vicious circle not only undermines the effectiveness of the president as a policy maker but also threatens his ability to survive politically.

This reciprocal relationship and the vicious circle that it produces are at least partially responsible for the observation in recent scholarship on the presidency that the office has been in a period of crisis since the late 1960s. It is a crisis whose consequences include uncoordinated policy making, institutional deadlock, nondecisions, and increasing reliance on dramatic political events (e.g., Hodgson, 1980; Light, 1982). It is not coincidental that recognition of these problems by presidential scholars and the development of vicious circles in public support have arisen at roughly the same time.

To avoid entrapment in zone 3, a president can essentially choose between a long-term strategy (improve the quality of outcomes) or a short-term strategy (engage in high politics). The president faces a dilemma in this choice, however. The long-term approach will direct the president's actions and energies toward the solution of principal problems of the day. This approach requires substantial capital. If approval declines, the policies directed at quality of life concerns are not likely to yield comprehensive and innovative solutions but instead are likely to be incremental modifications of existing programs or piecemeal attempts to solve broad-based problems. To the extent that such attempts fail to solve problems, the president's resource reservoir will become increasingly shallow as the vicious circle begins to undermine his influence on the policy process. This explains the attractiveness of the short-term approach. The president is relatively unconstrained in relying upon political drama and will welcome the bursts in support which actions on the political stage trigger. However, the impact of such actions are short-lived and, by themselves, can do little but provide bumps and wiggles on the downward course of approval. Therein lies the dilemma.

The prospects for avoiding such a state of affairs are not encouraging. What is required is a comprehensive strategy for avoiding the problems associated with zone 3. There are several premises upon which such a strategy must be constructed. First, it must be realized that continuous scrutiny and evaluation of presidential performance is an integral and inescapable part of modern presidential government. Second, the major result of this scrutiny—the level of public support—is a key presidential resource. Its impact is felt throughout the term and it is the sine qua non of effective presidential government. Third, the protection of this resource must be recognized as a critical instrumental goal in the president's strategic calculations. There are times when a president must adopt a pure short-term, resource enhancement strategy to accumulate the capital necessary to maintain influence over the policy-making process. Thus, political drama is a method that can provide the increases in support needed to replenish presidential influence and avoid the ravages of zone 3. Fourth, reliance on political drama is not a solution in itself. It can be used to create "windows of opportunity" and leverage for the passage of policies designed to have a long-term impact. Because the president is ultimately held responsible for outcomes, however, exclusive reliance on a short-term strategy offers few prospects for success.

The president must, therefore, develop a coherent mix of long and short-term strategies. Because of their inherent controversy and the resource demands placed on the president, attacks on fundamental problems must be limited in number, cautiously chosen, and well-timed. Political drama then serves as a useful device for providing needed bursts of support, articulating priorities, and focusing or diverting public attention. Although difficult and not without distasteful implications, it is possible for a president to avoid the vicious circle; he will remain in zone 1 or 2 only if he is able to fashion his choices in a manner that influences the standards on which he is judged, the relative salience of these performance dimensions, and the outcomes connected to those standards.

## The Reagan Presidency: Escape from Zone 3

At the outset of this discussion, we observed that public support for President Reagan from 1981 to 1983 was, in a comparative sense, highly unusual. Table 7 displays the Reagan approval ratings along with a listing of several measures and events identified in our analysis as important determinants of public support. During 1981 and 1982, support for the president followed the expected pattern of decline, albeit more rapidly than the erosion experienced by Reagan's predecessors. Support for Reagan in 1983 was even more atypical. The decline was arrested and zone 3 escaped as public support rose from 35 percent in January to 55 percent in December.

There are several factors that can be used to explain this recovery. The first is an improved economy. As table 7 shows, the quality of economic outcomes were mixed during the first two years of the administration. The inflation rate peaked at 10.6 percent in June 1981 but thereafter declined in dramatic fashion

TABLE 7
Public Support and the Reagan Presidency: A Summary

| Date | Approval | Unemployment Rate (monthly) | Inflation Rate (monthly) | Economy Most Important | Foreign Most Important | Event |
|------|----------|------------|------------|-----------|-----------|-------|
| 1/81 | 51.0% | 7.5% | 9.9% | 64% | 8% | |
| 2/81 | 53.0 | 7.4 | 9.6 | 81 | 5 | |
| 3/81 | 60.0 | 7.3 | 9.1 | | | |
| 4/81 | 67.0 | 7.2 | 10.0 | | | Assassination attempt |
| 5/81 | 68.0 | 7.5 | 10.1 | 74 | 10 | |
| 6/81 | 58.7 | 7.4 | 10.6 | | | |
| 7/81 | 58.7 | 7.2 | 10.5 | | | |
| 8/81 | 60.0 | 7.4 | 9.6 | | | |
| 9/81 | 52.0 | 7.6 | 8.8 | | | |
| 10/81 | 54.5 | 8.0 | 6.9 | 71 | 11 | Libyan Air skirmish |
| 11/81 | 52.0 | 8.3 | 5.3 | | | |
| 12/81 | 49.0 | 8.6 | 3.1 | | | Richard Allen scandal |
| 1/82 | 48.0 | 8.6 | 3.1 | 77 | 11 | |
| 2/82 | 47.0 | 8.8 | 4.0 | | | |
| 3/82 | 46.0 | 9.0 | 5.5 | | | |
| 4/82 | 44.0 | 9.3 | 6.1 | 68 | 11 | |
| 5/82 | 44.5 | 9.4 | 6.6 | | | |
| 6/82 | 44.5 | 9.5 | 6.9 | 64 | 13 | Reagan tours Europe |
| 7/82 | 41.5 | 9.8 | 7.2 | | | |
| 8/82 | 41.3 | 9.9 | 5.1 | 68 | 10 | |
| 9/82 | 42.0 | 10.2 | 2.3 | | | |
| 10/82 | 42.0 | 10.5 | 1.4 | 79 | 6 | |
| 11/82 | 43.0 | 10.7 | 0.4 | | | |
| 12/82 | 41.0 | 10.8 | 0.5 | | | |
| 1/83 | 35.0 | 10.4 | 0.8 | | | |
| 2/83 | 40.0 | 10.4 | 1.9 | | | |
| 3/83 | 41.0 | 10.3 | 2.9 | | | |
| 4/83 | 42.0 | 10.2 | 3.4 | 71 | 16 | |
| 5/83 | 44.0 | 10.1 | 4.7 | | | |
| 6/83 | 45.0 | 10.0 | 5.4 | | | |
| 7/83 | 43.0 | 9.5 | 4.8 | | | |
| 8/83 | 43.5 | 9.5 | 4.8 | | | |
| 9/83 | 47.5 | 9.3 | 6.0 | 64 | 23 | Lebanon/KAL 007 |
| 10/83 | 45.0 | 8.7 | 4.8 | | | |
| 11/83 | 53.0 | 8.4 | 3.6 | 44 | 37 | Lebanon/Grenada |
| 12/83 | 55.0 | 8.2 | 3.6 | | | |

to an annual rate of less than 1 percent at the end of 1982. The political benefits stemming from the reduction of inflation were offset, however, by the rise in unemployment; the jobless rate increased from 7.2 percent in April 1981 to 10.8 percent in December 1982. The economic track record in 1983 was not as ambiguous. Inflation held steady in the 4 to 5 percent range while unemployment dropped from its high of 10.8 percent to 8.2 percent in December 1983. Whether due to the Reagan fiscal policy or not, the conditions that prevailed during 1983 represented an improvement in the economic outcomes experienced by the public.

Second, the adverse impact of economic problems in general was further reduced due to a marked shift in public concerns. Between March and December 1983, the proportion of the public citing the economy as the most important problem dropped from 79 percent to 43 percent while the percentage identifying foreign affairs rose from 6 percent to 37 percent. This shift in public attention was not due solely to changing economic conditions. The president's use of rhetoric and the political stage provided a stimulus as well. For example, the mean value of presidential rhetoric and action toward the Soviet Union was −6.8. This indicates that the Reagan administration adopted a substantially more visible posture and aggressive tone toward the Soviets than any president since Kennedy. Further, eight of Reagan's national television addresses during these years were devoted to foreign policy concerns with specific messages castigating the Soviets on arms control, Poland, and the downing of the Korean jetliner.

Third, several crises in late 1983—the Soviet downing of KAL 007, U.S. military action in Grenada, the dispatch of marines to Lebanon and the subsequent bombing of their barracks—triggered a substantial rally effect. Again, the dramatic impact of these events was enhanced by the president's use of the political stage. Reagan's televised speeches during 1983 were exclusively devoted to foreign affairs with emphasis placed on Lebanon and Grenada.

In sum, Reagan's recovery of popular support in 1983 can be attributed to improved outcomes in the economic realm, a shift in public attention from domestic issues to foreign affairs, the rally effect, and what even opponents of the president consider to be an adept use of the political stage. The result of these developments was to create a political context which is more reminiscent of the Eisenhower-Kennedy years than the atmosphere in which Reagan's more immediate predecessors operated.

## NOTES

1. The source of the public opinion data employed in this analysis is the Gallup poll. See Ostrom and Simon (1984) for a discussion of how the monthly measure of popular support was constructed.

2. For example, during Reagan's first twenty-eight months in office, his general job performance was evaluated forty-four times by Gallup, twenty-four times by Harris, and twelve times by CBS/New York Times (*Public Opinion*, April/May, 1983).

3. Essentially, long-term attitudes such as political efficacy operate as a "discount factor" or measure of credibility applied to presidential policy initiatives and successes in the Congress. See Ostrom and Simon (1984) for an elaboration of this argument.

# REFERENCES

Abramson, Paul. 1983. *Political Attitudes in America*. San Francisco: Freeman.

Abramson, Paul, John Aldrich, and David W. Rohde. 1982. *Continuity and Change in the 1980 Elections*. Washington, D.C.: Congressional Quarterly Press.

Azar, Edward. 1982. *Conflict and Peace Data Bank (COPDAB), 1948–1978: Daily Aggregations*. Inter-University Consortium for Political and Social Research, ICPSR 7767.

Azar, Edward, and T. Havenar. 1976. Discontinuities in the symbolic environment: A Problem in scaling events. *International Interactions* 2:231–46.

Brody, Richard A. 1983. That special moment: The public response to international crises. Paper presented at the annual meeting of the Western Political Science Association, Seattle.

Cronon, Thomas E. 1980. *The State of the Presidency*. 2d ed. Boston: Little, Brown.

Dennis, Jack. 1975. Dimensions of public support for the presidency. Paper presented at the annual meeting of the Midwest Political Science Association, Chicago.

Edwards, George C., III. 1980. *Presidential Influence in Congress*. San Francisco: Freeman.

———. 1983. *The Public Presidency*. New York: St. Martins.

Fiorina, Morris P. 1977. *Congress: Keystone of the Washington Establishment*. New Haven: Yale University Press.

Fishel, Jeffrey. 1979. From campaign promise to presidential performance. Paper presented at the Woodrow Wilson International Center for Scholars, Washington, D.C. 20 June.

Greenstein, Fred I. 1982. *The Hidden-Hand Presidency*. New York: Basic Books.

Hibbs, Douglas A., Jr. 1982a. On the demand for economic outcomes. *Journal of Politics* 44:426–62.

———. 1982b. The dynamics of political support for American presidents among occupational and partisan groups. *American Journal of Political Science* 26: 312–23.

Hodgson, Godfrey. 1980. *All Things to All Men*. New York: Simon and Schuster.

Kernell, Samuel. 1978. Explaining presidential popularity. *American Political Science Review* 72:506–22.

Light, Paul C. 1982. *The President's Agenda*. Baltimore: Johns Hopkins University Press.

MacKuen, Michael. 1983. Political drama, economic conditions, and the dynamics of presidential popularity. *American Journal of Political Science* 27:165–92.

Miller, Arthur. 1974. Political issues and trust in government. *American Political Science Review* 68:951–72.

Miller, Arthur, Jeffrey Brudney, and Peter Joftis. 1975. Presidential crises and political support. Paper presented at the annual meeting of the Midwest Political Science Association, Chicago.

Nathan, Richard. 1983. *The Administrative Presidency.* New York: Wiley.

Neustadt, Richard. 1960. *Presidential Power.* New York: Wiley.

Ostrom, Charles W., Jr., and Brian L. Job. 1982. The president and the political use of force. Paper presented at the annual meeting of the American Political Science Association, Denver.

Ostrom, Charles W., Jr., and Dennis M. Simon. 1983. Managing popular support: The presidential dilemma. Paper presented at the annual meeting of the American Political Science Association, Chicago.

————. 1984. Promise and performance: A dynamic model of presidential popularity. Paper presented at the annual meeting of the Midwest Political Science Association, Chicago.

Page, Benjamin I. 1978. *Choices and Echoes in Presidential Elections.* Chicago: University of Chicago Press.

Parker, Glenn. 1977. Some themes in congressional unpopularity. *American Journal of Political Science* 21:93–109.

Pious, Richard. 1979. *The American Presidency.* New York: Basic Books.

Rohde, David W., and Dennis M. Simon. 1983. Presidential vetoes and the congressional response. Paper presented at the annual meeting of the American Political Science Association, Chicago.

Roll, Charles W., Jr., and Albert H. Cantril. 1972. *Polls.* New York: Basic Books.

Simon, Dennis M. 1981. Presidential management of public support. Ph.D. diss., Michigan State University.

Stokes, Donald E. 1966. Spatial models of party competition. In *Elections and the Political Order,* ed. A. Campbell, et al. New York: Wiley.

Sundquist, James L. 1981. *The Decline and Resurgence of Congress.* Washington, D.C.: Brookings Institution.

Tufte, Edward. 1978. *Political Control of the Economy.* Princeton: Princeton University Press.

John P. Burke

# Presidential Influence and the Budget Process: A Comparative Analysis

The annual process through which the federal budget is adopted has emerged as one of the most significant political dramas in American politics. For the economy, the fiscal policies that result from the budget process have direct impact upon its stability and well-being; witness, for example, the increasing share of federal spending as a percentage of GNP and the impact of mounting deficits upon interest rates and the supply of borrowable funds. For the Congress, the way the budget process presently is undertaken is instructive about the success and pitfalls of reform. What in the 1950s and 1960s resulted from a disjointed, fragmented, incremental process (Wildavsky, 1964), now comes about through comparably more integrated and centralized procedures adopted in the mid 1970s by a reform-minded Congress (see Havemann, 1978; Ellwood and Thurber, 1977; Schick, 1980; LeLoup, 1980; Ellwood, 1982; and Hartman, 1982). For the president, the federal budget has always been a necessary fiscal means to policy ends, but in the 1980s the budget has become an even more central part of his agenda. Mounting budget deficits were a central theme in the 1984 presidential campaign, and from 1981 through 1984, Ronald Reagan wagered the success of his administration upon achieving the most radical shift in the nation's economic agenda since the New Deal. Attaining significant reductions in nondefense spending coupled with lower tax revenues was central to the "supply-side" economic program he proposed upon taking office. As a result, the annual budget process provided the obvious terrain for an ongoing political battle that preoccupied the administration and Congress beginning in 1981 and persisting through 1982, 1983, and 1984, even as the White House abandoned some of the more dogmatic facets of the supply side formula.

Analysis of the budget process is instructive, however, not only about a phenomenon affecting the American political economy, as a tale about congressional reform, or as a gauge to measure Ronald Reagan's partisan successes or failures. For scholars of the presidency, the politics of the budget process are highly consequential and distinctively important for what they tell us about presidential influence. Since the budget process is an arena in which both the president and the Congress exercise their political wills, it is an important source for understanding the operations, dynamics, and character of executive-congressional relations and—from the perspective of the presidency—for assessing the relative merits of different styles and strategies for exercising presidential influence. Furthermore, analysis of successive budget cycles not only provides a useful empirical perspective for understanding how, in a descriptive way, the president influenced Congress, but it also allows us to assess the impact of various causal factors upon the policy process. Successive political conflicts in the same policy areas with different episodes of presidential success and failure not only permit us to see how presidential influence waxes and wanes, but also encourage us to make empirical observations about what factors are causally significant in this relationship.

The range of complex variables that potentially affect the president's role in the policy process might be usefully sorted out by employing the notion of a "funnel of causality," which arrays these causal factors from the distal to the more proximate. Using this approach, we might make five major distinctions concerning the effects of: (1) broader political and economic factors on the international or national levels such as political economic structures (Miroff, 1976 and 1979; Wolfe, 1981), political culture, political cleavages, and a weak party system (Rockman, 1979); (2) the formal-legal and constitutional powers and prerogatives the president possesses (Corwin, 1957; Pious, 1979) and other institutonal constraints such as the effects of policy cycles (Bunce, 1981; Shull, 1983), types of policy (Lowi, 1964 and 1972; Wildavsky, 1966; Kessel, 1974; LeLoup and Shull, 1979; Light, 1981; Spitzer, 1983; Shull, 1983; Hill and Plumlee, 1984), the differing perspectives of presidential appointees compared to those of the permanent civil service bureaucracy (Heclo, 1977), and the presence of bureaucratic politics in the budget process (Wanat, 1975); (3) differing organizational forms within the administration (Light, 1982), especially those of the White House staff (Thomas, 1970; Johnson, 1974; Hess, 1976; George, 1980; and Salamon, 1981) or legislative liason operations (Wayne, 1978; Davis, 1979); (4) factors arising from the political context such as shared party affiliation (Cooper and Bombardier, 1968; LeLoup, 1982), shared policy preferences, congressional efforts to dominate policy initiation (Sundquist, 1968; Moe and Teel, 1970), public popularity (Edwards, 1980), interest group support, electoral success, and discrete political events and crises; and (5) the internal, personal resources the president as a strategic actor might exercise such as an ability to control the political agenda (Light, 1982), create trust and personal identification (Sperlich, 1969), and exploit external resources through a recognition of his political "stakes," employment of skill

in legislative bargaining, and effective use of public prestige (Neustadt, 1960; also see Cronin, 1979).

Each of these factors can affect the ability of the president to influence the Congress, and the analysis of the budget cycles from 1981 to 1984 that I will present may shed some light on the relative contributions of these factors. This effort to make causal determinations is particularly important in the case of personal factors (the fifth set in the list), since they are often assumed to be most significant yet are not subject to rigorous testing against competing explanations. As Pika (1981, p. 23) has pointed out, "The personal dilemmas, decisions, and conduct [of the presidency] . . . are most often explained, quite naturally, in relation to personal attributes," with the result, according to Pika, of implicitly and unjustifiably "washing out" the nonpersonal.

Analysis of the budget process enables us to avoid these omissions and allows us to consider the significance of other, nonpersonal factors, to "wash back in" a wider range of hypotheses and competing explanations. But, as I shall argue, it also provides evidence of the importance of personal factors to policy outcomes. Thus, those variables emphasizing the president's personal political skills and his role as a strategic actor, the fifth set of factors, mediated through his ability to exploit his strengths in the external political context, the fourth set, are most significant in explaining the variance in budgetary politics and outcomes in this case study.

Furthermore, in addition to what this analysis suggests about the relative strengths of causal factors, it is useful for what it tells us about the president's personal skills and resources. The pattern of presidential influence that Reagan exhibited largely fits the description of presidential strategy that Neustadt (1960) presented in *Presidential Power:* a president who recognizes his "power stakes" in dealing with Congress, appeals to his prestige with the general public, and engages in persuasion and bargaining to gain congressional support. Subsequent modifications and refinements of Neustadt's analysis, such as fostering trust and loyalty among key advisers (Sperlich, 1969) and effectively using communicative skills—the bully pulpit (Neustadt, 1983)—in building support among the general public, also played an important role. In addition, then, to a model of presidential influence relying on bargaining and direct persuasion, Reagan also exhibited traits of a more "plebiscitary" model (Seligman, 1980) of presidential influence: appealing to the public over the heads of the Congress.

Although this mode of exercising presidential influence served Reagan well in early 1981, it became increasingly ill-suited to achieving his goals. This, in turn, allows us to discern what elements of the personal factor, the particular way the president chooses to exercise influence, contribute to presidential success or failure. It also invites us to consider alternatives to the Reagan case. I will thus conclude by presenting an alternative conception of presidential influence in the budget process drawn from the experience of the Eisenhower administration. The Eisenhower example, as a comparative case, also illustrates the importance of the president's personal role in the budget process, but it also shows how that role and the strategies and tactics of presidential influence that are a part of it can be defined in a different (and perhaps more successful) fashion.

## Budgetary Politics, 1981–1984

### Round I: Seeming Success in 1981

Before we consider the particulars of how Reagan sought to exercise presidential influence, it is useful to reconstruct briefly the landmark events and outcomes of each successive budget cycle from 1981 to 1984. In 1981, the first year of the new administration, Reagan experienced initial success, although in the latter months of 1981 Congress grew restive about giving the president what he wanted. The reconciliation resolution (H Con Res 115, commonly called Gramm-Latta I) that Congress approved in June cut approximately $36.6 billion from fiscal 1982 outlays, a figure close to Reagan's proposed reductions. Reagan's initial success in winning most of his requested cuts startled long-time observers who expected the Congress to deal the administration a swift defeat.

The budget guidelines set by this resolution then underwent the new reconciliation process to square them with existing entitlements and law. Again a coalition of Republicans and conservative Democrats joined to pass the reconciliation bill (HR 3982, commonly called Gramm-Latta II) by a 217–211 vote. The House bill cut $37.3 billion from the budget, most of which was in accord with the administration's request. The Congress thus rejected the work of its own authorizing committees, reconciled appropriations and authorizations, changed entitlement rules, and even rewrote major parts of substantive law having no significant impact on the budget, all in accord with the administration's fiscal program. Following House-Senate conference, the final budget measure reduced fiscal expenditures by $35.2 billion.

In September the rosy picture began to change as projections indicated deteriorating economic conditions and forecasts of deficits in the $100 billion range. In response, Reagan proposed a new round of cuts in domestic spending of $13 billion. These proposals ran into stiff opposition, and neither reductions in entitlement programs nor "revenue enhancement" of $3 billion garnered sufficient congressional support. The stalemate resulted in a showdown. After several late-night sessions, House and Senate conferees, meeting with OMB Director David Stockman, thought they had White House support for a compromise package. Reagan, however, vetoed it (Cohen, 1981). Reagan also rejected a conciliatory bid by moderate Senate Republicans to launch another reconciliation effort that would push for further cuts but also significantly increase revenues.

Reagan's tactics did not succeed. In November, he retreated from his September requests and postponed budget savings until the next year, but this failed to end the impasse. Since final appropriations for the fiscal year (which began in October) had yet to be approved, continuing resolutions were necessary to keep the government in business. Moreover, Reagan's stance generated increasing congressional hostility: Democrats charged that the veto was a political tactic aimed at shoring up the president's image in the face of mounting economic difficulties, and members viewed Reagan's budget policies as increasingly unpopular and perhaps even unworkable (Cohen, 1981). The year ended without a second resolution. Both houses simply ratified the figures contained in the first resolution, "even though everyone knew they were wildly inaccurate" (LeLoup, 1982).

*Rounds II, III, and IV: Congressional Resurgence*

In 1982 and 1983, the pattern that developed in late 1981 continued and Reagan's position weakened. In both years, the president's January budget proposals fell on deaf congressional ears and alternative budgets were proposed from within the Congress and subsequently passed.

In January 1982, Reagan's initial budget generated little enthusiasm on Capitol Hill among Republicans or Democrats (C.Q., 1982e, 1982f). Reagan proposed continued support for the 25 percent tax reduction package, increased defense spending, and more reductions on the domestic side. Instead of the promised balanced budget, the administration projected a deficit of $100 billion (a figure that was soon to double). Each of these was politically and ideologically incompatible for the majority in the Congress, even in the Republican-controlled Senate.

In the ensuing weeks, congressional leadership developed alternative proposals. Republican Senate Budget Committee Chairman Pete Domenici (R-NM) was silent, refusing to make anything but perfunctory comments about the president's initial request. In the House, GOP leaders notified the president that they wanted "running room" to develop their own alternatives, while House Budget Committee Chairman Jim Jones (D-OK) announced "that both political parties were in a state of paralysis, and nothing even the semblance of a consensus existed" (C.Q., 1982b). Initiative on the budget passed from the administration's hands to the Congress.

Reagan subsequently gave qualified endorsement to a proposal that Domenici crafted, and he at least participated in attempts to reach bipartisan agreement. Privately, Reagan indicated to key staff members that he would scale down his military request by $10 billion and accept limited tax increases if significant cuts were made in domestic programs (Barrett, 1983). The negotiations of the so-called Gang of 17, however, proved unproductive. Democrats were incensed about Reagan's unwillingness to compromise significantly on taxes and especially to accept bipartisan responsibility for limits on social security cost-of-living increases. Reagan deflected compromise, choosing to preserve his popularity and avoid blame for reductions in social security.

On 21 May, the Senate, acting largely independently of the White House, pushed through a fiscal 1983 budget by a vote of 49–43. The White House agreed to some concessions only after the Senate Budget Committee unanimously rejected Reagan's initial request and prepared to report a resolution the administration did not support (C.Q., 1983). In the House no fewer than eight budgets were proposed and came up for a vote on 27 May, but each was defeated. Finally, working independently of the White House, but under Republican auspices, the House passed a compromise measure by the narrow margin of 220–207. Reagan had reservations about the extent of the proposed cuts but said he would tacitly support the proposal if some of the objectionable reductions were restored in conference. Reagan's proposed restorations were not made.

The third year of the Reagan administration repeated the politics of the second, as power over the budget passed increasingly to the Congress. Reagan's problems were compounded by a twenty-six seat decrease in House Republican membership, yet he failed to modify his strategy to compensate for this shift in his political fortunes. As a result, the final 1983 budget not only bore the marks of being a congressional rather than a presidential document, it also was now more decidedly a Democratic one. In the House not only was the president a less central figure, as he had been in 1982, but Republican influence over the budget was not as strong as it had been the year before. In the Senate, despite continuation of their majority, Republicans were divided and could only reach agreement by making concessions that ran against the administration's wishes.

Initially, Reagan proposed a budget that included $245 billion for defense and $603 billion for nondefense expenditures. In the House Budget Committee, the conservative chairman, Jim Jones, was initially willing to compromise with Reagan as he had unsuccessfully attempted to do in 1981 and 1982, yet this proved unnecessary. Congressional Republicans did not even offer an alternative of their own. The result was that, on 23 March, the House passed (by a 229–196 margin) a Democratic budget resolution that rebuked the president by cutting defense spending to $235 billion, increasing nondefense expenditures to $635 billion, and raising revenues by $30 billion.

In the Senate disarray prevailed, particularly over the size of defense expenditures and tax increases. Reagan finally assented to a compromise fashioned by Domenici and the Senate Republican leadership, but liberal Republicans did not support it. On 19 May, the Republican leadership again presented a compromise budget with larger tax increases and a reduced defense increase. This again failed. Finally, a bipartisan compromise was offered which, with the support of Majority Leader Howard Baker, passed 50–49.

The final 1983 budget resolution contained no significant reductions in domestic spending and lower levels of increases in military outlays (a 5 percent increase rather than the administration's requested 10 percent). It also called for $73 billion in tax increases over the next three years. Significant differences with the administration over the level of military spending and the tax increases necessary to reduce the deficit thus prevailed.

From June through October, several of the appropriation bills necessary to fulfill the terms of the budget resolution were passed, but a complete budget including a deficit reduction package proved elusive. In October, two continuing resolutions were necessary to keep the federal government in operation. The tax component of the original budget resolution proved especially sticky. Reagan strongly opposed the tax increase, and Congress itself could not agree on a revenue figure that would take effect in an election year despite several congressional attempts to pass a deficit reduction package. In September, for example, Robert Dole (R-KAN) and other members of the Senate Finance Committee proposed a bipartisan $150 billion package equally divided between spending reductions and tax increases. Reagan, however, refused to consider the proposed revenue figures, while Speaker Thomas P. O'Neill refused to exert pressure on House Democrats unless Reagan showed some willingness to go along with Congress's proposed tax increases and reductions in military spending. The problem of coping with the deficit was pushed forward to 1984.

In early 1984, some hope for an accommodation between the White House and the Congress seemed possible. In January, Reagan proposed a budget of $925 billion with a projected deficit of $180 billion, but in his State of the Union message to Congress he also proposed a bipartisan effort to make a $100 billion ''down payment'' on the deficit over the next three years. Reagan's proposal put the Democrats on the defensive since they would share the blame for any tax increases and, if they failed to reach agreement, Reagan could pin the deficit problem on them.

The administration proved to be its own undoing. Several meetings of a bipartisan White House and congressional deficit reduction committee were held, but negotiations broke down. The president demanded that the group reach agreement first and then present its package to the administration, a stance that would weaken Congress's bargaining position. Congressional negotiators also feared a political trap. In the words of one participant, the administration's ''whole strategy is to do a little package of reductions, put it on a fast track, pass it apart from anything else, have a big White House signing ceremony and defuse the issue politically in 1984'' (*New York Times,* 1984).

In March, several leading Republicans on the budget, appropriations, and finance committees met independently of the bipartisan effort and crafted a new $150 billion proposal that included new tax increases coupled with a 7.8 percent increase in military spending (as contrasted with the administration's request for a 13 percent increase). An accord with the White House was reached; Reagan agreed to back the proposal if the Senate Republicans would not press for further cuts in military spending.

The accord presumably was an attempt to isolate key Senate Republicans from any moves to make further cuts. However, it did not end the attempts of other members of Congress to seek reductions. In the weeks following its announcement, the House voted in favor of a Democrat-sponsored deficit reduction package of $185 billion, which roughly matched the Senate Republican-White House tax increase figure ($50 billion for the Democrats over three years versus $47 billion for the Republicans) but more than doubled the proposed reductions in Reagan's defense request ($95.7 billion versus $40 billion).

Reagan struck a deal with key members of Senate committees, but he also committed himself to hefty tax increases and significant reductions in military expenditures. While this proved successful in gaining the approval of the Senate, it did not serve him well in his negotiations with the Democrat-controlled House. His agreement with Senate Republicans about an expenditure floor in effect became a ceiling in his negotiations with House Democrats. With respect to defense, for example, the Congress finally passed a budget bill in October that included only $293 billion in military appropriations. This figure represented only a 5 percent increase in defense expenditures, not the 13 percent Reagan originally requested or the 7.8 percent in his compromise with Senate Republicans. The bulk of budget initiative once again passed to the Congress.

## Explaining Budget Outcomes: The Effect of Different Causal Factors

Turning now to the empirical question of what accounts for this pattern of presidential influence and, specifically, which of the five general causal determinants of president influence best explains performance and outcome, we find that both Reagan's initial success and the difficulties he began to experience in late 1981, extending through 1982, 1983, and into 1984, can be best attributed to his particular style and strategy for exercising influence. This is not to claim that other factors did not influence the budget process, but only that the president's role as a strategic actor and the particular strategies and tactics he chose to employ are particularly important in explaining variance in those years.

The first three dimensions of presidential power outlined above, structural, formal-legal/institutional, and organizational, did not shift markedly from 1981 through 1984. Broader configurations of politics and economics remained

stable. On the formal-legal dimension, no legal powers or constitutional prerogatives figured significantly in the budget process, save the threat of a
presidential veto in 1983. Institutionally, the comprehensiveness of the new
budget procedures compared to the previous fragmented, incremental state
(Wildavsky, 1964) did enhance opportunities for exercising presidential influence. However, as a constant during each of these years, this factor alone
cannot account for variance in performance and outcome. Types of policy under
consideration undoubtedly affect political configurations and the interactions of
participants. The nonincremental nature of Reagan's budget proposals may
have increased the costs for exercising presidential influence (Light, 1981), but
these and other policy characteristics—for example, their distributive, regulatory, and redistributive character (Lowi, 1964 and 1972; Hill and Plumlee,
1984)—were basically constant over the four years. Reagan generally pursued
spending reductions in the same domestic policy areas, while he consistently
sought increases in other areas, principally in defense. Budget outcomes,
however, varied in each of the four years.

The cycle of the president's term in office may have affected policy, particularly during the "honeymoon" days of 1981 and again in late 1983 and in 1984
with the prospect of an impending presidential election (Light, 1982; Bunce,
1981), yet there is a distinct pattern that persists from mid-1981 through 1984
that cannot be explained through appeal to some theory of institutional cycle.
With respect to organizational factors, the formal structure of the legislative
liaison unit remained stable over time, and while the structure of the White
House staff and personnel changes may have affected the administration's
policy-making and executing capabilities, it too remained largely unchanged.[1]

The fourth set of factors, the effects generated by a president's more immediate external political environment such as particular political events,
partisan composition of Congress, and public popularity, did shift over time.
However, these factors did not operate as external aggregates that add or
subtract from the president's "political capital" (Light, 1982). For example,
congressional Republicans were particularly cohesive in key votes in 1981, and
some analysts (LeLoup, 1982) have suggested that simple partisan composition
can explain presidential support: there was an increase in Republican seats in
1980 that gave the conservative coalition the margin needed for victory. However, although this might explain both the success of early 1981 and reversals in
1983, when Republican membership in the House declined by twenty-six seats,
it cannot account for Reagan's reverses starting in late 1981 and continuing
through 1982, when Republican membership is constant. Similarly, in the
Senate, partisan balance cannot explain variance in presidential support since
the number of Republican seats remained roughly the same over the four years.

Immediate political events, such as the Lebanon crisis, activity in Central
America, the economic downturn in 1981 and 1982, or the MX missile con-

troversy, may also have affected the tenor of executive-legislative relationships. However, emphasis on these contextual events cannot account for crucial episodes in the budget process that contributed to presidential success or failure, such as the breakdown of negotiations with the "Gang of 17" in 1982 or the collapse of the bipartisan efforts of 1984.

Other external resources such as shared policy preferences, intrainstitutional pride, interinstitutional competition, and public popularity do appear to have greater effect upon Reagan's success, as Light (1982) and Edwards (1980) have suggested about presidential influence in general. In 1981, conservative "boll weevil" Democrats provided the margin of victory on key votes, and as Reagan's popularity declined, his defeats became more frequent. However, the linkage between cause and effect is a complex one in which Reagan played an important role through his attempts to exploit the political environment, thus indicating the importance of his place as a strategic actor—the fifth dimension of presidential power.

*President as Strategic Actor*

What were these personal skills and what resources did they exploit? One component that was manifest early involved Reagan's skill in controlling the political agenda. This especially worked to his advantage in 1981. According to Light (1982), presidents can maximize their personal resources by presenting their most important piece of legislation early on in the first year, keeping the agenda simple, and concentrating political efforts upon it. The Reagan administration did precisely this: it knew what it wanted and worked fast, simply, and directly to win support. Reagan quickly presented his fiscal package to Congress in the early weeks of his new administration. He did not wait until the new fiscal cycle to present a Reagan budget. Quickness was complemented in turn by limiting the agenda to the budget and not clogging it with a welter of proposals. Reagan thus avoided the unnecessary political crosscurrents and legislative complexities that beset Carter's more ambitious first-year agenda. Finally, he concentrated his efforts on the budget issue, enabling him to control the agenda before opponents had a chance to mobilize. Specifically, he focused upon broader fiscal goals and avoided consideration of their particular impact upon beneficiaries. His simple, fast, and direct attack also permitted him to benefit from the erratic leadership and divided troops among Democrats and to capitalize on the cohesiveness of Republican support (LeLoup, 1982).

Other personal resources and skills that Reagan employed complemented his control of the agenda and parallel Neustadt's (1960) emphasis upon personal contacts and bargaining with individual legislators and an ability to use and trade upon public support in gaining congressional assent (also see Light, 1981). Although it is difficult to measure the effects of Reagan's actions on congressional support, he did target wavering legislators and strike bargains with them, and they voted in favor of his program. For example, Reagan retained sugar price supports in his budget, thus enlisting the support of several additional Louisiana congressmen; he increased funds for Medicaid and Conrail, thus keeping several Northeastern liberal Republicans in line; and he retained appropriations for the controversial Clinch River Project, which happens to be located in Tennessee, the home state of then Senate Majority Leader Howard Baker. Much of Reagan's persuasive efforts, however, avoided controversial details and compromises that would weaken his fiscal aims (Ornstein, 1982). The president did some horse trading at the margins but gave up very little (C.Q., 1982a). This ability to bargain at the margins was possible in 1981, but began to prove costly in 1982 as the bargains that would have to be struck penetrated more deeply into the administration's fiscal package. Thus, although Neustadt (1960) and Light (1981, 1982) are correct about the importance of legislative lobbying and bargaining as a part of presidential influence, these techniques were used less extensively in Reagan's case and proved increasingly costly to his spending goals.

These bargaining tactics also were effective in 1981 because they were complemented by skillful use of public support—another major component of Reagan's exercise of influence, but one that also proved less enduring over time. According to Neustadt (1960), presidents can enhance their bargaining abilities with Congress if they exploit the perception of public support. Reagan did precisely this. In fact, the importance of preserving the appearance of the president's strength through association with an election mandate, public support, and a string of legislative victories was consciously articulated in memoranda circulated in the White House during his first months in office (Barrett, 1983). Furthermore, throughout 1981, whenever his program ran into difficulty, Reagan went over the heads of Congress and took his case to the public. This not only attempted to reinforce Congress's perception of his public support, but, as Neustadt (1983) has recently noted, it serves to build support that can be directly brought to bear on the Congress. There is then a plebiscitary side to presidential influence that, while reinforcing the lobbying position and resources the president might possess as a bargainer (Neustadt, 1960), provides an avenue of appeal when bargains fail.

Reagan also undertook selective lobbying efforts that were directed at special groups. He tapped into his network of conservative activists, with Lyn Nofziger focusing upon fifty-one swing districts, 45 percent of them in the South (Smith, 1981). At the same time, Reagan avoided a backlash by groups adversely affected by his proposals. He sought reductions that would negatively affect various groups and interests, but in pursuing his fiscal ends he used the phrases and code words that would not agitate or politically mobilize those who might be disadvantaged (Schick, 1982).

How did this strategic stance fare over time? Although it is difficult to measure the precise effects of presidential activity upon congressional decision making, Reagan's strategy does correlate with his success in 1981. However, this relationship seems to hold only to the extent that the requisites for each part were present, complementing and reinforcing the other parts, and were skillfully used. The appeal to the public was effective in gaining congressional approval as long as Reagan was perceived as enjoying mass popularity that could affect congressional electoral outcomes. Bargaining was possible as long as the bargains struck were not at the expense of the ideological core of Reagan's program. Subtle rhetoric could convey the right message as long as affected groups were unmobilized and unaware. Fast, simple, direct attempts to push the budget agenda through Congress were possible as long as the opposition remained unprepared to do serious battle.

Each of these aspects of Reagan's stance as a strategic actor worked in his favor in early 1981. However, beginning in mid-1981 and continuing through 1982 and 1983, the conditions underlying each facet of his strategy slowly deteriorated, yet Reagan failed to modify his stance accordingly. This inflexibility, in turn, offers useful lessons about the president's role as a strategic actor.

With respect to the appeal to public prestige, for example, the bloom on the supposed Reagan mandate faded as popular support proved increasingly shallow. Public opinion dropped precipitously from its high of 68 percent in May 1981 to a low of 49 percent in December (*Gallup Report*), leveling off to about 45 percent approval, 45 percent disapproval in 1982 and 1983. This decline coincides with increasing congressional reluctance to support Reagan's program. Reagan, however, continued to appeal to the public as his budget encountered resistance, yet his weakening popularity and worsening economic conditions did not provide Congress with sufficient incentives to guarantee legislative support. Crucial "boll weevil" and "gypsy moth" support particularly declined. In late 1983 and early 1984 Reagan's popularity began to rise, but an increase in congressional support, particularly among the opposition during an election year, did not follow.

Reagan's support among special interest groups also declined. Lobbies and affected groups that had been caught by surprise in 1981 were mobilized for action in 1982 and 1983 (C.Q., 1982c). Support among the president's allies, by contrast, weakened. For example, as the weak consensus among monetarists, supply-siders, and fiscal conservatives split apart, the business community began to drift away (Barrett, 1983; Levitan and Cooper, 1984, pp. 59–61). The influential Business Roundtable, for example, publicly criticized the high deficits and called for a slowing of the defense buildup (C.Q., 1982d).

Within the Congress, other factors tended to reduce presidential support. Many members viewed the reconciliation process and a strong presidential role in it as a temporary expedient and one averse to the folkways of the institution (Schick, 1981b). Republicans, weary of continuous battle, wanted compromise, not further confrontation (Schick, 1982). Democrats were open to compromise, only to find Reagan inflexible (Cohen, 1982).

Reagan's response, however, was not to move toward bipartisanship but to grow more intractable and to rely on the approach he had already used: the appeal to prestige and limited bargaining. However, the conditions necessary for these to work had weakened (electoral pressure and the appeal to public support) or had worn thin (limited bargaining).

Especially with respect to bargaining, Reagan's initial steamroller tactics, his willingness to bargain when encountering opposition, but his increasing practice of deciding to fight and take his case to the people when the bargains began to encroach on the ideological core of his program "severely damaged his credibility as a trustworthy negotiator." For example, during the ill-fated negotiations of the "Gang of 17," the chairmen of the House budget and ways and means committees refused to push ahead until the president unequivocally stated that he would support the group's compromise (C.Q., 1982e). Ways and Means Chairman Dan Rostenkowski specifically cited the absence of mutual trust as a stumbling block in the group's ability to negotiate (Barrett, 1983). Reagan's unwillingness to compromise his personal prestige complemented this absence of trust as an impediment to bipartisan accommodation. During the "Gang of 17" negotiations, for example, there was no Democratic consensus on social security decreases, and the issue was ripe for compromise if the president had been willing to share in the responsibility for reductions. This he would not do, and in fact as negotiations foundered, the White House began to view the goal of the process as putting the Democrats on the public relations defensive, not striking a last-minute bargain (Barrett, 1983). Similar problems beset the bipartisan "down payment" efforts of 1984. Democrats feared a political trap, not a forum for compromise and accommodation. Neither side was willing to negotiate seriously.

Reagan also failed to develop a positive relationship with key actors who might have been useful allies or willing negotiators. The conservative chairman of the House Budget Committee, Jim Jones, provides a good case in point. Jones had offered to work with Reagan in the salad days of 1981, and Jones's own proposals were not markedly different from Reagan's (LeLoup, 1982; Barrett, 1983). Reagan, however, spurned compromise and failed to develop the ties that might have borne fruit in future years. Reagan was also often inflexible in his dealings with the Senate leadership of his own party. In late 1981, he rejected a compromise package that Domenici, ten of twelve Budget Committee Republicans, and Senate Majority Leader Baker had worked out. According to the *New York Times* (1983), Senate Republicans went against the president because he had "refused to give one inch," especially on military spending. Reagan, for his part, resorted to his old tactic of appealing to the public, although now the media was blamed for his setbacks.

Finally, Reagan's ability to move directly and control the agenda, which had given the administration a fast break in 1981, proved less effective as he failed to adapt to a changing political context that provided diminished opportunities for the direct and bold exercise of influence. Both Democrats and liberal Republicans reasserted their own ideological and institutional priorities. The Congress also learned how to deal with Reagan and the new budget procedures. In 1981, Carl Perkins (D-KY), the House Education and Labor chairman, compromised key programs such as Head Start, student loans, and impact aid with the assurance that he could later obtain floor amendments. Weeks later, however, the bill appeared under a closed rule (Peters, 1981). In 1982, Perkins's compromises were not repeated. Reagan's ability to gain reductions without mobilizing the opposition also faded as rising budget deficits indicated the need for further cuts. These cuts would have to come in more politically volatile entitlement programs like Medicare and social security.

Several lessons about the personal and strategic dimensions of presidential influence can be drawn from the Reagan experience. First, the case obviously indicates the importance of the president as a strategic actor. Other factors such as party composition and public popularity matter but they are mediated through his personal skills. Secondly, our standard understanding of presidential "power" (Neustadt, 1960) should be modified. While bargaining is important, it was less central to Reagan's dealings with Congress than tapping public support and properly timing his efforts. The elements that make up the president's role as a strategic actor thus may need to be reordered. Third, while presidential influence depends on the incumbent's ability to exercise personal skill, it also depends on the existence of resources available for exploitation. As his popularity declined, as bargains struck more deeply into his program, and as the first six months of the new presidential term passed into history, Reagan encountered increasing opposition, yet he did not alter his dealings with Congress to reflect these changes in his political fortunes. This indicates that the political context surrounding the policy process should be taken into account in ascertaining the particular kind of presidential influence that is feasible. It also indicates that the "textbook" advice about presidential power may not only need reordering and reconceptualization, but it may be limited in its applicability to a short span of time during the initial months of the president's first year in office.

## An Alternative Model of Presidential Influence

Did Reagan have alternatives? At least two possibilities stand out. First, he might have attempted to strike more frequent and direct deals with Congress, heeding more closely the counsel of Neustadt (1960) and other advocates of bargaining-cum-persuasion modes of presidential influence. This alternative generally seeks to induce legislators to believe that what the president wants is in their interest or posits some ability to exchange between them. However, given legislators who may be ideologically unwilling to accept the president's policy proposals, and given a president who may be unable, in the interest of preserving the purity of his program, to compromise major parts or seek new increments in other federal programs, the probability of exchangeable resources will likely be low.

Presidential influence may be constrained by the presence of other political actors in the policy process and the need to bargain or in other ways deal with them, but this does not mean that presidential efforts to attain policy ends are necessarily futile or condemned to failure. There are alternative models of presidential influence. The principal features of one of them can be discerned through a comparative case study of President Eisenhower's attempts to control federal spending in the 1957 budget process (Burke, 1985). Although the political context, both inside and outside of Washington, of the mid-1950s differs from that of the 1980s, and the budget processes each president could use and exploit are not identical, Eisenhower and Reagan share a concern for holding the line on federal spending, while selectively seeking increases in limited areas. Both presidents enjoyed at least initially strong popular support and recent electoral victories. Each also faced a Congress that was less than agreeable to do their bidding.

In contrast to Reagan, Eisenhower followed an indirect strategy to achieve his fiscal ends. This alternative style of presidential influence has been observed (Greenstein, 1982) at work in the Eisenhower presidency generally, but its use and success can be specifically evaluated and compared by examining its presence in the budget process.[2] The politics involved in the 1957 process are particularly interesting since it is often conventionally held that Eisenhower failed to exercise an adequate type and degree of presidential influence that year (Neustadt, 1960). Recently declassified documents and other evidence that were not available to earlier scholars indicate, however, that Eisenhower did generally attain what he wanted and exercised presidential influence in the process. It is, however, a type of influence that differs from the activist, wheeling and dealing, "textbook" exercise of presidential power. The main components of this alternative approach are: (1) bipartisanship and a president perceived as above the political fray; (2) a more flexible, indirect bargaining stance highly attentive to variations in the political context surrounding different parts of the budget process; and (3) less frequent appeals to public prestige.

## Bipartisanship

Like Reagan, Eisenhower faced potentially strong partisan opposition, but unlike his successor, he attempted to strike a bipartisan and ostensibly cooperative pose in his dealing with Congress. In the 1957 budget process, this meant weekly meetings with the Republican leadership of both houses and key committees and (generally) monthly meetings with a bipartisan leadership group. Eisenhower also attempted to be conciliatory in dealing with congressional demands and to seek reasonable compromises. With respect to military appropriations, for example, the president wanted to maintain current levels of appropriations, avoiding demands for either reductions or increases. Many Democrats and some Republicans, especially among congressional leaders, wanted reductions. Eisenhower's response was to maintain that the budget was a sound one, yet also to indicate that he would consider some reductions. He offered, for example, to delay procurement of more B-52 bombers until 1959, and he proposed cuts of $200 million in army public work projects and another $500 million in weapons procurements. In addition to responding to demands for further cuts, these proposals carried implicit political warnings of the effects of reductions on home districts.

Reagan, in contrast to Eisenhower, attempted to form a highly partisan and ideological coalition of Republicans and conservative Democrats. This stance eked out a narrow victory in 1981, but as motivations for identifying with Reagan's ideology and partisanship among some members weakened, this margin disappeared. A bipartisan approach that did not compromise key essentials of Reagan's program was, however, feasible. James Jones, the conservative House Budget Committee chairman was repeatedly willing to deal, yet his offers were spurned by the White House. Jones, in fact, drew a precise parallel with the bipartisanship of the Eisenhower era: ''I had hoped to have another experience similar to Eisenhower's, where the leaders of both parties, in an effort to build a national consensus, were able to compromise their differences'' (C.Q., 1982g).

An earlier effort on Reagan's part to compromise and strike a less partisan tone might have won him less credit in 1981, but would have built trust and bridges for compromise that could have been used in subsequent years. From the perspective of the White House, compromise might have given too much away. However, as the negotiations in 1982 and again in 1984 indicated, compromise failed not on policy substance but on who would get public credit or blame. A bipartisan approach had, in fact, been successfully employed in the gasoline revenue, jobs, and social security reform bills. Moreover, the ''Gang of 17'' negotiations in 1982 and the bipartisan meetings of 1984 indicated that forums were readily available for such efforts.

*Flexible and Indirect*

The second characteristic of an alternative model of presidential influence is a flexible approach in the selection of a proper strategy coupled with indirect attempts to exercise influence. Not only did Eisenhower strike a bipartisan pose, compromising when necessary and giving Congress its due, he selectively and indirectly attempted to channel the congressional response to his proposals in preferred directions.

This selective approach to exercising influence has not been noted by scholars who have analyzed presidential power. Discussions of influence have generally focused on a kind of undifferentiated, unqualified need for presidential activism (Neustadt, 1960; Burns, 1966; Light, 1982) and the requisites of that activism. There have been more recent analyses of the effects of timing (Light, 1981; Bunce, 1981) and policy type upon policy outcome both generally (Lowi, 1964 and 1972; Hill and Plumlee, 1984) and with particular respect to the presidency (Wildavsky, 1966: LeLoup and Shull, 1979; Light, 1981; Spitzer, 1983; Shull, 1983). There has been, however, with only a few exceptions (Johannes, 1972; Lowi, 1972) less focused attention upon the variations in the political context that implicitly seem to underlie this attention to typological differences. Furthermore, with the possible exception of Lowi's (1972) findings about the presence of presidential activism in redistributive policy arenas, there has been almost no discussion of the implications of these respective differences in policy types and contexts for the issue of presidential influence, influence that is exercised across a range of policy types and arenas.

While one case study cannot definitively analyze this facet of presidential power, it can at least begin to focus attention upon these critical issues and suggest some tentative observations. In the Eisenhower example, three patterns of influence that are attentive to variations in political context are discernible: active leadership where little political support is present; careful lobbying where pressures from conflicting political quarters exists; and covert nonsupport in the face of popular agenda items that the president opposes.

With respect to the first of these patterns Eisenhower, like Reagan, sometimes took a more active leadership role that complemented private lobbying with overt, often public attempts to build a political clientele. However, Eisenhower did this selectively, restricting these efforts to programs that had little support, such as foreign aid. Here he did not have to worry about pressures for additional expenditures or reductions, and he could thus be direct and open in his support. He also recognized that in this policy area it was up to the president to take an active leadership role in building support both in Congress and among the public.

In building support for foreign aid appropriations, Eisenhower directly appealed to the public, making several televised addresses in which he tried to emphasize the cost effectiveness of foreign aid as contrasted with military assistance and to defuse the charge that the program was a mere "giveaway." He also lobbied successfully to enlist the support of senators normally critical of the program such as William Knowland (R-CALIF), Homer Capehart (R-IND), and Styles Bridges (R-NH). The transcript of one meeting with Bridges, held after the senator had publicly criticized the president's proposal, illustrates the approach at work. The record shows Eisenhower carefully explaining in detail the advantages of foreign aid for American security interests, particularly its cost efficiency compared to military assistance. The appeal was framed in terms convincing to the fiscally conservative Bridges, and the meeting ended with the senator offering to make a public tour extolling the virtues of the president's aid program.

In other political contexts, Eisenhower employed alternative means to achieve his ends. Where he faced demands for cuts by some but pressure for increases by others, as in defense, he pursued a careful course that sought to avoid threats from both sides. He concentrated his lobbying efforts on key congressional leaders and committee members, and he presented his arguments in a way that would forestall demands for reductions yet not fuel calls for increases. For example, he continually pointed to his care in preparing the budget and defended the increases that he sought, yet he coupled this appeal with examples of where further reductions were possible as both a conciliatory gesture to the economizers and as a sign of his own fiscal concerns to those advocating further increases. He also emphasized that Congress itself bore responsibilities for adequately funding proposals since the appropriations process only sought to fund what Congress had authorized.

Where Eisenhower opposed a popular program like aid to education, he publicly echoed support but avoided even simple actions that would have secured passage. Federal aid to education was part of the convention platforms of both parties in the 1956 election, and the president himself had gone on record in support of aid. Other analyses of the 1957 budget process (Neustadt, 1960) have noted the absence of Eisenhower's effort to support the federal aid bill as a prime example of his strategic failure. However, evidence indicates that Eisenhower's lack of action may itself have been strategically shrewd and deliberate. Public support for aid began to drop in 1957, opposition among the party leadership increased, and the administration's initial proposal had been changed by the Democrats in Congress from a need-based formula to general subsidies and with the period of aid extended from four to five years. These political developments parallel private memoranda and transcripts that show Eisenhower increasingly opposed to the aid bill. Thus it should come as no surprise that Eisenhower occasionally stated, when queried, that he supported some form of federal aid, yet that he took no steps to lobby for the bill then under consideration. His action (or rather covert inaction) with respect to the aid bill thus provides an example of presidential influence in dealing with a popular agenda item to which a president may be publicly committed but privately opposed.

Eisenhower also gave Congress leeway to act but coupled it with indirect attempts to channel the result. For example, in his foreign aid proposal, he replaced the controversial grant-in-aid provision with a development loan fund, and he lobbied committee chairmen of both the Senate and House to prevent the separation of funding for military assistance from that for economic aid, a separation that would have jeopardized the latter. He engaged in instrumental use of language, such as when he deliberately feigned ignorance of steps he could have taken to secure passage of aid to education or when he rhetorically played upon his own military experience in defending military and foreign aid outlays. Other presidents, Reagan included, have made rhetorical appeals. Their use of rhetoric, however, seems more symbolic and emotional in its purposes and thus less closely connected to indirect approaches for attaining presidential ends. Eisenhower also deemphasized his own direct political involvement by working through other actors. In 1957, as we have seen, he enlisted Knowland, Capehart and Bridges, prominent critics of foreign aid, to defend his aid program on the Hill.

*Public Prestige*

The third major component of this alternative model of presidential influence concerns Eisenhower's use of public popularity and prestige. For both Reagan and Eisenhower, the president's standing with the public is an important resource in gaining congressional assent. But the two cases differ in its occasions and use. Reagan has appealed to his popularity frequently, often as a counter to resistance on Capitol Hill. This has, however, been of limited utility over time since he has drawn continually upon a decreasing reservoir of public support. In 1984, his popularity began to climb again, but there has been no appreciable difference in his congressional support, save perhaps among Senate Republicans. Eisenhower, by contrast, carefully husbanded his position among the general public. He did make public appeals, but only when absolutely needed, as he did in bolstering his foreign aid request. However, he did not do this often and was generally perceived as above the political fray. This in turn enhanced his abilities to project a bipartisan stance and to pursue his political will selectively and indirectly. It also enabled him to maintain his popularity. Effective use of presidential prestige, in turn, also contributes to the president's success with Congress. While not all factors affecting prestige are subject to presidential control, empirical data indicate that members of Congress of both parties respond favorably to presidential popularity, with the response strongest where popularity among their own electoral supporters is highest (Edwards, 1980).[3]

## Conclusion

Reagan surely cannot be "another Ike," and the purpose of this comparison is not to suggest that he should be; the kind of public prestige each enjoyed and the tenor of the times differ. Moreover, Congress as an institution has changed.

Dole and O'Neill preside over bodies that are more independent and tied to constituency interests and less bound by institutional hierarchy and tradition than did Lyndon Johnson and Sam Rayburn in the 1950s. However, elements of the style and strategy for exercising presidential influence that the Eisenhower case illuminate remain applicable despite these differences. Even in a more fragmented and decentralized Congress, a comparably more centralized process exists in areas such as budget legislation; selective lobbying with key leaders like Domenici and Jones thus matters. Furthermore, the need for a selective approach attuned to differences in political context remains relevant for complex legislation like the annual budget. Elements of the Eisenhower example, thus, might have served Reagan well.

A bipartisan, selective approach might also better serve the Republic. It posits neither purely presidential nor congressional leadership in the policy process bur recognizes that presidential influence should be tailored to the design of a political system where different institutions share power. Many alternative channels for encouraging more effective government, such as constitutonal reform, "responsible" parties along European lines, or some form of congressional government based on a parliamentary model, are politically infeasible or ill-advised (Sundquist, 1981). Given our present constitutional structure of formally separate branches, the informal relations between the president and Congress provide the basis for cooperation and compromise necessary to achieve policy results. Properly defined, the president's role as a strategic actor could bridge this institutional gap and prove that "comity within the system" necessary for efficient, representative, and responsible governing.

## NOTES

I would like to thank Fred I. Greenstein, MacAlister Brown, Gary Jacobsohn, George Marcus, Jeffrey Tulis, and the editors of this volume for their helpful comments and criticisms.

1. Reagan's use of a troika did prove increasingly maladapted to the personalities involved and to effective decision making (Barrett, 1983).
2. A lengthier discussion of the Eisenhower case (as well as relevant archival documentation) can be found in Burke (1985).
3. Presidential popularity among the general public is probably less important among House Budget Committee members since they tend to be more ideological and partisan and more concerned with policy and the integrity of the budget process (LeLoup, 1979, 1980). The House Budget Committee is not a "constituency" committee, to use Fenno's (1973) typology. Thus a president might want to emphasize other elements in his strategic repertoire, such as shared ideology and party identification with members of his own party (LeLoup, 1982), shared ideology with like-minded members of the opposition, and indirect tactics aimed at encouraging bipartisan support for those whose policy and party preferences differ from his own.

# REFERENCES

Barrett, Laurence I. 1983. *Gambling with History: Reagan in the White House.* New York: Doubleday.

Bunce, Valerie. 1981. Policy cycles and the American presidency. Paper presented at the annual convention of the Midwestern Political Science Association, Cincinnati, Ohio.

Burke, John P. 1985. Political context and presidential influence. *Presidential Studies Quarterly* 15:301–19.

Burns, James MacGregor. 1966. *Presidential Government.* Boston: Houghton Mifflin.

Cohen, Richard E. 1981. If you thought the fiscal 1982 budget battle was over, take another look. *National Journal*, 19 December, 2245–47.

———. 1982. Congress and White House play a waiting game in 1983 budget. *National Journal*, 20 March, 488–93.

Congressional Quarterly. 1982a. Budget experts warn process could fail. *Congressional Quarterly Weekly Report*, 23 January, 115–18.

———. 1982b. Congress balks at '83 budget with cuts and huge deficits, *Congressional Quarterly Report*, 13 February, 223–24.

———. 1982c. Congress facing budget cuts, recognizing Reagan can be beaten. *Congressional Quarterly Weekly Report*, 20 February, 305–06.

———. 1982d. Presidential strategy for budget under fire. *Congressional Quarterly Weekly Report*, 6 March, 506.

———. 1982e. Budget rules reflect unique political and economic brew. *Congressional Quarterly Weekly Report*, 24 April, 901–03.

———. 1982f. Budget battle erupts on Hill as compromise talks fizzle. *Congressional Quarterly Weekly Report*, 1 May, 967–69.

———. 1982g. Rep. Jones: Beleaguered budget chairman. *Congressional Quarterly Weekly Report*, 19 June, 1447–49.

———. 1983. Reagan support fades in key votes in 1982. *Congressional Quarterly Weekly Report*, 15 January, 117.

Cooper, Joseph, and G. Bombardier. 1968. Presidential leadership and party success. *Journal of Politics* 30:1012–27.

Corwin, Edward S. 1957. *The President: Office and Powers, 1787–1957.* New York: New York University Press.

Cronin, Thomas. 1979. Presidential power revised and reappraised. *Western Political Quarterly* 32:381–95.

Davis, Eric. 1979. Legislative liaison in the Carter administration. *Political Science Quarterly* 95:287–301.

Edwards, George C. 1980. *Presidential Influence in Congress.* San Francisco: W. H. Freeman.

Ellwood, John. 1982. How Congress controls expenditures. In *Reductions in U.S. Domestic Spending*, ed. J. Ellwood, pp. 21–32. New Brunswick, N.J.: Transaction Books.

Ellwood, John, and James Thurber. 1977. The new congressional budget process: The hows and whys of House-Senate differences. In *Congress Reconsidered*, ed. L. Dodd and B. Oppenheimer, pp. 163–92. New York: Praeger.

Fenno, Richard. 1973. *Congressmen in Committees.* Boston: Little, Brown.

Fisher, Louis. 1981. In dubious battle? Congress and the budget. *The Brookings Bulletin* 17:6–10.

*Gallup Report.* 1982. No. 203. August.

George, Alexander. 1980. *Presidential Decisionmaking in Foreign Policy: The Effective Use of Information and Advice*. Boulder, Colo: Westview.

Greenstein, Fred I. 1982. *The Hidden-Hand Presidency: Eisenhower as Leader*. New York: Basic Books.

Hartman, Robert W. 1982. Congress and budget making. *Political Science Quarterly* 97:381–402.

Havemann, Joel. 1978. *Congress and the Budget*. Bloomington: Indiana University Press.

Heclo, Hugh. 1977. *A Government of Strangers*. Washington, D.C.: The Brookings Institution.

Heclo, Hugh, and Rudolph Penner. 1983. Fiscal and political strategy in the Reagan Administration. In *The Reagan Presidency: An Early Assessment*, ed. F. I. Greenstein, pp. 21–47. Baltimore: The Johns Hopkins University Press.

Hess, Stephen. 1976. *Organizing the Presidency*. Washington, D.C.: The Brookings Institution.

Hill, Kim Q., and John Patrick Plumlee. 1984. Policy arenas and budgetary politics. *Western Political Quarterly* 37:84–99.

Johannes, John. 1972. When does the buck stop: Congress, president, and the responsibility for legislative initiation. *Western Political Quarterly* 25:396–415.

Johnson, Richard Tanner. 1974. *Managing the White House*. New York: Harper and Row.

Kessel, John H. 1974. Parameters of presidential politics. *Social Science Quarterly* 55:8–24.

LeLoup, Lance. 1979. Process versus policy: The U.S. House Budget Committee. *Legislative Studies Quarterly* 4:227–53.

————. 1980. *The fiscal congress: Legislative control of the budget*. Westport, Conn.: Greenwood Press.

————. 1982. After the blitz: Reagan and the U.S. congressional budget process. *Legislative Studies Quarterly* 7:321–39.

LeLoup, Lance, and Steven Shull. 1979. Congress versus the executive: The "two presidencies" reconsidered. *Social Science Quarterly* 59:704–19.

Levitan, Sar, and Martha Cooper. 1984. *Business Lobbying: The Public Good and the Bottom Line*. Baltimore: The Johns Hopkins University Press.

Light, Paul. 1981. Passing nonincremental policy: Presidential influence in Congress, Kennedy to Carter. *Congress and the Presidency* 9:61–82.

————. 1982. *The president's agenda: Domestic policy choice from Kennedy to Carter*. Baltimore: The Johns Hopkins University Press.

Lowi, Theodore. 1964. American business, public policy, case-studies, and political theory. *World Politics* 16:677–715.

————. 1972. Four systems of policy, politics, and choice. *Public Administration Review* 32:298–310.

Miroff, Bruce. 1976. *Pragmatic Illusions*. New York: McKay.

————. 1979. Beyond the Washington establishment: A broader theory of the presidency. Paper presented at the annual convention of the American Political Science Association, Washington, D.C.

Moe, Ronald, and Steven Teel. 1970. Congress as policy maker: A necessary reappraisal. *Political Science Quarterly* 85:443–70.

Neustadt, Richard E. 1960. *Presidential Power: The Politics of Leadership*. New York: John Wiley.

————. 1983. Presidential leadership: The clerk against the preacher. In *Problems and Prospects of Leadership in the 1980s,* ed. J. S. Young, pp. 1–36. Lanham, Md.: University Press of America.

*New York Times.* 1983. Signs of mutiny among Reagan's good soldiers. 18 April.

————. 1984. Deficit talks begin but meeting fails to resolve key differences. 8 February.

Ornstein, Norman J. 1982. Reagan's coming collison with Congress. *Fortune,* 8 February.

Pechman, Joseph, et al. 1983. *Setting National Priorities: The 1983 Budget.* Washington, D.C.: The Brookings Institution.

Pika, Joseph. 1981. Moving beyond the Oval Office: Problems in studying the presidency. *Congress and the Presidency* 9:17–36.

Pious, Richard. 1979. *The American Presidency.* New York: Basic Books.

Peters, Jean. 1981. Reconciliation, 1982: What happened? *PS* 14:732–38.

Rockman, Bert A. 1979. Constants, cycles, trends and persona in presidential governance: Carter's troubles reviewed. Paper presented at the annual convention of the American Political Science Association, Washington, D.C.

Salamon, Lester M. 1981. The presidency and domestic policy. In *The Illusion of Presidential Government,* ed. L. Salamon and H. Heclo, pp. 177–202. Boulder, Colo.: Westview.

Schick, Allen. 1980. *Congress and Money.* Washington, D.C.: The Urban Institute.

————. 1981a. *Reconciliation and the Congressional Budget Process.* Washington, D.C.: American Enterprise Institute.

————. 1981b. In Congress reassembled: Reconciliation and the legislative process. *PS* 14:748–52.

————. 1982. How the budget was won and lost. In *President and Congress: Assessing Reagan's First Year,* ed. N. Ornstein, pp. 14–43. Washington, D.C.: American Enterprise Institute.

Seligman, Lester. 1980. On models of the presidency. *Presidential Studies Quarterly* 10:353–63.

Shull, Steven A. 1983. *Domestic Policy Formation: Presidential-Congressional Partnership?* Westport: Greenwood.

Smith, Hedrick. 1981. Taking charge of Congress. *New York Times Magazine,* 9 August, pp. 12ff.

Sperlich, P. W. 1969. Bargaining and overload: An essay on presidential power. In *The Presidency,* ed. A. Wildavsky, pp. 168–92. Boston: Little, Brown.

Spitzer, Robert. 1983. Presidential policy determinance: How policies frame congressional response to the president's legislative program. *Presidential Studies Quarterly* 13:556–74.

Sundquist, James L. 1968. *Politics and Policy: The Eisenhower, Kennedy, and Johnson Years.* Washington, D.C.: The Brookings Institution.

————. 1981. *The Decline and Resurgence of Congress.* Washington, D.C.: The Brookings Institution.

Thomas, Norman C. 1970. Presidential advice and information: Policy and program formulation. *Law and Contemporary Problems* 35:540–72.

Wanat, J. 1975. Bureaucratic politics in the budget formulation arena. *Administration and Society* 7:191–212.

Wayne, Stephen W. 1978. *The Legislative Presidency.* New York: Random House.

————. 1982. Congressional liaison in the Reagan White House: A preliminary assessment of the first year. In *President and Congress: Assessing Reagan's First Year,* ed. N. Ornstein, pp.44–65. Washington, D.C.: American Enterprise Institute.

Wildavsky, Aaron. 1964. *The Politics of the Budgetary Process.* Boston: Little, Brown.

―――. 1966. The two presidencies. *Trans-action* 4:7–14.

Wolfe, Alan. 1981. Presidential power and the crisis of modernization. *democracy* 1:19–32

M. Stephen Weatherford and Lorraine M. McDonnell

# Macroeconomic Policy Making Beyond the Electoral Constraint

The literature on the political business cycle has sensitized political scientists to the importance of elections as constraints on macroeconomic policy. Combining the conventional wisdom that politicians manipulate the economy to win elections with the reasonable assumption that politicians are vote maximizers, researchers have outlined a set of patterns in which major economic policy decisions are strongly influenced by electoral considerations. This research carries forward both an old theme among postwar political commentators as well as the more recent line of "economic" or "spatial" models of party competition (cf. Kramer, 1971; Keech, 1980, for reviews of this literature). But it stands quite separate from the well-established tradition that views macroeconomic management as the outcome of an elite-level governmental policy process rather than as a direct aspect of party competition (Stein, 1969; Flash, 1965; Porter, 1980). For this second school, the primary determinants of economic policy are to be found in the interplay among national political forces between elections, not in the campaign itself. These authors do not neglect the influence of elections entirely, but they give the electoral constraint minor billing.

This essay is part of a larger research project that attempts to place this apparent disagreement into a broader perspective. Our goal is to formulate a theoretical framework into which both the causal hypotheses of the political business cycle approach and those of the traditional policy process approach can be included as separate components. From economic models we take the notion that the formation of macroeconomic policy can be best understood in terms of an abstract model. The major components of this model are the *goals* of presidential economic policy; the *options,* opportunities, and resources afforded by economic conditions, the state of political and economic knowledge, and the president's own ability to assemble and utilize the tools of economic management; and the *constraints* on the president's ability to pursue those goals through the political process. The model takes from the policy process approach the conviction that neither economic goals nor the choice of instruments is determined by the need to win elections. We envision the electoral constraint as one among several, and probably not the most important, of forces impinging on government economic policy decisions. In this essay, we concentrate on the president's economic policy goals, suggesting that an important source of nonelectoral goals is the president's economic ideology. Our ideas are illustrated by brief case studies of economic policy making in the Eisenhower and Kennedy administrations.

## The President and Economic Policy Making: Options and Constraints

The assumption that politicians are vote maximizers is generally true but always a simplification of reality. Although it is obviously necessary to win a plurality in order to pursue other goals, there remains a great deal of variation among politicians in their willingness to trade off popularity against ideological purity, and especially in their willingness to take actions once in power that might endanger their party's short-term electoral chances. Economic policy making is an arena in which we should expect the president's deepest and most strongly held conceptions of the social good to come into play, so it is certainly worth investigating the assumption than other goals are automatically subverted to the maintenance of an electoral majority. Moreover, even if the president is intent on assuring success in the next election, he is not free to choose any strategy or policy combination to achieve that goal: a politician with a well-established record, strong ideological principles, and firm policy predilections may have very little spatial mobility in attempting to approach the median voter (Stokes, 1966). Finally, the president's goals are pursued within the bounds of an economy over which he has only partial control. His ability to pursue these goals is conditioned by the limits of knowledge and understanding, as mapped by his advisors and by current macroeconomic theory and research.

By placing primary emphasis on the electoral goal, the vote-maximizing assumption lumps together as *ceteris paribus* a multitude of other factors that constrain presidential choice. These factors cannot be counted on to cancel out in the real world, so a theory is needed to elaborate more precisely the notion of nonelectoral constraints. The anticipated reactions of voters are an important constraint, but the actions and anticipated reactions of other political elites are also critical to the formation of national economic policy. These include:

> executive actors in addition to the president (most notably the Federal Reserve and its chairman, but also cabinet officers from State, Treasury, Commerce, Labor, and possibly other departments, and the Council of Economic Advisors);

powerful members of Congress, especially committee chairmen, and patterned executive-legislative relations involving not only the president, but also the long-standing ties among agencies, legislative committees, and Office of Management and Budget staff (after 1974, the new congressional budget process is the most visible, if not the most important such constraint);

extragovernmental demands for particular economic policies and budget allocations (e.g., from government program clients and other interest groups, party activists, and in advice from "economic notables" in the business and intellectual communities).

These constraints circumscribe the president's ability to use his powers to pursue his party's electoral goals or, indeed, or focus his administration's economic policy narrowly on any simple objective. In the next section we propose the notion of presidential economic ideology as a way of understanding how the president might resolve the demands of multiple goals.

## The President's Economic Ideology

Quantitative studies of the correlation between elections and economic policy are necessarily limited to analyzing those indicators for which reliable time-series data can be assembled. These comprise a small set: indexing unemployment, inflation, disposable income, and a few other economic aggregates. Presidents obviously have economic goals that go beyond a concern for unemployment, inflation, or growth rates and for which these indicators are not appropriate substitutes. Moreover, although these economic goals may be pursued in some measure because they enhance the president's electoral chances, they also spring from personal and partisan conceptions of the role of the state in the national economy. In this sense, economic goals are ends in themselves and cannot be understood simply as components of an electoral strategy.

The notion of presidential economic ideology is intended to summarize the goals that animate the administration's program of macroeconomic management. Journalistic shorthand references to Reagan's "supply-side economics" or Kennedy's "new economics" serve this sort of summary function, but they do so in an unsystematic and often misleadingly simplified way. For the concept to be usable in scholarly discourse, two important requisites must distinguish it from this informal usage. First, the term must be given a denotation that is sufficiently abstract for comparison and generalization while still pointing to the way in which economic and political goals are melded in specific policies. Second, it must be operationally precise enough to guide the interpretation of presidential economic activities.

At its most general, the administration's economic ideology proposes answers to questions about the interaction between private and public economic power and the ends to which governmental economic activity is directed. Borrowing from the economic literature on public finance, we can distinguish three broad policy objectives:

> the *allocation* function—"the provision for social goods or the process by which total resource use is divided between private and social goods and by which the mix of social goods is chosen";

> the *distribution* function, concerned with adjusting the distribution of income and wealth accruing to individuals or groups in the population;

> the *stabilization* function—"the use of budget policy as a means of maintaining high employment, a reasonable degree of price level stability, and an appropriate rate of economic growth [and] stability in the balance of payments" (Musgrave and Musgrave, 1973, p. 8; cf. Musgrave, 1959).

The president's beliefs and preferences about the appropriate government role in each of these policy domains comprise his economic ideology. These ideas will influence his perception of economic conditions and his interpretation of ambiguous economic indicators; his selection of particular policies from the menu of available options in any given situation; and his preference for specific policy instruments to achieve a given macroeconomic goal. Moreover, as the administration's economic ideas take shape and the president's sense of mastery in the economic realm grows, his economic ideology will also channel his selection of advisors and narrow the sources of influence and advocacy to which his decision-making procedures are most open (Flash, 1965; Stein, 1969; Norton, 1977; Porter, 1980).

The president's economic ideology is, of course, not independent of his conceptions of the policy agenda for which the voters chose him (and hence of the standards by which they will judge his performance at the next election), nor of the interest groups, congressional factions, and party coalitions to which he feels closest. But at any given time his ideology is not a proxy for those influences. It is, rather, a tool that allows him to select from their demands, to meld them, or to adopt a novel option. And in a crisis or ambiguous situation, the president's own economic lodestone will be the surest guide among a set of alternatives whose future effects can be only dimly gauged.

Presidents do not often develop new policy ideas once in office. Given the complexity of the policy-making process and inevitable emergencies requiring immediate response, the administration's time and energy are often stretched thin managing the implementation of prior goals. The president's economic ideology maps such a set of policy aspirations, and to this extent it stands *ex ante* as the guide to a host of later goals and actions pursued during the term. But economic events are also the source of many of the most pressing short-term demands on the administration's attention. To the extent that the president ends up articulating his economic policy vision in response to short-term stabilization problems, his economic ideology will be worked out through a process of successive approximation. Policy ideas will be tried out and compared for their consistency with the president's broader purposes and commitments; their ability to survive a policy environment in which powers are shared between legislator and executive; and their ability to ameliorate the economic problems toward which they are directed. "Ideology" at this pole is close to what political scientists generally refer to as "strategy" (cf. Neustadt, 1980, for such a definition of presidential ideology), and it may be quite distinct from the notion of ideology as a relatively fixed set of prior beliefs.

When will presidential economic ideology resemble the conception of a stable, far-ranging core of fundamental beliefs and when will it more closely match Neustadt's "strategic" image? Three conditions determine variation along this continuum: (1) the strength or intensity of the president's initial economic beliefs; (2) the content of those beliefs, particularly the extent to which his goals can be fulfilled by maintaining the status quo versus the degree to which his ideology requires substantial changes in the role of government or the operation of the economy; and (3) the magnitude and frequency of external shocks to the macroeconomy. In this essay, we compare two presidents distinguished clearly on the second of these characteristics, although both were strongly committed to their economic beliefs. Moreover, we choose two administrations occurring contiguously in time in order to control, as much as possible, for the potentially confounding influences of exogenous changes in the national and international economic environment.

## Economic Ideology and Economic Policy

The president might take the macroeconomy largely as he finds it, attempting to guide it according to either of the following approaches:

(1) Pursue a simple political business cycle strategy, stimulating economic activity just prior to the election, then putting on the brakes for the next year or so in order to push the inflation rate back down to tolerable levels.

(2) Strive for a smooth economic growth path, using discretionary and automatic stabilizing policies whenever indicated by macroeconomic conditions, regardless of the timing of elections.

These two options leave the determination of allocative and distributive outcomes up to the market (or, more specifically, to the operation of the market within the parameters established by existing government regulations). They take the composition of the national product and the distribution of income as given, and specific policies implemented in pursuit of these goals would attempt to avoid placing new, governmentally created advantages or disadvantages into the flow of market transactions. These are the sorts of policies that commentators have in mind when they surmise that bipartisan subscription to the Employment Act of 1946 entails that both parties will pursue the same economic policy goals (e.g., Stigler, 1973; Stein, 1969). For political science, the critical aspect of these two economic management strategies is that they could be pursued by either party, with only efficiency considerations distinguishing one party from the other.

Most presidents, however, do not seek a socially or economically neutral role for the state (cf. Nordlinger, 1981). The typical president would be much more likely to direct his efforts toward policy goals like the following:

(3) Attempt to serve the short-term interests of his partisan or socioeconomic constituency or to serve the short-term interests of potential converts from opposition parties or groups.

(4) Pursue the long-term allocative goals of party or presidential economic ideology, for instance, by seeking to diminish/increase the share of government as a proportion of aggregate demand or to diminish/increase the federal share of total governmental expenditure.

(5) Pursue the long-term distributive goals of party or presidential economic ideology, for instance, by using tax or expenditure policies to alter the distribution of income toward/away from greater equality.

The distinguishing feature of these three policies is their unmistakable partisan bias. Not only is it clear *a priori* whether left or right parties would adopt each option, but it is also the case that none of these policies would have neutral effects across socioeconomic classes: they are the stuff of party competition (Pomper, 1972; Page, 1978, 1983).

A sixth option, intermediate between these two groupings, is possible. This policy would concentrate on "expanding the pie," rather than on altering current shares. Because the underlying growth rate of the economy can be shifted upward only by increasing the efficiency of productive capacity, the primary short-term thrust of policy will inevitably favor investment at the expense of consumption. The partisan character of a growth-enhancing policy will be clear only from the context of other economic and social programs with which it is linked. If the gains from any resulting expansion remain in the hands of investors, management and unionized labor, then the political implications of the policy are quite different from the situation in which increased growth fosters "human capital" investment like expanded education and training programs, redistributive tax policies, or a poverty program.

One final distinction among these policy paths is worth noting, this one distinguishing the latter two from the others. While the first three policy paths focus attention on short-term economic stabilization, only the fourth and fifth options envisage the president's use of his powers to achieve allocative or distributive goals. Similarly, these two options shift the time horizon from short-term "fire-fighting" to the pursuit of medium- or long-range ends. Our inclusion of these two policy paths in the depiction of presidential ideology marks a clear departure from the political business cycle literature, which is characterized in all its versions by the presupposition that short-term goals dominate economic policy choices.

No administration is allowed the luxury of single-mindedly pursuing its conception of the ideal use for governmental economic power. All modern presidents have been bound to consider the international strength of the dollar and the balance of payments; none can afford to ignore the movement of some important economic indicator into the crisis range (cf. Frey, 1978); and their pursuit of any one goal is circumscribed by the vague but deeply held sense of fairness implied by the Employment Act of 1946. Hence, for instance, price stability cannot be sought by inducing a depression, and if some exogenous shock threatens prevailing levels of employment or capacity utilization, then the administration may have to abandon its other goals temporarily to work at restoring stability. Both the press of short-run economic "emergencies" and the weight of convention and expectations about the government's traditional economic role diminish party differences and hence the unique impact of presidential ideology.

At the same time, however, it must be noted that these bounds are neither narrow nor inflexible. They are set largely by historical experience and they are open to change. An activist president, or one confronting an especially difficult situation for which conventional remedies seem inadequate, can alter the context in which policy options are defined and actions evaluated. The Reagan administration's first two years show the spaciousness and permeability of conventional limits on presidential actions in pursuit of economic goals.

## Economic Ideology and Policy in the Eisenhower Administration

When the Eisenhower administration took office, the Federal Reserve was pursuing a tight credit policy, largely in response to the exuberant monetary expansion of the previous two years. The new administration, believing a serious threat of inflation existed, reinforced this policy through Treasury operations in the bond market, by reducing government expenditures, and by opposing tax cuts. The latter involved the active intervention of the administration in securing congressional assent to retention of the Excess Profits Tax scheduled to expire automatically in June 1953. The critical aspect of this initial economic policy was that the president's belief in the importance of fighting inflation brought him into direct conflict with the business interests at the center of his party's constituency (cf. Stein, 1969; chap. 11), as well as with other moderate Republicans. Nevertheless, the administration maintained its belief that demand was generally excessive and that the danger of inflation was immediate (Humphrey, 1954, pp. 204–07; Martin, 1954, pp. 7–8; cf. Schlichter, 1956).

Although tight monetary conditions ensured that smooth, nonrecessionary adjustment would be difficult in the face of any fiscal shock, they merely formed the background for the 1954 recession. The primary cause of the recession was the administration's purposeful and dramatic reduction of federal expenditures. Eisenhower, pledged to end the Korean conflict, immediately cut defense expenditures projected in the Truman budget and reduced them further with the July 1953 truce. This is unquestionably the most significant fiscal policy action of the Eisenhower years, amounting to a decrease of nearly 20 percent in federal expenditures—3 percent of GNP—over a period of less than one year (*Economic Report*, 1956, tables D-1, D-11, D-12; Kramer, 1956; Gordon, 1980, p. 116). Severe problems of readjustment were readily foreseeable from a shift of this magnitude.

If the post-Depression commitment to activist fiscal stabilization policy marks the "fiscal revolution," then the 1954 recession is, as Stein (1969) notes, a critical test case in deciding whether the Republican party had accepted the change or not. How active was the administration's commitment to smoothing the path of economic growth?

In the broadest sense, government fiscal policy was the primary *destabilizing* force in the first Eisenhower administration, with the great magnitude of the cut in defense expenditures being the dominant source of fluctuations in aggregate demand. Even on a narrower definition of fiscal policy, treating defense spending as an exogenous impact on the economy, the picture is only slightly more positive.

The president's budget message of January 1954, for instance, shows no recognition at all of the developing recession, and the counsel of Arthur Burns for the quick application of stimulative fiscal policy to halt the decline is in a distinct minority (Stein, 1969, p. 301). The *Economic Report* gives more attention to the recession, but it is vague about specific countercyclical policies and portrays the administration's tax proposals not as a response to the recession but as part of a long-range program to promote economic growth by reducing taxes on private sector investment resources. As Stein summarizes the impression as of early 1954, "the administration's fiscal policy to counter the recession was to carry on despite the recession with the course that would have been followed if there had been no recession" (1969, pp. 301–02).

The president and others averred frequently that they were amenable to spending on public works if conditions became sufficiently serious and that they were compiling a list of federal projects that could be commenced if the need arose (*Economic Report*, 1954, p. iv; U.S. Congress, 1955, p. 23). There is little evidence that this commitment to large federal expenditures as a countercyclical device went beyond rhetoric, however, and even so sympathetic an observer as Stein concludes that "there is reason to doubt that either the administration or the government then had an effective policy for fiscal measures in a more severe recession" (1969, p. 306). In spite of administration claims that federal spending on public works was prepared for implementation if the need arose, the estimates of Lewis and others indicate that bureaucratic and organizational obstacles would have prevented this from being more than a miniscule and tardy stimulus (Lewis, 1962, pp. 164, 184).

Even the Eisenhower administration's claim to have stimulated the recovery by cutting taxes in 1954 is in need of severe qualification. Of the $7.4 billion of revenue reduction, $5 billion was automatic, having been mandated by earlier Revenue Acts. The Excise Tax Reduction Act of 1954 released another $1 billion into the economy, but the administration opposed this reduction. Finally, the Revenue Act of 1954 reduced taxes by some $1.4 billion, with three-quarters of the reduction directed toward corporations and high-income individuals (U.S. Congress, 1956, pp. 30–31). In sum, the revenue act provided little stimulation of the recovery. The administration argued successfully against the increase in personal tax exemptions urged by the Democrats and concentrated most of the tax cut on corporate investment in heavy equipment. These investment-oriented tax cuts, however, had little short-term stimulative effect, both because of the long planning horizon of business fixed investment and because the recession's depressing effect on consumer demand made businessmen pessimistic about the payoff from investing in new plant and equipment (*Economic Report*, 1956, table D-7; Kramer, 1956)

In short, neither the administration's pronouncements nor its few positive actions had any substantial influence on the timing or the strength of the recovery. That was effected by two factors of economic policy over which the president and his administration exercised no direct control. The primary route out of the 1954 recession was the effective work of the automatic stabilizers that had become law in the New Deal. As economic activity declined and unemployment increased, federal revenues fell and entitlement expenditures increased, helping to sustain private consumption and business investment. In addition, recovery was abetted by a well-timed change in the growth rate of the money supply by the Federal Reserve in mid-1953. This policy was more a reaction to the overly tight credit conditions of the previous months than a far-sighted stabilizing program, but it did coincide closely with the dramatic cut in defense spending (Samuelson, 1956, pp. 371–72).

The automatic stabilizing programs produced recovery, however, only because the administration tolerated the federal budget's sharp swing into deficit, and this is the primary implication of the recession for the "fiscal revolution." The 1954 recession showed that, even under a Republican adminisration strongly commited to fiscal probity, stabilizing budget policy would not be defeated by raising taxes in a recession. And this, as Stein (1969, p. 306) notes, could not have been taken for granted, even as late as the fall of 1953.

It is important, however, to be clear about exactly what this implies about the countercyclical policy commitments of the Republican party. The body of Keynesian ideas that emerged from the Depression comprised a proscriptive part and a prescriptive part. It proscribed the annually balanced budget and simply dictated that the government do nothing to frustrate the automatic stabilizing effect of compensatory revenue and expenditure changes during recessions. The Eisenhower administration adhered to this passive part of its stabilization policy role. That is, the core of the New Deal economic ideas that the president accepted were those that, relying on policies already in place, would be implemented without his active intervention. The positive or prescriptive part of the government's post-Depression stabilizing role entailed the commitment to take effective action to hasten the upturn or to strengthen and sustain the recovery. "The administration also claimed that it was prepared to move on this second part if necessary. This, although not tested in 1954, was doubtful" (Stein, 1969, p. 308).

What explanation can be given for the Eisenhower administration's passive response to its stabilizing budget responsibilities? Although the question has not been discussed at length by economic historians, it is generally implied that the explanation is unproblematical. It amounts to little more than a restatement of Eisenhower's moralistic conservatism about budget balancing, a conservatism greatly strengthened by Humphrey and then Anderson at the Treasury and, after 1956, by Saulnier at the Council of Economic Advisors. Democratic partisans have tended to make much of Eisenhower's apparent hesitancy and unsureness in economic affairs and of his unsophisticated and occasionally ill-informed rhetoric on budget matters (cf. Harris, 1962); centrists and conservatives have agreed with his economic policy actions and forgiven his rhetorical excesses (Schlichter, 1956; Fellner, 1956). Both these interpretations suggest that the president's statements be largely ignored; he was, after all, "economically illiterate" when he entered the White House and domestic economic policy never enjoyed a priority high enough to require his deep involvement in the area (cf. Larson, 1968; Greenstein, 1982). Moreover, both explanations abjure searching among the policy choices and outputs themselves for the sort of thematic coherence we expect of Kennedy's or even Johnson's macroeconomic management.

This posture raises important questions about presidential accountability for economic policy making. By focusing only on the president's actions in response to short-term crises, both approaches obscure the broader context within which economic policy decisions are made, and they imply that economic policy is essentially a series of more or less ad hoc responses to particular episodes of deviation from the path of stable growth.

In proposing a reinterpretation of Eisenhower economic policy, we concur with recent revisionist treatments of his presidency which argue that Eisenhower had distinct policy goals and that the leadership style through which he pursued them was more subtle and effective than contemporary commentators realized (Larson, 1968; Rovere, 1969; Alexander, 1975; Greenstein, 1982). To the extent that these studies have focused on substantive policy rather than on leadership style or on the organizational aspects of Eisenhower's presidency, they have skirted domestic and especially economic issues and concentrated on foreign policy and international relations. This is logical from the perspective of the president's own priorities (cf. Larson, 1968, p. xii; Greenstein, 1982, chap. 1), but it leaves unexplained and ill-understood Eisenhower's contribution to the development of an identifiable Republican approach to economic management after Hoover.

Eisenhower's approach to guiding the economy is not simply a minor variation on the consensual theme of the Employment Act, but neither can it be easily categorized as the antithesis of enlightened liberal economics (cf. Canterbury, 1968, p. 58 ff.). It is most distinctly characterized by its orientation toward the long-term condition of the economy. From this, and from the traditional conservative belief in the primacy of the market, there follow broad policy prescriptions in each of the three areas of presidential economic ideology.

On questions of allocation, the consistent goal is to resist the expansion of the public sector and to decentralize as many aspects of economic decision making as possible. On issues of distribution, the president firmly believed that Democratic taxes on corporate profits and on high incomes were excessive and that economic growth could be assured only if they were reduced. At the same time, however, the administration was open to (if not enthusiastic about) increasing the minimum wage and expanding unemployment coverage. On issues of economic stabilization, the overriding concern was with inflation and, more broadly, with the government's role in maintaining economic "confidence" by portraying an image of self-discipline and prudence designed to stifle the development of inflationary expectations. These three economic themes implied a concerted policy to withhold government action in response to short-term fluctuations, at least until their severity made the justification of some activism unambiguous. By allowing the federal budget to move into deficit, Eisenhower conceded that an all-out assault on inflation would violate the Employment Act. At the same time, he resisted, albeit mainly by inaction, the call to expand the government's role by increasing federal expenditures or for weakening its revenue base by emergency alterations in tax rates (cf. Adams, 1962).

The most significant implications of this aversion to activist stabilization policy are clear only in an economic downturn more severe than could be readily reversed by the automatic stabilizers alone. In this case, the administration's unwillingness to take early action left it with the unfortunate choice between dramatic intervention and nothing at all. Four years later, faced with just such a situation in the 1958 recession, Eisenhower took a similar stance of "watchful waiting," allowing the automatic stabilizers to draw the government into deficit without the administration's taking explicit action. Then, however, both Democrats and moderate Republicans in Congress found his assurances unconvincing, and they pushed through a variety of ameliorative measures that went directly counter to the administration's preferences. In this more serious recession, then, the outcome of a passive policy stance was to succeed in blocking only the most liberal-activist proposals. More importantly, however, this cautious, relatively inflexible economic ideology led quickly to the loss of White House leadership over short-term countercyclical policy in general (Lewis, 1962; Sundquist, 1968).

Eisenhower's conception of the government's proper role in economic stabilization and his deep commitment to stimulating private sector investment and keeping a tight rein on public sector growth are not the accidental outcomes of an inactive president, however. They represent a conscious decision to trade short-term costs for long-term benefits. The trade-off was eased by Eisenhower's relative lack of concern for the electoral implications of his economic policies (Larson, 1968, pp. 34–40; Nixon, 1962, pp. 309–11), but the strength of these economic beliefs led to his conclusion that immediate electoral gains could justly be endangered for the sake of long-term economic goals.

## Economic Ideology and Policy in the Kennedy Administration

With perhaps the exception of Ronald Reagan, Kennedy more than any other postwar president shaped economic policy according to a clearly articulated ideology. At the heart of his New Economics was a strong belief that government should play an active role in stimulating long-term, stable growth. Kennedy's economic ideology differed from that of past Democratic administrations in his conviction that fiscal policy should do more than just combat fluctuations in the business cycle; that a long-term expansion in capacity is as important to economic growth as increased aggregate demand; and that growth can be accelerated through tax policies which directly encourage business investment. Although evolving over time and circumstance, Kennedy's economic ideology went beyond mere public rhetoric to serve as a continuous guide for his actions and policies.

Although his use of tax policy as a means of stimulating sustained economic growth did not emerge until later, Kennedy was an activist in economic policy from the beginning of his administration. Four legislative initiatives form the core of Kennedy's policy actions:

> the use of traditional countercyclical measures to end the 1960–1961 recession, including the temporary extension of unemployment payments, liberalized social security benefits, an increase in the minimum wage and extension of its coverage, revision of the federal Aid to Dependent Children program, passage of the Area Redevelopment Act, and accelerated federal procurement;

> investment tax credit legislation enacted in 1962 that permitted a tax credit of up to 7 percent of the cost of new business assets as a means of encouraging new plant and machinery;

> the Trade Expansion Act of 1962 that gave the president five-year authority to negotiate reciprocal tariff reductions, particularly between the United States and the Common Market;

> the Revenue Act of 1964, proposed by Kennedy but not enacted until after his death (through a change in tax rates, this legislation reduced the tax liabilities of both individuals and corporations).

Kennedy's economic policy during his first year in office was firmly rooted in the Keynesian tradition. When Kennedy assumed office in January 1961, the country was in the midst of its fourth postwar recession. Unemployment had increased from 5.1 percent in May 1960 to 6.6 percent by January. Gross national product, corrected for price changes, had decreased 1 percent between the second and fourth quarters of 1960, and almost a fifth of the nation's manufacturing capacity lay idle. Still, this recession was shallower than the previous three and recovery was faster. Unemployment had fallen to 6.1 percent by December 1961 from a high of 6.8 percent, and the GNP had grown from $501 billion (annual rate) in the first quarter of 1961 to $542 billion by the last quarter. This growth narrowed the gap between actual and potential GNP from approximately 10 to 15 percent, and about half the plant capacity that lay idle at the beginning of 1961 was in use by the end of that year. The consensus is that Kennedy's countercyclical measures and the unexpected increase in defense spending resulting from the Berlin crisis helped speed the recovery considerably (Canterbury, 1968, pp. 107–09).

However, recovery did not mask the fact that, as Paul Samuelson noted in a preinaugural task force report for Kennedy, the recession had "been superimposed upon an economy which, in the last few years, [had] been sluggish and tired" (1961, p. 25). Recovery from the 1957–1958 recession had been "anemic," and the period of expansion between 1959 and 1960 had not only been shorter than the earlier postwar recoveries, but had also not raised the economy to its previous high levels of employment and capacity utilization. Kennedy had, in effect, inherited an economy primed for expansion. Not only was its productive potential underutilized, but prices were relatively stable (increasing only slightly more than 1 percent annually). Thus, a president interested in an activist fiscal policy had considerable manuevering room for stimulating aggregate demand and investment without fear of overheating the economy.

Kennedy could take advantage of the opportunity economic conditions presented him for two major reasons. The first was his own economic ideology. Several chroniclers of the Kennedy presidency have noted that, prior to his selection, Kennedy held no firm beliefs about economic policy and showed little interest in the subject (Stein, 1969; King, 1983). Upon taking office, Kennedy's views on fiscal policy were still "lightly held" (Stein, 1969, p. 374), but he, nevertheless, was commited to strong presidential leadership in economic policy. This firmly held belief in an activist fiscal policy, along with somewhat more embryonic ideas about broadening the definition of what constitutes a balanced budget and the need to address both issues of aggregate demand and increased supply, were gradually shaped into a coherent ideology through the influence of a second major force in Kennedy's economic policy making, his advisors. These advisors—on the CEA, in the Treasury, and at the Bureau of the Budget—were not only competent and innovative thinkers, but they also functioned as effective advocates, presenting a set of policy options that fit Kennedy's own predilections as well as current economic conditions.

To argue that the Kennedy administration evidenced a stong link between economic ideology and policy is not to argue that the path from the first to the second was a smooth, or even a direct, one. Although Kennedy proposed the investment tax credit within three months of assuming office, his acceptance of the need for a major tax cut was much slower. It would take more than another year before Kennedy would fully accept the idea that the current tax structure was exerting too heavy a fiscal drag on the economy, thus curbing long-term economic growth, and that planned budgetary deficits were an effective mechanism for addressing the problem.

Part of the reason Kennedy was slow to extend his belief in the need for an active governmental role in stimulating economic growth to include the use of planned budgetary deficits was that he faced strong political constraints. Not only did his slim electoral majority deny him a coattail effect in Congress, but he was also dogged by a widespread belief that although federal deficits may be generated as a result of downswings in the business cycle, no president should intentionally plan to create one. The federal budget, like individual household accounts, should be balanced except in unusual circumstances—a notion strongly espoused by Kennedy's predecessor.

These constraints affected not just the length of time Congress spent in enacting Kennedy's tax cut proposals, but also the way the administration and its supporters packaged the proposal. The administration portrayed the tax cut as a reform of oppressive tax rates left over from the Korean war (Tobin, 1974, p. 14). Wilbur Mills, chairman of the House Ways and Means Committee and the administration's most influential congressional supporter, turned the budget deficit argument on its head by portraying the tax cut as an antispending and antideficit measure. According to his reasoning, a temporary deficit was necessary to achieve a balanced budget later, and it was better to incur a deficit through tax reduction than through increased government spending (Sundquist, 1968, p. 50). The administration was also assisted by the support of corporate leaders who were less wedded to a balanced budget ideology than those in Congress, and by the fact that fiscal orthodoxy, as practiced by Eisenhower and carried on to some extent by Kennedy, had not worked to assure economic growth. These arguments were persuasive enough to secure congressional passage of the tax cut. However, as James Tobin wrote several months after the legislation was enacted, "there is not a Keynesian majority in Congress, and conscious deficit finance is still not respectable" (1964, p. 14).

Kennedy's ideology led him to focus on augumenting economic growth and to make redistributive issues secondary. As his remarks to the U.S. Chamber of Commerce indicate, he believed that everyone would benefit from a healthier economy: "In short, our primary challenge is not how to divide the economic pie, but how to enlarge it" (Kennedy, 1962, p. 352). This assumption led him to emphasize measures that would benefit business investors, on the assumption that all would gain from a growing economy and that, in its absence, few purely redistributive measures would make any difference in helping the poor. At the same time, Kennedy by no means ignored redistributive policy, as his espousal of an increase in the minimum wage, manpower training programs, and area redevelopment indicate.

Two other caveats must be made about Kennedy's seeming lack of attention to redistributive issues. Revisionist historians have argued that in proposing the investment tax credit, Kennedy was emphasizing supply-side subsidies for investors at the expense of consumers and traditional Democratic constituents (King, 1983). However, we would argue that such a view neglects the fact that Kennedy proposed tax reform as an integral part of his tax cut proposals. Although he was unsuccessful in obtaining their congressional passage, Kennedy presented these proposals as two parts of a whole. One was designed to stimulate economic growth and would benefit business investors most directly, but the other would broaden the tax base and most adversely affect the affluent who were the primary beneficiaries of most tax loopholes. The criticism, then, is not that Kennedy was insensitive to average working people, but rather, like presidents before and after him, that he lacked the political capital to counter the myriad interests that oppose any significant tax reform.

A second caveat speaks more to what Kennedy intended than to what he actually did. Although it cannot be proved conclusively, it is very likely that had Kennedy lived he would have proposed most of the same Great Society programs that Lyndon Johnson did. At the president's request, Walter Heller and his CEA colleagues were already working at the time of Kennedy's death on the proposals that would become part of the War on Poverty. With a growing economy and a wider electoral margin in 1964, Kennedy would have been able to turn much more of his attention to distributive issues without risking his stabilization goals.

The policies generated by Kennedy's ideology were certainly not without their problems and mistaken assumptions about how economics and politics intersect. Despite these weaknesses, that were not to become apparent until well into the Johnson administration, Kennedy still stands as a model of how much the president can do to shape economic policy if he uses the resources at his disposal well. Kennedy's policy leadership demonstrates the importance of a well-defined ideology as an overarching guide for economic policy decisions; competent advisors; and a course of action flexible enough to be adjusted for either political or economic reasons, but complete enough to begin implementation immediately upon assuming office.

## Conclusion

This essay has suggested that presidential policies can be understood as springing in part from economic ideology. These beliefs about allocation, distribution, stabilization, and economic growth contribute to the way in which a chief executive perceives economic problems, seeks advice about their solution, and chooses among policy options. If strongly held, as they were by Eisenhower and Kennedy, these beliefs establish economic goals that take precedence over considerations of short-term electoral gains.

This research began as a response to the assumption that presidents are motivated primarily by considerations of short-term vote maximization, an assumption common to the political business cycle literature. Neither of these presidents ignored the electoral constraint. Eisenhower, for instance, was an effective campaigner on economic issues and his stump speeches against inflation were some of his most influential, especially during the early years of his presidency. Kennedy, elected with a slim electoral mandate, was painfully aware that his ability to effectuate major changes in economic policy was severely constrained. Moreover, the activism of his policy goals brought him into visible conflict with political elites whose ideas and interests were threatened by a dramatic new approach. It is clear from these cases, however, that presidents pursue multiple goals through economic policy. Forced to choose among these, the president will look to certain long-held personal and partisan conceptions of the economic role of the state. This ideology will seldom rank vote maximization at the head of the president's list of economic goals.

The fact that an economic ideology helps to organize our understanding of Eisenhower and Kennedy economic policy is encouraging, but therein lies its most serious limitation. How readily can the explanatory notion of economic ideology be generalized? Three considerations circumscribe theoretical generalizations from these cases, just as they condition the application of presidential ideology to macroeconomic management. First, these two presidents considered economic policy to be one of the primary tasks of their job as national leader, and both carried into office a strongly held conception of the direction in which the country's economy ought to move. Other presidents have taken less interest in economic management and have held less clearly formulated economic policy goals. The less clear the president's economic ideology and the more inclined he is to abandon its pursuit in the face of short-term pressures, the less any consistent direction will be discernible in the succession of an administration's economic policies. Second, in retrospect it is possible to see that these two presidents enjoyed the relative luxury of managing an American economy protected in many respects from the supply shocks and destabilizing international trade and capital movements which have become familiar since the mid-1970's. Their sharing this blessing increases our warrant for comparing one administration to the other, but it must also caution generalizing about the role of economic ideology without taking careful account of the changed circumstances facing later administrations.

If the similarity of Eisenhower and Kennedy in terms of our first two considerations warns against generalizing from case studies of limited variability, then we have stronger external validity in respect to the third criterion. Here, the influence of presidential economic ideology can be seen clearly across a range of partisan goals. Although Eisenhower clearly rejected any serious attack on the ameliorative programs of the New Deal, he perceived an economy constantly in danger of overexuberant expansion, in which the government's job was to intervene as little as possible, but to concentrate its effort primarily on the fight against inflation. Kennedy and his advisors, on the other hand, perceived a chronically underemployed economy in which both investment and consumer demand were deficient. And although the active implementation of traditional Keynesian stabilization policies could remedy the recession

Kennedy faced on taking office, the longer run health of the economy would be ensured best by deemphasizing inflation and unemployment and concentrating on investment and growth.

An economic ideology like Eisenhower's, that calls for "holding the line,"requires relatively little cooperation from economic conditions or even political elites: it requires clear-eyed perseverance, but little more to be implemented in a political system with multiple veto points. An economic ideology like Kennedy's is more broadly activist, threatening both the economic status quo and its underpinning of ideas and economic myths; its successful pursuit requires tractable economic conditions and the assent of congressional and private decision makers. With a narrow electoral mandate, a suspicious Congress, and the business community skeptical of the desirability of his goals, Kennedy's accomplishment of even a substantial portion of his aspirations is attributable to the strength of his economic ideology and his skill in marshaling resources in its pursuit.

The generalizability of the notion of presidential economic ideology must be assessed in further research. In the meantime, however, this approach to explicating the nonelectoral goals of national economic policy should introduce a useful elaboration of current models of macroeconomic management.

## REFERENCES

Adams, Sherman. 1962. *Firsthand Report*. New York: Harper.

Alexander, Charles C. 1975. *Holding the Line*. Bloomington: Indiana University Press.

Canterbury, E. Ray. 1968. *Economics on a New Frontier*. Belmont, Cal.: Wadsworth.

*Economic Report of the President as Transmitted to the Congress*. 1954; 1955; 1956. Washington, D.C.: U.S. Government Printing Office.

Fellner, William. 1956. The economics of Eisenhower: A symposium. *Review of Economics and Statistics* 38:373–75.

Flash, Edward S., Jr. 1965. *Economic Advice and Presidential Leadership*. New York: Columbia University Press.

Frey, Bruno S. 1978. *Modern Political Economy*. Oxford: Martin Robertson.

Gordon, Robert J. 1980. Postwar macroeconomics. In *The American Economy in Transition* ed. Feldstein, pp. 101–62. Chicago: University of Chicago Press.

Greenstein, Fred I. 1982. *The Hidden-Hand Presidency*. New York: Basic Books.

Harris, Seymour E. 1962. *The Economics of the Political Parties*. New York: Harper.

Humphrey, George. 1954. *Annual Report of the Secretary of the Treasury for the Fiscal Year 1953*. Washington, D.C.: U.S. Government Printing Office.

Keech, William R. 1980. Elections and macroeconomic policy optimization. *American Journal of Political Science* 24:345–67.

Kennedy, John F. 1962, 1963. *Public Papers of the Presidents of the United States: John F. Kennedy*. Washington, D.C.: U.S. Government Printing Office.

King, Ronald Frederick. 1983. From redistributive to hegemonic logic: The transformation of American politics, 1894–1963. *Politics and Society* 12:1-52.

Kramer, Gerald. 1971. Short-term fluctuations in U.S. voting behavior, 1896–1964. *American Political Science Review* 65:131–45.

Kramer, R. 1956. A review of employment trends in 1954 and 1955. *Monthly Labor Review* 78:1105–11.

Larson, Arthur. 1968. *Eisenhower.* New York: Scribner's.

Lewis, Wilfred, Jr., 1962. *Federal Fiscal Policies in the Postwar Recessions.* Washington, D.C.: Brookings.

Martin, William McChesney. 1954. *Hearings of the Economic Stabilization Subcommittee of the Joint Committee on the Economic Report* (December 6, 1954). Washington, D.C.: U.S. Government Printing Office.

Musgrave, Richard A. 1959. *The Theory of Public Finance.* New York: McGraw-Hill.

Musgrave, Richard A., and Peggy B. Musgrave. 1973. *Public Finance in Theory and Practice.* New York: McGraw-Hill.

Neustadt, Richard E. 1980. *Presidential Power.* New York: Wiley.

Nixon, Richard M. 1962. *Six Crises.* New York: Doubleday.

Nordlinger, Eric. 1981. *The Autonomy of the Democratic State.* Cambridge, Mass.: Harvard University Press.

Norton, Hugh. 1977. *The Employment Act and the Council of Economic Advisors, 1946–76.* Columbia: University of South Carolina Press.

Page, Benjamin I. 1978. *Choices and Echoes in Presidential Elections.* Chicago: University of Chicago Press.

———. 1983. *Who Gets What from Government?* Berkeley: University of California Press.

Pomper, Gerald M. 1968. *Elections in America.* New York: Dodd Mead.

Pomper, Gerald M. 1975. *Voter's Choice.* New York: Harper.

Porter, Roger B. 1980. *Presidential Decision Making: The Economic Policy Board.* Cambridge, Mass.: Harvard University Press.

Rovere, Richard. 1956. *Affairs of State.* New York: Farrar, Straus and Cudahy.

Samuelson, Paul A. 1956. The economics of Eisenhower: A symposium. *Review of Economics and Statistics* 38: 4 (November):371–73.

———. 1961. Economic frontiers. In *New Frontiers of the Kennedy Administration* (The Texts of the Task Force Reports Prepared for the President) (Washington, D.C.: Public Affairs Press), pp. 24–38.

Schlichter, Sumner H. 1956. The economics of Eisenhower: A symposium. *Review of Economics and Statistics* 38:365–71.

Stein, Herbert. 1969. *The Fiscal Revolution in America.* Chicago: University of Chicago Press.

Stigler, George. 1973. Aggregate economic conditions and national elections. *American Economic Review* 64:160–67.

Stokes, Donald E. 1966. Spatial models of electoral competition. In *Elections and the Political Order,* ed. A. Campbell, et al., pp. 161–179. New York: Wiley.

Sundquist, James L. 1968. *Politics and Policy.* Washington, D.C.: Brookings Institution.

Tobin, James. 1964. Tax cut harvest. *The New Republic,* 7 March, 14–17.

———. 1974. *The New Economics One Decade Older.* Princeton, N.J.: Princeton University Press.

U.S. Congress. Joint Committee on the Economic Report. 1955. *Hearings on the Economic Report of the President.* 84th Cong., 1st sess. Washington, D.C.: U.S. Government Printing Office.

———. 1956. *Hearings on the Economic Report of the President.* 84th Cong., 2nd sess. Washington, D.C.: U.S. Government Printing Office.

Ryan J. Barilleaux

# Evaluating Presidential Performance in Foreign Affairs

The president is the director of American foreign policy, and as such he is said to "bear the burden" for foreign affairs. He is not only the central decision maker but also the chief spokesman, and his performance is continually judged the Congress, by public, the press, and international observers. Yet, by what standards is he judged? Concomitantly, how accurate are those standards for evaluating his performance?

These questions are the concern of this study. Its aim is to develop a clear idea of current evaluative standards, to examine them in the light of historical experience, and thus to aid in refining the criteria for presidential evaluation. In essence, it will be the first step toward an empirical theory of presidential performance in policy making.

Such a theory is relevant to both the presidency and the policy area of foreign affairs. American democracy places primary responsibility for foreign policy in the hands of the president, so it is important that evaluative standards in this area be thoughtful and realistic. Moreover, foreign policy is a distinct area for analysis and for presidential policy making: presidential power in domestic and foreign affairs is uneven. As Wildavsky (1966) demonstrated and Shull (1979) and Shull and LeLoup (1981) have confirmed, presidential influence and power is greater in foreign than in domestic policy, thus making his performance particularly relevant to that area of public policy.

## Presidential Policy Making: The Conventional Wisdom

Few president watchers deal explicitly with evaluation (see Buchanan, 1981; Edwards, 1983; Hargrove and Nelson, 1984; Wayne, 1982; and Shull, 1979). Scholars, editorialists, and the public all judge presidents, but they seldom identify the criteria by which they choose to evaluate incumbents. Moreover, as

114

Shull (1979) has noted, presidents themselves take little time for reflection or evaluation. For the most part, discovering a guide to evaluation involves gleaning evaluative criteria from various observers' more general comments on the presidency or foreign policy.

Nevertheless, it is possible to identify the standards by which presidents are evaluated. In effect, presidential assessment appears to be governed by the view that the most important factors in presidential foreign policy performance are the elements of the decision process. This view focuses on how well the president handles policy processes and devotes less attention to the outcomes he is able to achieve. Consequently, the conventional wisdom on presidential evaluation suggests that good processes will yield good outcomes.

Of course, it is not the message of the conventional wisdom that the president is omnipotent. Rather, by focusing their attention on process-based criteria for assessment, most president watchers underestimate the importance of circumstantial factors affecting outcomes. In doing so, however, they undertake flawed evaluations of presidential performance—assessments based primarily on the president's effectiveness in policy formation and decision making.

This view is manifested throughout the writing and comments of president watchers, whether stated explicitly or implicitly. As a review of public opinion research, eight major editorialists on the presidency and foreign affairs, and thirty-five scholars of foreign affairs and the presidency reveals (see References for a complete listing), president watchers clearly focus their attention on processes, to the point of implying a causal relationship between policy process and policy outcomes. In essence, the conventional wisdom's concentration on processes is built of two components: a concern for outcomes in evaluating presidents and the assumption that the processes of policy making are the most significant factors affecting outcomes.

More specifically, this view is based on a few broad criteria for evaluating presidential performance in foreign affairs. Although these observers do not share a set of clear, consistent, and well-defined standards of presidential appraisal, they agree on which factors are important in assessing performance. According to the conventional wisdom, five criteria are relevant to presidential evaluation.[1]

1. *Policy Direction and Design.* The president's performance in foreign affairs is to be judged according to his ability to provide policy direction and design. This criterion includes the development of foreign policy goals for the nation, unified through a comprehensive design that guides policy formation and action by providing a sense of priorities, policy coordination and coherence, perspective for individual issues and cases, and the capacity for future planning.

This criterion calls upon the president to have, at minimum, a clear notion of the policies he wants to pursue. In other words, it is the president's responsibility to point a direction in which policy ought to go: as Reedy (1970) put it, "he must resolve the policy questions that will not yield to quantitative, empirical analysis." Beyond this, however, the president is expected to produce a comprehensive design that will shape and guide foreign policy. Such phrases as "grand design," "world view," "global policy," and "moral compass" are all used to describe this requirement. But he must also be able to provide coherent perspectives on individual issues, policies, programs, and decisions. This means that he must be able to articulate (to whomever it is necessary to do so) how the matter at hand (whether a crisis in Central America or a new international trade bill) relates to his grand design and how it is to be handled.

2. *Organization and staffing*. The president's performance in foreign affairs is to be judged according to his ability to effectively organize and staff the foreign affairs government. This judgment is based on the quality and effectiveness of the organizational scheme the president establishes for handling foreign affairs, his ability to work within that scheme, and the individuals he chooses to make it work.

This criterion has two features. First, the president must develop an organizational structure to facilitate policy making, and he must, as George (1980) argues, "learn to define his own role in the policymaking system." Second, he must animate the structure with effective and useful subordinates, who can help him achieve his goals and offer him what Koenig (1981) calls a high "quality of counsel."

3. *Management and Oversight*. The president's performance in foreign affairs is to be judged according to his management and oversight of the information and decision processes of foreign policy, his subordinates, and policy implementation. The president must insure that policy is consistent with his comprehensive design, that all necessary work is properly carried out, and that the mechanisms and personnel of his administration are coordinated in their operations. He must also make provisions for crisis management.

This criterion, which has received the most attention from the observers of conventional wisdom, requires the president to effectively manage the mechanisms, personnel, and processes of the foreign policy government. Moreover, he must pay particular attention to decision process management, which George (1980) describes as having five components: (1) ensure that sufficient information about the situation at hand is obtained and analyzed; (2) facilitate consideration of all major values and interests affected; (3) assure a search for a relatively wide range of options and a reasonably thorough evaluation of the expected consequences of each; (4) provide for considerations of implementation problems that may arise under each option; and (5) maintain receptivity to indications of difficulties with current policies and cultivate a capacity for learning from experience. Finally, the president must engage in oversight, that is, he must ensure that all necessary work is done, and done properly. The president, whom Hilsman (1971) describes as the "ultimate coordinator" of the government, is held responsible for following through on management by overseeing the work of his subordinates.

4. *Consensus-building*. The president's performance in foreign affairs is to be judged according to his ability to build and maintain a consensus in support of his policies and decisions. A president should possess the requisite political skills to seek out, establish, and maintain the limits of his consensus.

This criterion is part of the conventional wisdom for two reasons. First, it grows out of the understanding that without consensus of some sort, the president is limited in his ability to implement his policies and decisions. Neustadt (1980) captured this point in his remark about the "power to persuade." At a higher level, many observers see consensus as important because foreign policy is the policy of a nation, so unless it is based on a consensus, it may be divisive.

Yet the president must also master the techniques of consensus-building. To do so involves a variety of political skills, ranging from what Hughes (1972) calls a "sense of timing," to what others describe as skills in anticipating and overcoming opposition, coalition-building, and mastering the arts of both public and private persuasion.

Beyond these points, however, the conventional wisdom is not much more specific. None of the observers offer very explicit guidelines for how a president is to build consensus or how he is to develop the necessary skills to do so. This standard is thus simultaneously vague and demanding.

5. *Achievements/Outcomes*. The president's performance in foreign affairs is to be judged according to the outcomes he achieves. This criterion is a central one for most observers, whether scholars, commentators, or the general public. It is a judgment based not on outputs, on what the president and his administration do, but on outcomes: the results and consequences of presidential policy making (Shull, 1979). The conventional wisdom views these outcomes in terms of what the president achieves: success, failure, victory, or defeat.

Yet the conventional wisdom's emphasis is on how policy processes affect these outcomes. Most evaluators underestimate the importance of situational factors affecting presidential achievement, thus implying that good outcomes will follow from good processes. The conventional wisdom fails to balance its assessment of processes with an assessment of circumstances in evaluating presidential performance.

This lack of balance needs correction, for it affects current evaluations of presidential policy making. Achieving that correction can best be accomplished by examining presidential performance in the light of the realities of the foreign affairs presidency. For in doing so, it will be possible to demonstrate the importance of situational factors to outcomes.

## Methodology

Since the conventional wisdom focuses on how the policy process affects policy outcomes, an examination of this view requires a comparative study of presidential policy making in circumstances of both success and failure. In this way, it will be possible to isolate the role of the four "process" criteria in determining outcomes and to assess what situational factors influenced achievement. Although such a study should not be seen as conclusive or definitive, it will provide a means for the historical record to inform assessments of presidential performance.

This requires a series of case studies undertaken in the "disciplined-configurative" mode of analysis. In this mode, several cases are examined in terms of the same general and theory-related variables (Eckstein, 1975; George, 1980; Thomas, 1983). To employ this mode of analysis requires a guiding theory to organize analysis (the conventional wisdom), a "class" of cases relevant to that theory, and a selective, focused treatment of cases. In this last matter, as long as the researcher is sensitive to the circumstances of each case, he is less interested in its idiosyncrasies than in how the case illuminates the theory under scrutiny.

As for the cases to be studied, a definition of the relevant class is in order. This study will examine episodes in foreign affairs that can be identified as successes or failures for the president. An episode can be defined as an identifiable incidence of presidential foreign policy making, whether it be the management of a particular crisis, a major policy decision (or group of related decisions), attempts to obtain or block passage of foreign policy legislation, or attempts to obtain ratification of a treaty. "Episode" refers to a study of something more coherent and discrete than amorphous bodies of policy and entire presidencies: the Bay of Pigs crisis, the ratification of the SALT treaty, the decision on whether to deploy the MX missile, the issue of the AWACS sale to Saudi Arabia, or attempts to pass new international trade legislation. Such incidents are identifiable subunits of foreign policy on which president watchers focus much of their attention.[2]

Episodes are useful not only because they are common to the judgments of the conventional wisdom, but also because they are focused enough to allow a close examination of presidential performance. By examining episodes, such as the case of SALT I, it is much easier to assess presidential success and failure, how the process criteria were relevant to that outcome, and what other factors affected it, than it is to address either question with an issue such as Mr. Nixon's entire defense policy. Focusing on episodes makes sense because the conventional wisdom already does so and because foreign policy is "lumpy"—it is certainly more than merely discrete episodes, but such episodes are common, coherent, and more amenable to focused analysis than are larger units of analysis.[3]

## The Cases

In order to select cases, we must develop a typology of foreign policy episodes which identifies the various types of problems and thus makes it possible to match similar episodes (comparability) and cover the range of episodes (variety) arising in foreign affairs. The typology provides the framework for analysis (illustrated in figure 1). It contains three issue areas.

1. *Crises.* We define crises in this study as those situations of high threat to national security in which the president and other decision makers perceive a threat and feel they are under great time pressure to respond effectively to it. Perception is important as a determinant of foreign policy crises, because how the president perceives the nature, gravity, and urgency of a case will greatly influence how he will behave in response to that situation. The second factor in this definition is time urgency, because threat and urgency combine to yield situations that demand, or that the president believes demand, a quick and effective response (compare Hermann, 1969).[4]

In the Taiwan Strait crisis (1954–1955), President Eisenhower was successful in his attempt to defend American interests in the Far East, project American power abroad, and maintain the security and morale of Taiwan while avoiding war with China (Rushkoff, 1981; Eisenhower, 1963).[5] In the Cuban missile crisis, President Kennedy achieved his goal of forcing the Soviet Union to remove missiles it was emplacing in Cuba, while avoiding nuclear war (Allison, 1971; George and Smoke, 1974). In the Bay of Pigs crisis (1961), Kennedy met defeat in his attempt to defend American interests and project national power. This case is a clear failure of policy making (Wyden, 1979; Wills, 1981).[6] In the Berlin crisis of 1961, Kennedy failed in his efforts to deter Soviet aggressiveness (George and Smoke, 1974).

2. *Noncrisis Security Issues.* This category contains those cases that are not

FIGURE 1
Framework for Analysis
(asterisked cases are examined in the text)

| | Crises | Noncrisis Security Issues | Noncrisis Non-Security Issues |
|---|---|---|---|
| Success | Taiwan Strait*<br>Cuban Missiles*<br>Lebanon, 1958<br>Mayaguez | SALT I*<br>North Atlantic Treaty<br>Test Ban Treaty* | Trade expansion act, 1962*<br>GATT<br>Camp David accords<br>Foreign assistance act, 1967* |
| Failure | Bay of Pigs*<br>Berlin, 1961* | SALT II*<br>Skybolt<br>Open Skies* | Trade act of 1970*<br>Jackson-Vanik amendment* |

crises, but that directly involve defense and security issues: arms control, weapons systems, security alliances, and military readiness. Security issues are readily distinguishable, but this category includes those cases not of the same threat and urgency as crises.

This study will examine the cases of the two SALT treaties as well the first arms limitation treaty and an early nuclear arms control proposal. In the case of SALT I, President Nixon was able to achieve his goal of concluding and ratifying an arms agreement with the Soviet Union (Kissinger, 1979; Newhouse, 1973; Platt, 1978). In the Partial Test Ban Treaty, Kennedy was able to achieve the first arms control treaty (Seaborg, 1981). President Carter achieved a second arms treaty with the Soviet Union in SALT II, but he was unable to obtain approval for it in the Senate (Brzezinski, 1983; Talbott, 1979). In the case of Eisenhower's Open Skies proposal, an early arms control initiative was rejected by the Soviet Union (Rostow, 1982).

3. *Noncrisis Nonsecurity Issues.* This category includes those cases that involve neither crises nor are directly related to defense and national security. In one sense, this is a ''remainder'' category, but in another sense the issues included here are related: issues that often receive less attention than crises and questions of security but that nevertheless fall in the realm of foreign affairs. Issues such as those of international trade policy, diplomacy, and foreign aid tend to be seen as qualitatively different from security affairs.

This study examines cases of international trade and of foreign aid. In the trade expansion act (1962), President Kennedy obtained passage of a major initiative in trade policy: one that increased presidential authority to negotiate tariff reductions and ushered in the Kennedy Round in international trade talks (Pastor, 1980). The foreign assistance act (1967) marked a victory for President Johnson's proposal in the face of strong criticism (Berkowitz, Bock, and Fuccillo, 1977). In the case of the trade act of 1970, President Nixon failed either to renew lapsed provisions of the 1962 act or to move toward more free trade (*Congressional Quarterly Almanac 1970*). In the case of the Jackson-Vanick amendment, Nixon again failed in his attempt to shape American trade policy (Kissinger, 1982b).

## Findings

The twelve case studies provide some interesting results regarding the accuracy of the conventional wisdom (see figure 2). It is clear that presidential performance according to the conventional wisdom's process criteria does not generally explain the outcomes of the cases. Except in the Bay of Pigs crisis, there is little significant difference between cases of success and failure. Consequently, although the conventional wisdom focuses on important and

FIGURE 2
Results of the Case Studies: Did the president meet the requirements of the conventional wisdom in each case?

| | Criterion | | | | |
|---|---|---|---|---|---|
| | Policy Dir. & Design | Organization & Staffing | Management & Oversight | Consensus-building | Other Factors |
| **Cases of Success** | | | | | |
| Taiwan Strait | Yes | Yes | Yes | Mixed | U.S. power |
| Cuban Missiles | Mixed | Yes | Yes | Mixed | U.S. nuclear superiority |
| SALT I | Mixed | Yes, w/reservations | Yes, w/reservations | yes | Domestic political climate |
| Test Ban Treaty | Yes | Yes | Yes | Yes | Domestic and internat'l political climate |
| Trade expansion act | Yes | Yes | Yes | Yes | Domestic and internat'l political climate |
| Foreign assistance act | Yes | Mixed | Mixed | Mixed | Domestic political climate |
| **Cases of Failure** | | | | | |
| Bay of Pigs | Yes | No | No | Yes, w/reservations | Bureaucratic "slippage" |
| Berlin, 1961 | Yes | Yes | Mixed | Mixed | Soviet power predominance |
| SALT II | Yes | Yes | Yes | Yes | Issues of SALT, dom. and intnt'l political climate |
| Open Skies proposal | Yes | Yes | Yes | Mixed | Adversary motivations |
| Trade act of 1970 | Yes | Yes | Yes | Mixed | Domestic politics |
| Jackson-Vanik amendment | Yes | Yes | Yes | Mixed | Domestic politics |

perhaps necessary criteria for presidential achievement, fulfillment of those process criteria is insufficient for producing success.

Yet the outcome of these cases cannot be explained as merely due to chance. Rather, there is a pattern to the conditions affecting success and failure: outcomes can be explained as the results of the complex interaction of presidential performance with certain external circumstances.

In the cases of success, the president generally fulfilled the conventional criteria and in doing so took advantage of auspicious circumstances. President Eisenhower's performance in the Taiwan Strait crisis met the requirements of the conventional wisdom, but his success can be explained only by reference to American power predominance over China. In the same way, American nuclear superiority was crucial to Kennedy's success in the Cuban missile crisis. For those cases that involved legislation, presidential success was based on a favorable domestic political climate (such as strong sentiment for arms control in the case of SALT I) and, in at least two cases (trade expansion act and Test Ban Treaty), an international political climate conducive to the results the president desired. Presidential performance did not dictate outcomes.

In the cases of failure, only one case can be attributed to the president's failure to fulfill the requirements of the process criteria: the Bay of Pigs. Kennedy's failure to meet the requirements of the Organization and Staffing and Management and Oversight criteria ushered in disaster: he established a collegial system for decision making, but failed to properly manage that system and oversee his subordinates. Moreover, his fulfillment of the criterion of consensus-building, at least regarding his advisors, actually contributed to his failure. Kennedy's ability to achieve an easy consensus among his advisors underscores the ambiguity of this standard: in living up to its demands, he achieved the opposite of what he wanted.

The other failures demonstrate the insufficiency of the process criteria for explaining outcomes, for in these cases presidential performance was generally good. To explain the president's failure requires reference to the circumstances of each case. In the Berlin crisis of 1961, presidential action had little effect in the face of Soviet power in the region. In the case of SALT II, the complexities of arms control delayed conclusion of the treaty, which in turn undermined the president's consensus-building efforts. So did the Soviet invasion of Afghanistan. In the cases of the trade act of 1970 and the Jackson-Vanik amendment, President Nixon was defeated by domestic politics: in the first, a wave of protectionism in Congress killed the president's proposal; in the second, the weakening of the presidency by Watergate decreased Nixon's ability to negotiate a favorable outcome. Finally, the Open Skies proposal failed because of international tensions and the motivations of the Soviet leadership. In all these cases, the president involved performed at a level on par with the levels of performance in cases of presidential success. With some reservations, it is possible to say that they met the demands of the conventional wisdom. Yet they failed.

## Toward More Effective Evaluation

The case studies point to a number of changes that ought to be made in the assessment of presidential policy-making performance. They also suggest how the whole concept of evaluation might be modified.

First, the cases have exposed significant conflicts and trade-offs among the criteria of the conventional wisdom. As the Bay of Pigs case demonstrates, there is a significant conflict between the idea of consensus-building and the need for effective management of the decision process. Kennedy's easy consensus among his advisors impaired the process for realistically examining the CIA's invasion proposal.

At the same time, consensus-building may be undercut by policy design. The conventional wisdom shows no sensitivity to the problems encountered in SALT II, the 1970 trade act, and the Jackson-Vanik amendment. In each case, the president's design was a source of his troubles: in SALT II, Carter's design of arms control without linkage to Soviet behavior around the world directly contributed to his difficulties in building a consensus because the Senate still adhered to the Nixon-Kissinger notion of linkage; in proposing the trade act of 1970, Nixon had a clear design of free trade but with protection for the Southern textile industry, yet it was this design that opened his proposal to claims for recognition from other interest groups seeking protection (e.g., the footwear industry) and ultimately killed the bill; and, in the case of Jackson-Vanik, linkage was used against Nixon. In each case, the president diminished his chances for consensus by meeting the requirements of Policy Direction and Design.

Because of these conflicts and trade-offs, a more effective scheme of evaluation ought to include an understanding of the need to strike a balance among competing objectives. The conventional wisdom does not do so.

Second, the conventional wisdom does not include any consensus on the importance of democratic accountability. Yet it is clear from the cases that accountability is a relevant issue: Nixon's broad delegation of SALT issues to Kissinger, as well as his circumvention of Congress and the State Department in policy making, raises this issue, while Kennedy's actions in the Bay of Pigs crisis, stifling dissent and preventing relevant experts and congressional leaders from participating in or influencing his decision, also raises the question of accountability.[7]

Because of the importance of these matters, a pair of new criteria ought to be added to the evaluation of presidential policy making.

1. *Democratic Accountability.* The president's performance in foreign affairs

should be judged according to his ability and willingness to act in a manner consistent with the requirements of democratic government. These include adherence to constitutional ethics, public discussion and debate of policy and actions, and consultation with executive, congressional, and other public leaders.

There is no consensus supporting this criterion in the conventional wisdom, but the case studies have demonstrated its importance. For the president is the leader of a democratic republic, and as such is an accountable official. Evaluation of his performance thus requires some assessment of his behavior in this regard.

2. *Striking a Balance*. The president's performance in foreign affairs should be judged in light of the necessity to balance the conflicting demands and trade-offs among the various criteria of presidential performance.

It is difficult to give greater definition to this criterion, except to note that realistic evaluation ought to include a sensitivity to the competing demands of the other criteria. As the cases have shown, presidents can fail because fulfillment of one criterion inhibits achievement of another. So presidents and president watchers must be aware of the need to balance the various aspects of presidential policy making.

The case studies have also revealed that situational factors are important determinants of outcomes. Process alone is insufficient for explaining outcomes, and concentrating on them leads to flawed evaluations of presidents. Both process and circumstances must be included in assessments of presidents.

In this regard, a more effective scheme for presidential assessment would employ a two-stage system for evaluation, one that includes both process and circumstances affecting achievement. In the first stage, presidential effectiveness should be assessed according to the four process criteria and the additional criteria described above. In the second stage, presidential achievement should be assessed with outcomes measured in light of contextual factors (power predominance, domestic political environment, etc.) affecting achievement. Employing a conceptual scheme such as this, and it is intended only as a conceptual scheme, would provide for more thoughtful and accurate evaluation of presidential policy making than does the conventional wisdom's focus on process alone.

The essential point, then, is that evaluators must regard both process and circumstances as important to evaluating presidents. Focus on one to the exclusion of the other is misleading and perhaps dangerous, which is why this study has sought to balance current assessments by drawing attention to the importance of situational factors. Such factors as power relationships (among allies, between adversaries, etc.), domestic politics, economic conditions, bureaucratic politics, and the limits of presidential power (both at home and in world politics) all affect outcomes and must be included in assessments of presidential performance. The two-step evaluative scheme outlined above is aimed at balancing these factors and can serve as a model for better evaluations in the future.

## Where Do We Go from Here?

This study is only the first step toward an empirical theory of presidential foreign policy performance. It identified the conventional wisdom on evaluation and employed a series of case studies in order to scrutinize that wisdom. The results have been far from definitive, but the cases have demonstrated the importance of including situational factors in assessments of presidential achievement. In short, this work has demonstrated the need for a more balanced view of presidential performance.

The evaluative scheme sketched above represents a move in the direction of a more balanced view, but it is limited by the scale of this study. It must be pursued on a more ambitious scale: more cases are needed in order to cover the large number of cases of presidential foreign policy making since World War II. These studies should include cases with indeterminate or mixed outcomes so as to provide a more comprehensive analysis of presidential performance and a better understanding of the circumstances affecting outcomes. A number of additional case studies would provide a better data base for examining the various components of presidential performance, developing a typology of the factors affecting achievement, and exploring the relationship between process and circumstances.[8]

Along with the inclusion of additional case studies, research should be directed toward developing better indicators for the various evaluative criteria and for outcomes. Studies on presidential policy making (e.g., Wildavsky, 1966; Shull, 1979 and 1983; George, 1980) and implementation (e.g., Edwards, 1979) can inform this effort, which could result in the development of a more rigorous data base for studying presidential performance and achievement.

Yet the research agenda should not end with a refinement of this model. Indeed, research is needed in a number of other relevant areas: the domestic and international constraints on the president; the requirements of presidential accountability; the nature of presidential decision making and implementation; and changing expectations of the president and American power.

In the future, research also ought to go beyond discrete cases to examinations of larger policy issues (e.g., security issues, or even arms control) and whole presidencies in order to broaden this analysis and provide better means for evaluating performance.

At the same time, empirical research is needed for policy areas other than foreign affairs. Some studies have looked at presidential policy making in domestic policy (Thomas, 1979; Miroff, 1979; Lynn and Whitman, 1982) and economic policy (Stein, 1984), but empirical analyses of evaluation in these areas are also in order. What is the conventional wisdom on presidential economic policy making? Domestic policy making? Is it realistic? These are important questions, like that of foreign policy evaluation, and ones open to investigation. This study has suggested how such questions might be approached. In its own tentative way, it has also suggested that their answers may be significant.

## NOTES

1. Although there may be overlapping of these components in practice, the five criteria are analytically distinct in the conventional wisdom and in fact: e.g., although staffing might affect policy design, the two remain analytically distinguishable.
2. The question of success or failure does not lend itself to easy quantification, but it is possible to make a distinction. In this study, success or failure is determined by two criteria: (1) whether there is a clear and general interpretation of the case as a success or failure; and (2) whether the outcome met with the president's goals in that case.
3. There is no claim here that a focus on episodes will capture the entirety of presidential performance in foreign affairs. Nevertheless, such a focus will facilitate focused and rigorous analysis. Moreover, because episodes are highly visible and, as noted above, frequently observed and commented on by president watchers, focus on them is not a significant distortion of the reality of presidential evaluation.
4. Hermann adds the element of surprise to his definition of crisis, but begs the question of just what is a surprise. For, even if decision makers know that trouble may be looming on the horizon, the actual occurrence of even expected trouble may very well be perceived as a crisis. It is therefore extremely difficult to operationalize and measure surprise, so this study will employ the definition stated in the text.
5. Despite the fact that the affair dragged on for several months, it is clear that Eisenhower, his advisors, and U.S. allies all perceived this case to be a crisis of high threat and great time urgency. See Eisenhower (1963) and Rushkoff (1981).
6. As Sorensen (1965) makes clear, Kennedy acted in response to what he believed was a crisis: high threat (Castro's Cuba growing in strength) and time urgency (Cuba would soon have sufficient military power, and Castro's regime would have consolidated its control over the island, so as to make Cuba invulnerable to all force save full-scale war).
7. For a discussion of how Kennedy stifled dissent and excluded relevant experts and congressional leaders, see Wyden (1979).
8. The number of additional cases needed is not clear, but thirty or more cases would provide some compelling results and perhaps allow the calculation of low-order statistical inferences.

## REFERENCES

Allison, Graham T. 1971. *Essence of Decision*. Boston: Little, Brown.
Bailey, Thomas A. 1978. *Presidential Greatness*. New York: Irvington.

Barber, James D. 1977. *The Presidential Character*. 2d. ed. Englewood Cliffs, N.J.: Prentice-Hall.
Berkowitz, Morton, P. G. Bock, and Vincent J. Fuccillo. 1977. *The Politics of American Foreign Policy*. Englewood Cliffs, N.J.: Prentice-Hall.
Berman, Larry. 1982. *Planning a Tragedy*. New York: Norton.
Broder, James. 1980–1984. Columns in *Washington Post*.
Brzezinski, Zbgniew. 1983. *Power and Principle*. New York: Farrar, Straus and Giroux.
Buchanan, Bruce. 1981. *Assessing Presidential Performance: Can We Do Better?* Paper presented to the American Political Science Association, New York, New York. Mimeographed.
Burns, James MacGregor. 1973. *Presidential Government: The Crucible of Leadership*. Boston: Houghton-Mifflin.
*Congressional Quarterly Almanac 1970*. Washington, D.C.: Congressional Quarterly, Inc.
Corwin, Edward S. 1957. *The President: Office and Powers*. 4th. ed. New York: New York University Press.
Cowhey, Peter F. and David D. Laitin. 1978. Bearing the burden: A model of presidential responsibility in foreign policy. *International Studies Quarterly* 22:267–96.
Cronin, Thomas E. 1980. *The State of the Presidency*. 2d. ed. Boston: Little, Brown.
Destler, I. M. 1974. *Presidents, Bureaucrats, and Foreign Policy*. Princeton: Princeton University Press.
———. 1980. Altering the security job. *New York Times*. 25 March, A19.
———. 1981. National Security II: The Rise of the Assistant (1961–1981). In *The Illusion of Presidential Government*, ed. H. Heclo and L. Salamon, pp. 263–85. Boulder, Colo.: Westview.
Donovan, Hedley. 1981. Fluctuations on the presidential exchange. *Time*, 9 November, 121–22.
———. 1982. Job specs for the Oval Office. *Time*, 13 Devember, 20–29.
Eckstein, Harry. 1975. Case study and theory in political science. In *The Handbook of Political Science* VII, ed. F. Greenstein and N. Polsby, pp. 79–137. Reading, Va.: Addison-Wesley.
Edwards, George C., III. 1979. Problems in presidential policy implementation. In *The Presidency: Studies in Policy Making*, ed. S. Shull and L. LeLoup, pp. 271–94. Brunswick, Oh.: King's Court.
———. 1980a. *Implementing Public Policy*. Washington, D.C.: Congressional Quarterly.
———. 1980b. *Presidential Influence in Congress*. San Francisco: W. H. Freeman.
———. 1983. *The Public Presidency*. New York: St. Martin's.
Eisenhower, Dwight D. 1963. *Mandate for Change*. Garden City, N.Y.: Doubleday.
Fisher, Louis. 1972. *President and Congress: Power and Policy*. New York: Free Press.
George, Alexander. 1972. The case for multiple advocacy in making foreign policy. *American Political Science Review* 66:751–85.
———. 1980. *Presidential Decisionmaking in Foreign Policy: TheEffective Use of Implementation and Advice*. Boulder, Colo.: Westview.
George, Alexander, and Richard Smoke. 1974. *Deterrence in American Foreign Policy*. New York: Columbia University Press.
Greenstein, Fred I. 1982. *The Hidden-Hand Presidency*. New York: Basic Books.
Hargrove, Erwin C. 1974. *The Power of the Modern Presidency*. New York: Alfred A. Knopf.

Hargrove, Erwin C., and Michael Nelson. 1984. *Presidents, Politics, and Public Policy.* New York: Alfred A. Knopf.

Heclo, Hugh. 1977. *Studying the Presidency.* A report to the Ford Foundation. New York: Ford Foundation.

Heclo, Hugh, and Lester Salamon. 1981. *The Illusion of Presidential Government.* Boulder, Colo.: Westview.

Hermann, Charles F. 1969. International Crisis as a Situational Variable. In *International Politics and Foreign Policy,* ed. J. Rosenau, pp. 409–21. New York: Free Press.

Hilsman, Roger. 1971. *The Politics of Policy Making in Defense and Foreign Affairs.* New York: Harper and Row.

Hodgson, Godfrey. 1980. *All Things to All Men.* New York: Simon and Schuster.

Hoxie, R. Gordon. 1980. The not so imperial presidency: A modest proposal. *Presidential Studies Quarterly* 10:194–210.

Hughes, Emmet John. 1972. *The Living Presidency.* New York: Coward, McCann and Geohagan.

Hunter, Robert E. 1982. *Presidential Control of Foreign Policy.* Washington Paper 10, no. 91. New York: Praeger.

Janis, Irving L. 1972. *Victims of Groupthink.* Boston: Houghton-Mifflin.

Kernell, Samuel. 1978. Explaining Presidential Popularity. *American Political Science Review* 72:506–22.

Kissinger, Henry. 1979. *White House Years.* Boston: Little, Brown.

———. 1982a. First, coherent policy. *New York Times,* 18 January, A35.

———. 1982b. *Years of Upheaval.* Boston: Little Brown.

Koenig, Louis W. 1981. *The Chief Executive.* 4th ed. New York: Harcourt, Brace and World.

Kraft, Joseph. 1980–1984. Columns in *Washington Post.*

———. 1980. The Post-imperial presidency. *New York Times Magazine,* 1 November, 31–95.

Laski, Harold. 1980. *The American Presidency.* New York: Universal Library.

Lewis, Flora. 1980–1984. Columns in *New York Times.*

Light, Paul. 1983. *The President's Agenda.* Baltimore: Johns Hopkins University Press.

Lynn, Laurence E., Jr., and David F. Whitman. 1982. *The President as Policymaker.* Philadelphia: Temple University Press.

Miroff, Bruce. 1979. The presidency and social reform. In *The Presidency: Studies in Policy Making,* ed. S. Shull and L. LeLoup, pp. 174–94. Brunswick, Oh.: King's Court.

Neustadt, Richard E. 1980. *Presidential Power.* Rev. ed. New York: Wiley.

Newhouse, John. 1973. *Cold Dawn.* New York: Holt, Rinehart and Winston.

Pastor, Robert A. *Congress and the Politics of U.S. Foreign Economic Policy, 1929–1976.* Berkeley and Los Angeles: University of California Press.

Pious, Richard M. 1979. *The American Presidency.* New York: Basic Books.

Platt, Alan. 1978. *The U.S. Senate and Strategic Arms Policy.* Boulder, Colo.: Westview.

Reedy, George E. 1970. *The Twilight of the Presidency.* New York: World Publishing.

Reston, James. 1980–1984. Columns in *New York Times.*

Rockman, Bert A. 1981. America's *Departments* of State: Irregular and regular syndromes of policy making. American Political Science Review 75:911–27.

Rossiter, Clinton. 1963. *The American Presidency.* 2d. ed. New York: Time, Inc.

Rostow, Walt W. 1982. *Open Skies*. Austin: University of Texas Press.
Rushkoff, Bennett. 1981. Eisenhower, Dulles, and the Quemoy-Matsu Crisis of 1954–1955. *Political Science Quarterly* 96:465–80.
Sapin, Burton M. 1980. Isn't it time for a modest presidency in foreign affairs? *Presidential Studies Quarterly* 10:19–27.
Seaborg, Glenn. 1981. *Kennedy, Khrushchev, and the Test Ban*. Berkeley and Los Angeles: University of California Press.
Shull, Steven A. 1979. Presidential Impact: Foreign Versus Domestic Policy. In *The Presidency: Studies in Policy Making*, ed. S. Shull and L. LeLoup, pp. 295–306. Brunswick, Oh.: King's Court.
———. 1983. *Domestic Policy Formation*. Westport, Conn.: Greenwood.
Shull, Steven A., and Lance T. LeLoup. 1981. Reassessing the reassessment: Comment on Sigelman's note on the "two presidencies" thesis. *Journal of Politics* 43: 563–64.
Sidey, Hugh. 1980–1984. The Presidency. Regular column in *Time*.
———. 1980. Assessing a presidency. *Time*, 18 August, 10–15.
Sorensen, Theodore C. 1963. *Decision-making in the White House*. New York: Columbia University Press.
———. 1965. *Kennedy*. New York: Harper and Row.
———. 1984. *A Different Kind of Presidency*. New York: Harper and Row.
Spanier, John, and Eric M. Uslaner. 1982. *Foreign Policy and the Democratic Dilemmas*. 3rd. ed. New York: Holt, Rinehart, and Winston.
Stein, Herbert M. 1984. *Presidential Economics*. New York: Simon and Schuster.
Talbott, Strobe. 1979. *Endgame*. New York: Harper and Row.
Thomas, Norman C. 1979. The President and Education Policy. In *The Presidency: Studies in Policy Making*, ed. S. Shull and L. LeLoup, pp. 152–73. Brunswick, Oh.: King's Court.
———. 1983. Case Studies. In *Studying the Presidency*, ed. G. Edwards and S. Wayne, pp. 50–78. Knoxville: University of Tennessee Press.
Tugwell, Rexford G. 1960. *The Enlargement of the Presidency*. Garden City, N.Y.: Doubleday.
———. 1971. *Off Course: From Truman to Nixon*. New York: Praeger.
Vinyard, Dale. 1971. *The Presidency*. New York: Scribner's.
Wayne, Stephen J. 1978. *The Legislative Presidency*. New York: Harper and Row.
———. 1982. Great expectations: What people want from presidents. In *Rethinking the Presidency*, ed. T. Cronin, pp. 185–99. Boston: Little, Brown.
White, T. H. 1982. *America in Search of Itself*. New York: Harper and Row.
Wildavsky, Aaron. 1966. The two presidencies. *Transaction* 4:7–14.
Will, George F. 1980–1984a. Columns in *Newsweek*.
———. 1980–1984b. Columns in *Washington Post*.
Wills, Garry. 1981. *The Kennedy Imprisonment*. Boston: Little, Brown.
Wyden, Peter. 1979. *Bay of Pigs*. New York: Simon and Schuster.

Margaret Jane Wyszomirski

# The Roles of a Presidential Office for Domestic Policy: Three Models and Four Cases

During the past fifty years, the presidential role in policy making has expanded in terms of both the range of the president's policy responsibilities and the scope of his involvement in the policy process. This expansion has come to include all phases of the process (Jones, 1977; Shull, 1979) and not merely the explicitly executive function of implementation. Since 1939 presidents have, within the Executive Office of the President (EOP), acquired or developed a variety of institutional resources to assist them in their expanded policy role. Since 1970 a domestic policy office has been one of these resources.[1] Different presidents have called upon this office and its director (the presidential assistant for domestic affairs) to play different roles in the policy process. Each role reflects a different relational pattern among the president, the agency, and its director. In turn, each relational pattern exhibits different characteristics with regard to size, location, procedures, influence, and effectiveness of the domestic policy office.

This article proceeds in three major segments. First, it identifies three possible roles for a presidential domestic affairs office and the relational pattern inherent in each role. Second, it will employ these patterns to survey the roles into which the office and the presidential assistant for domestic affairs has been cast in the administrations of four presidents: Nixon, Ford, Carter, and Reagan. In each case, the performance of the agency and of the presidential policy assistant is assessed. Third, some generalizations concerning the organization, staffing, and functioning of a domestic policy office are presented The concluding section also considers the potential analytical utility of the relational patterns for the study of other agencies of the Executive Office of the President.

130

## Three Relational Patterns

Principles of agency law provide the basis for identifying three distinctive relational patterns that pervade bureaucratic administration.[2] These patterns can provide an analytical framework for the study of the interaction of presidents and other executive officials. The three patterns are those of (1) principal and agent; (2) master and servant; and (3) advisee and advisor. Each is distinguished by certain rights, responsibilities, duties, limitations, advantages, and liabilities.

An *agent* is one who is commissioned to transact business in the name of his principal. An agent is expected to perform loyally and competently, exercising whatever skills and discretion may be necessary to perform his charge. He must provide an account of his dealings. The principal is responsible for the actions and commitments that his agent makes pursuant to his commission. Depending upon the breadth of the commission, one can be a special or a general agent. The heads of the line agencies (executive departments and agencies) are a president's primary agents.

*Servants* or *administrative staff* perform operative, nondiscretionary tasks under the direct supervision (at least theoretically) of the master. Servants assist their master but they cannot act for him. A master is responsible for the activities of his servants, even if these contradict or exceed his directions. Thus, the president as master becomes politically accountable for the conduct of his staff "servants."

*Advisors* offer advice. They are selected for their special expertise or skill and are usually assigned specific, focused subjects for analysis and opinion. Advisors bear no responsibility for executing their recommendations. Advisees (in this case, the president) are under no obligation to accept or act upon advice that is tendered. Advisors may both inform presidential decision making and, by virtue of their expert reputations, help to legitimize policy decisions once they have been made. Nonetheless, expert advice is not always useful or costless (Thomas, 1972, pp. 119–20; Laski, 1960; Lyons, 1971). Professional expectations and norms may cause some expert recommendations to be substantively accurate but politically infeasible and, therefore, of limited utility. Although presidents are free to reject advice, they sometimes do so at the risk of seeing the scorned advisor return to private life where he may become a potent critic of presidential policy. These drawbacks are not, however, inherent in the advisory relationship itself. Rather they derive from differences between advisee and advisor in matters of personality, ideology, or perspective.

Both individuals and bureaucratic entities can be cast in any of these three roles. Presidential assistants can perform as administrators, advisors, or agents. Similarly, agencies within the EOP can be cast as advisors (e.g., the Council of

Economics Advisors or the Office of Science and Technology Policy), as administrators (e.g., the White House Office as it was originally conceived or the Office of Administration), or as agents (e.g., the Office of Economic Opportunity or the Office of War Mobilization and Reconversion). Collectively, the three relational patterns provide an analytical tool useful in identifying and comparing recurrent phenomena in what is essentially a discontinous institution.

In theory, each role is distinguishable from the others; in practice, the mutual exclusivity of each is more apparent than actual. Competent agents function as their own advisors and administrators. Administrators who exercise extensive discretion may become de facto agents. Advisors may be called upon to help implement their recommendations. Both individuals and offices may develop and draw upon a repertoire of roles, acting in different capacities under different circumstances. They may also be recast from one role to another. Thus, it is possible, perhaps likely, that presidential offices (as well as assistants) will fill more than one role, either concurrently or successively, within one presidency or through the course of many.

The EOP was established to provide presidents with help—meaning administrative staff. The relationship between the president and this staff was intended to be that of master and servant. Yet within a decade it was evident that the president needed another kind of help—expert advice. Hence, Roosevelt's experiments with a "brains trust" and a war council were subsequently formalized as advisory councils: the Council of Economic Advisors (CEA) and the National Security Council (NSC).

Much of the subsequent growth of the EOP has involved the addition of more staff and different types of advice. The institutionalized presidency began to emerge, and, as long as its components performed service or advisory roles, the public and other institutions of government perceived that development as legitimate.

This view rested on the assumption that staff and advisors did not expand the power or authority of the president but rather enhanced his ability to exercise that which he already held. Administrative staff were presumed to be dependent upon and directed by the president. Even if or when their actions exceeded the limits of service or were not at presidential direction, the responsibility for what the staff did remained with the president. Similarly, advisors could offer analysis and opinion, but the authority to make decisions and, hence, the responsibility for them was still the president's.

Within these limits, however, there was considerable flexibility, since the EOP had been designed to accommodate variations in presidential styles and goals. Individual EOP units also proved to be quite adaptable. Administrative units might develop special skills or competencies and, therefore, assume advisory functions. Similarly, advisory units might acquire administrative duties. Presidents might choose to diminish or dispense with certain kinds of advice or service. A unit could shrink, atrophy, expand, or diversify. As policy needs and preferences wax and wane, presidents experience a variable need for advice. As circumstances change, the need for service varies.

Customarily, the president's agents have been the political executives in the line agencies. These individuals are authorized to preside over policy implementation and have been variably involved in the formulation, enactment, and evaluation stages of the policy process. Few provisions were made for agents to be formally established in the EOP. Occasionally, however, the permanent executive bureaucracy seems too awkward, fragmented, or otherwise inadequate to address a pressing need. In such cases, Congress has, with or without presidential concurrence, authorized new executive agents and made them part of the EOP (e.g., the energy office, or the Council on Environmental Quality). The bureaucratic lifespan of such agents is generally short, troubled, and precarious. Few survive the duration of the critical issue that prompted their initial commissioning. In addition, some presidents have, in their search for the presumptive powers of the managerial presidency, attempted informally to turn servants or advisors into agents. Although some have secured such agents, the transformation is usually only temporary and achieved at significant political cost.

In large part, the roles that any given EOP unit plays will depend upon the differing needs of different presidents; upon the abilities of the personnel and directors of each unit; upon mutual compatability and trust among president, director, and agency personnel; and upon the influence or authority of other competing or interacting bureaucratic entities. The next sections will consider these conditions in the survey of the performance of the domestic policy office under Presidents Nixon, Ford, Carter, and Reagan.

## Presidential Agent: The Nixon Domestic Council

The Domestic Council (DC) was established by Executive Order 11541, pursuant to Reorganization Plan No. 2 of 1970. It was to be a two-tiered organization, created to preside over the domestic policy function as a bureaucratic counterpart of the NSC in national security affairs and of the Bureau of the Budget (BOB)/Office of Management and Budget (OMB) in budgetary management (Moe, 1976, p. 257).

Its first tier—the council—was to be chaired by the president. Its members included the vice-president; the attorney general; the secretaries of the departments of treasury, interior, agriculture, commerce, labor, HEW, HUD, and transportation; the chairman of the CEA; the director of the Office of Economic Opportunity; and the director and deputy director of OMB. An invitation to attend meetings or to otherwise participate in council activities could be extended to others as the need arose. The second tier was to consist of a support staff to be under the direction of the assistant to the president for domestic affairs.

Although the Nixon Domestic Council was soon reputed to be the "principal locus of domestic decision-making" (Kessel, 1975, p. 21), it was equally evident that the staff, rather than the interagency council, was performing this function. The council met very infrequently and seldom engaged in substantive policy debate. Rather, council meetings were, as Ehrlichman remarked, "largely show and tell."[3] In contrast, the staff was consistently and intimately involved in the domestic policy process, from formulation through implementation.

Organizationally, the staff was headed by a senior White House staff member (John Ehrlichman) who was assisted by a deputy director for day-to-day operations (Kenneth Cole) and six assistant directors (each of whom had responsibility for a flexible cluster of policy topics). Each assistant director had, in turn, a small staff. Overall, the staff size varied dramatically during the Nixon years, growing from fifteen in 1970 to fifty-five in 1973, then dropping to twenty-nine in 1974.[4]

Formally, the DC undertook its projects at the direction of the president and following consultation with the council (or some portion of it). Operationally, policy formulation and advice were coordinated through domestic council committees. These were chaired by a member of the DC staff and included the designated representatives of the departments/agencies (generally an assistant secretary) as well as personnel from other EOP units, notably top-level OMB staff (usually an assistant director or the relevant program associate director).

Each group would prepare a document describing the policy issue, presenting the relevant facts, advancing various options for action (or inaction), and analyzing the likely impact, political reception, and cost of each option. This system served the dual function of distancing (even isolating) cabinet and agency heads from policy formulation while also buffering the president from intra-administration debate. Ultimately, it also had the effect of minimizing presidential decision making, since President Nixon expected Ehrlichman to act, in large part, as his de facto general agent for domestic policy (Ehrlichman, 1982, p. 182).

The formal role of the DC staff was that of *administrator* charged with assisting in the coordination of domestic policy formulation. But it was also involved in the advocacy, monitoring, and evaluation of policy. Thus, in practice Ehrlichman became the president's general domestic agent while the DC staff provided him with administrative support. This role came complete with substantial policy discretion and de facto ability to direct and oversee the performance of department and agency executives. The assistant directors accomplished the administrative tasks by presiding over the working groups, which allowed them to determine the domestic policy agenda (within the limits set by presidential orientations), gather the facts, structure the options, and (through the assistant for domestic affairs) package the final decision.

Control over implementation, oversight, and evaluation were, in large part, realized in concert with OMB and subcabinet level departmental personnel. Ehrlichman, Deputy DC Director Cole, the assistant directors, and a half dozen top people from OMB met daily at 7:30 A.M. to coordinate afforts and exchange information. Top OMB staff were members of each Domestic Council committee and DC staff were invited to annual OMB budget review sessions with the departments and agencies (Waldmann, 1976, p. 264). Oversight and evaluation of policy implementation were routinely carried out by OMB (Kessel, 1975, pp. 100–02), although in some cases the DC staff would get involved directly.

Control at this level was premised upon the loyalty and commitment of the people involved. Middle-level staff at the Domestic Council, OMB, and the departments were all generalists, relatively young, of proven loyalty to the president, and often politically inexperienced. Ehrlichman recruited a staff that could organize, analyze, and "move quickly from one subject to another," and that, above all else, had the president's "confidence, whether [they] knew anything or not." Such a staff was both dependable and dependent upon presidential favor.

During his second term, President Nixon intended to use such personnel to implement a new strategy for achieving bureaucratic control. Having decided to abandon the White House counterbureaucracy approach as incapable of penetrating governmental operations deeply or systematically enough to control the policy setting and managerial processes concerning domestic affairs, President Nixon, instead, wanted to place a renewed emphasis on the line agencies and officers and to streamline the EOP (Nathan, 1983). However, to assure more dependable and loyal line agents "a deliberate strategy of colonization" was planned in which "super-loyalists"(some of whom had been DC assistant directors) were moved into the number two and three spots in many departments "to make sure that the new secretaries didn't marry the natives."

Although the attractions of a loyal and dependent DC staff were obvious to President Nixon, its disadvantages became apparent only later. It seemed to breed misunderstanding and distrust with others—Congress, the bureaucracy, the party, and the media. Furthermore, such a staff failed to provide the new agency with legitimate expert credentials to advise the president in substantive policy matters. In this sense the composition of the DC staff was in marked contrast to the membership of two other, more established presidential councils—the CEA and the NSC (Wyszomirski, 1982).

The results of this operational and staff system were paradoxical. On the one hand, the virtual exclusion of the cabinet and the substantive weakness of the

DC staff may have enhanced presidential control over domestic policy making. But as President Nixon himself had little interest in domestic policy, much of this increased control was, in practice, delegated to the unelected and unconfirmed White House assistant for domestic affairs. On the other hand, it also limited the efficacy of many of the administration's domestic policies by isolating them from other sources of bureaucratic, political, and substantive support.

From December 1972 to December 1974, the DC drifted in an ineffectual role. Following Ehrlichman's resignation from the administration, Deputy Director Cole was promoted to head the staff but was not made the president's domestic assistant. Instead, former cabinet member Melvin Laird was recalled from private life and appointed as domestic assistant. His actual function, however, was to act as a presidential emissary to Congress to contend with impending impeachment proceedings. With Laird a distracted intermediary and the president preoccupied with Watergate and impeachment, Cole found it increasingly difficult to gain access to, much less get answers or action from, the Oval Office. Thus, the council level was moribund and in distanced disarray; the staff level dwindled both in size and influence as it drifted into an ineffectual administrative role.

## Miscast and Cast Adrift: The Ford Domestic Council

President Ford's initial plan seems to have been to delegate the vice-president to be his chief agent for domestic policy. This was to be accomplished by appointing the vice-president as vice-chairman of the Domestic Council and by putting the council staff under his direction. Indeed, President Ford offered this arrangement to Nelson Rockefeller, who had a long and diverse history of involvement in domestic affairs, as an inducement to accept the vice-presidential nomination (Turner, 1982). Although Rockefeller accepted the offer and the arrangement, circumstances conspired against it being effectively implemented.

Months of controversy and delay over his confirmation kept Rockefeller out of the Ford White House during the crucial formative months of the new administration. When he finally did arrive in December 1974, he was perceived as a liability because of the controversial congressional hearings and as a potential threat to the ambitions of other administration officials, including those of the president.

Thus, when the vice-president came to claim control of the DC, he found that the president had become more self-confident and less willing to delegate broadly in domestic policy matters and that a White House system had evolved that included neither himself nor the Domestic Council (Turner, 1982; Light, 1984). Although Rockefeller succeeded in securing direction of the DC, it was at the expense of a bitter contest with the White House chief of staff, Donald Rumsfeld. As a result, Rumsfeld's antagonism toward the vice-president resurfaced time and again, soon becoming apparent with regard to both the staffing and the operation of the DC staff.

In terms of staff, Rockefeller secured the appointments of four individuals, but he was also "forced" to retain the remnants of the Nixon staff. James Cannon and Richard Dunham, both New York associates of the vice-president, were named as executive director and deputy director, respectively. Other former aides, Richard Parsons and Arthur Quern, were also brought in (Bonafede, 1975). A second deputy director, James Cavanaugh, was retained from the Nixon Domestic Council staff despite Rockefeller's objections that Cavanaugh was an ally of Rumsfeld's.

Thus, from the very beginning, the council staff was neither wholly Rockefeller's nor clearly part of the president's team. This schizophrenic situation was carried over into the organization of the staff by the establishment of a two-track division of labor between the deputy directors: Dunham was placed in charge of long-range policy planning and Cavanaugh was to administer day-to-day affairs. Rockefeller, who was well versed in bureaucratic politics, knew that operations were an important element of policy and felt that he had lost control of the staff to a significant degree. When Dunham resigned after only three months, it seemed to Rockefeller that even more control was lost.

With Dunham gone, Rockefeller tried to consolidate his hold over the DC staff by placing them in the awkward position of choosing between loyalty to him or to the president. When Director Cannon tried to defuse the issue by pointing out that they all (including the vice-president) worked for the president, Rockefeller felt betrayed. Ultimately, such efforts to draw the DC deeper into his sphere of influence did little to increase the vice-president's administrative control or policy impact, but it did tend to cost the DC staff the acceptance and trust of other White House staff members.

With their loyalty to the president in question, the DC director and staff were denied easy access to the president and, instead, were forced to rely on the vice-president as their major channel of information and communication. Since the vice-president had access to but little influence with the president, the DC staff had still less influence with the administration. As Rockefeller became disaffected from the DC, even this channel narrowed. Hence, with the critical relationship between the president, the leader of the DC, and the agency's staff so uncertain, the DC had little chance to develop an advisory role.

Other circumstances also hindered the possibility of the council staff developing into an advisor. One was the restrictive domestic agenda imposed by the president's tight budget policy. This severely limited the opportunities for the DC (or, indeed, anyone else) successfully to develop and advocate new domestic programs within the administration. Another problem was created by the DC's lack of allies within the EOP. Unlike the case of the Nixon Domestic Council staff (who worked closely with the OMB), in the Ford administration, the director of OMB (James Lynn) as well as the chairman of the CEA (Alan Greenspan) were in alliance with White House chief of staff Rumsfeld and, therefore, in opposition to the DC.

Alternatively, an effective administrative role was also denied to Rockefeller and the DC staff. Because they had joined the team late, both personal contact networks and a paper flow system had been developed without them. Given the suspicion and antagonism toward the vice-president within the EOP, little was done subsequently to include Rockefeller or his staff in the information system once they had come "on board." Without broad and timely access to information and to the decision-making process, the DC was foreclosed from performing an effective administrative role. Its ability to get even a single DC-developed domestic program placed in the 1976 State of the Union address was one measure of this failure (Light, 1984).

By early 1976, Rockefeller was frustrated by his ineffectiveness, convinced that he had lost control of the staff, and forced out of consideration as Ford's running mate in the coming election. He, therefore, requested that he be relieved of responsibilities for the operations of the Domestic Council. Since the administration had obviously developed other means and methods of managing and formulating domestic affairs, Rockefeller's withdrawal removed the DC's sole supporter within the EOP. Originally but unsuccessfully cast in an advisory role in support of the vice-president, the DC was now cast aside, bereft of any role within the waning Ford administration.

### Presidential Advisor: The Carter Domestic Policy Staff

Jimmy Carter come to office promising to reduce the size of government and to establish a more open style of governing. Pursuant to these ends, the DC was one of the first agencies he organized.

Reorganization Plan No. 1 of 1977 included three provisions that affected the structure and functions of the Domestic Council. Most significantly, the cabinet-level tier of the council was abolished. Consequently, the agency was redesignated the Domestic Policy Staff (DPS). This eliminated the large, unwieldy, and ineffectual council layer, while preserving an executive staff capability in domestic policy. In justifying these changes, the Carter administration emphasized the advisory role it envisioned for the new DPS. In congressional committee testimony, Domestic Policy Assistant Stuart Eizenstat stressed that the DPS would "coordinate the presentation of views to the President and not serve as a barrier to presentation of advice from the Cabinet and other agencies" (Eizenstat, 1977, p. 1034). Furthermore, he projected that the DPS, unlike the DC staff, would "not get involved consciously and purposively in any implementation of policy" (Eizenstat, 1978, p. 134). Official descriptions of the DPS focused on its "analysis" and "advice" functions as well as on multiphased policy coordination responsibilities that ranged from the formulation stage to strategic planning for legislative enactment.

The reorganization plan also abolished the Office of Telecommunications Policy and the Office of Drug Abuse Policy while transferring their advisory functions to the DPS. This had the dual advantages of reducing the size of the EOP as well as integrating these two issue areas into the general domestic policy process.

Operationally, the DPS worked through a system of interagency committees that bore a superficial resemblance to the council committees of the DC. Under the Carter Domestic Policy Review System, the agencies concerned in a policy issue would be brought together as a committee or task force. Although a member of the DPS staff (usually an associate director) was part of each committee, he did not always direct its operation. In addition, the DPS was also involved in other interagency councils concerned with policy advocacy or implementation (Bonafede, 1978, p. 680; Light, 1979, p. 2202). Thus, while the DPS was a participant in as wide a range of issues and in nearly as many stages of the policy process as the Nixon DC staff had been, its role was quite different. It acted as an advisor and as a coordinating support arm rather than as the directing force.

The agency was headed by Presidential Assistant for Domestic Affairs and Policy Stuart Eizenstat—a Georgian-born, Harvard-trained lawyer who had served as a speechwriter for Johnson, as research director of the 1968 Humphrey campaign, and as issues director for the Carter presidential campaign. He had two deputies: Bert Carp, who managed day-to-day affairs as deputy director of the DPS, and David Rubenstein, who acted as overall policy aid with the title of Deputy Assistant for Domestic Affairs and Policy.

Under Eizenstat, the DPS's administrative and advisory roles were carefully cultivated. Eizenstat's frequent, personal, and positive communications with cabinet members facilitated his acceptance as an honest broker regarding the advice and opinions of others. Furthermore, since he not only coordinated and presented information and advice from many sources but also assessed it as he passed it on to the president, his brokerage function shaded into an advisory one. Although Eizenstat did not have "expert" credentials in the form of advanced specialized training and degrees (as did the national security and CEA advisors), he was, nevertheless, recognized as able, informed, and experienced in the broad range of domestic affairs. As campaign issues director, he had gained breadth and exposure. His hardworking, low-profile style quickly earned him respect and distinction as one of the most competent members of the administration (Light, 1979, p. 2204). When combined with his daily access to and evident influence with the president, it is clear that this domestic policy assistant had both the close relationship and the personal ability conducive to an effective performance as administrator and advisor.

The DPS staff possessed qualifications and operated in a manner similar to Eizenstat and, therefore, supported his performance as advisor and adminis-trator.[5] Below the director and deputy directors were approximately a dozen associate directors, each of whom had a small staff of one to four people. In total, the staff numbered between forty and fifty. Although the staff members were mostly young generalists, virtually all had prior political experience, particularly in Washington (Bonafede, 1979). Such political background was in contrast not only to the Nixon DC staff but also to much of Carter's other White House staff. Thus, the DPS avoided a pitfall common among many presidential advisory units in that it offered advice informed both by subject matter analysis and by practical political calculation.

Although some members of the DPS staff, most notably Deputy Director Carp, had been recruited from the Mondale camp, this did not engender the tensions and rivalries that had characterized the appointment of the Rockefeller/Ford DC staff. In part, the difference may be attributed to the better and earlier integration of the Carter and Mondale staffs, to Mondale's avoidance of clear line responsibilities (unlike Rockefeller's vice-chairmanship of the DC), and to the precedent (and its growing acceptance) of a policy role for the vice-president (Light, 1984).

The effectiveness of the DPS director and staff was further enhanced by organizational structure and a relatively stable staff. Since the number of associate directors was nearly twice that of the DC staff, they could acquire a better substantive grasp of the issues to which they were assigned. On-the-job training was further facilitated by the continuity of the senior DPS staff: Eizenstat, Carp, and Rubenstein remained throughout the Carter presidency, and the average tenure among associate directors was nearly thirty months. Approximately half the junior staff were retained for two or more years.

These organizational assets did not, however, guarantee that DPS advice was always accepted or that domestic policy advisory and formulation pro-cesses were invariably channeled through that office. Indeed, Eizenstat's advise was rejected in several instances, for example, on real wage insurance, the proposed $50 tax rebate, changes in the minimum wage, and cargo preferences. On occasion, he and the DPS were circumvented from coordinat-ing or influencing policy, as they were by HEW Secretary Joseph Califano on welfare funding issues or by Attorney General Griffin Bell on most justice matters.

That Eizenstat and the DPS did not dominate the domestic policy process does not gainsay the fact that they exercised an important and influential role in domestic affairs. That role was, however, one of effective administrator and of contributing advisor rather than that of dominant advisor or general agent.

## Presidential Servant: The Reagan Office of Policy Development

Soon after the Reagan administration assumed office, it, like its predecessors, made changes in the domestic policy agency. By renaming it the Office of Policy Development (OPD), the new administration served notice that it would put its own and different stamp on domestic affairs (Kirschten, 1981, p. 826). The change also reflected the expectation that the office would expand into economic affairs (Gray, 1981)—a subject that was central to the new administration's priorities, was compatible with the expertise of the new presidential assistant for domestic policy, and had proven to be a concern of previous domestic policy offices.

During the first three years of the Reagan administration, the OPD had considerable personnel turnover throughout its ranks. Most significant was the succeson of presidential policy assistants: Martin Anderson (1981–1982), Edwin Harper (1982–1983), and John Svahn (1983–). Under each of these assistants, the office performed an administrative role, and only recently has it evidenced any potential for assuming an advisory role. Under each policy assistant, however, the role and performance of the OPD reflected presidential style, the character of the office's personnel, and the organizational dynamics of the EOP.

Since President Reagan is philosophically committed to the notion of cabinet government, he sought to develop a policy system in which department and agency heads were fully involved. By carefully screening appointees for ideological consistency, the president secured appointive executives who were, in general, dependable in their commitment to his programs and philosophy. To better use these agents, the department and agency heads were organized into a cabinet council system consisting of five to six councils. Each council was chaired by the president, or in his absence, by the cabinet secretary designated as chairman pro tempore. Council meetings were regularly attended by cabinet members, the vice-president, and members of the senior White House staff. The director or deputy director of OMB and the chairman of the CEA also attended often. Meetings were held frequently (191 between February 1981 and mid-May 1982) and presidential involvement was not unusual (President Reagan presided at twenty-six of these council meetings) (Newland, 1983, p. 6).

Under this system, OPD was cast in a supporting administrative role in collaboration with two other EOP offices.[6] Approximately one-quarter of the OPD staff (ten to twelve members) were designated as executive secretaries and assistants to the cabinet councils. In addition, an Office of Cabinet Administration (OCA) was created and charged with the tasks of assigning and tracking issues, as well as managing the flow of materials within and between councils. Although its five staff members were counted against OPD's personnel allocation, OCA reported directly to presidential counsellor Edwin Meese. Similarly, the four-member Office of Planning and Evaluation (OPE) reported to Meese and was staffed from OPD's personnel budget. This office assisted "in projecting strategic activities for the president, based on significant national, international, and political phenomena and conditions" (Newland, 1983, pp. 10–11).

Under the first policy assistant, Martin Anderson, OPD performed its administrative tasks at a distance from the president and in lackluster fashion. Although he had been Reagan's issues advisor during the 1980 campaign and seemed to act as the administration's ideological watchdog, Anderson was not an inner-circle confidant of the president. Furthermore, and unlike his predecessors in other administrations, he did not have direct access to the president; instead, he reported through another member of the senior White House Staff (Meese). Personally, Anderson acquired the reputation of being a passive, ineffectual manager "who lacked both the instinct and the inclination to play the pragmatic bureaucratic game" (Kirschten, 1983, p. 585). Thus, stylistically the domestic affairs assistant was ill-suited for a managerial role, and organizationally he was not positioned to direct an extensive administrative role.

The role of OPD is not, however, solely dependent upon the performance and position of the presidential assistant for policy development. Nonetheless, other organizational and political factors allowed the agency little opportunity to develop an alternative advisory role. First, the staff of OPD had neither the credentials nor the stability conducive to providing substantive expertise. Although Anderson himself had broad issue experience and expert credentials, his ideological rigidity diminished the scope and utility of his advice. His staff included many generalists who were veterans of Reagan's California statehouse but who were short on Washington experience. They were loosely organized into half-a-dozen, broadly defined issue areas. Individual staff members were considered generally interchangeable with respect to the issues they worked on (Kirschten, 1981, p. 825). Thus, many of the staff lacked policy expertise or Washington experience and, unlike the Carter DPS, they were deployed in a manner that hindered their ability to acquire substantive competence.

Furthermore, other EOP units had preempted OPD from assuming an advisory role in domestic affairs. Substantively, OMB Director David Stockman was a driving intellectual force behind the domestic policies of the administration (Kirschten, 1982, p. 588). He was also a presidential confidant who commanded bureaucratic resources that OPD could not begin to match. Meanwhile, political advice was coordinated by White House chief of staff James Baker III through the legislative strategy group. Thus, with a cabinet council system operating, OPD was not needed as a presidential agent. The preeminence of OMB and of the legislative strategy group foreclosed OPD from either a substantive or a political advisory role. Furthermore, given both the weak expertise of staff members and the siphoning of personnel to OCA and OPE, the office could not even seriously compete for an advisory role. OPD was, therefore, assigned an administrative role, which it shared with other units, performed at one step removed from the president, and discharged with impressive anonymity.

In February 1982, Anderson was replaced by Edwin Harper, the deputy director of OMB. Harper had a reputation as a nonideological conservative (Newland, 1983, p. 6) and as an experienced manager. He also had a doctorate in government and previous service on Nixon's Domestic Council as assistant director for budget and long-range planning. As deputy director at OMB, Harper had become familiar with OPD, having worked closely with his old friend, Martin Anderson. Thus, his appointment boded well for OPD's administrative role, through the promise of providing it with more effective and less ideological management.

Any prospect for developing an advisory role still encountered problems regarding access to the president, the competence of the staff, and the potency of bureaucratic competition. Although Harper was not a presidential confidant, he was regarded as a Meese loyalist, and Meese, it was rumored, might be supportive of a more assertive OPD since he had lost jurisdiction over the other major policy agency, the NSC. Thus, easier direct access or stronger support from Meese might be conducive to a closer presidential connection.

Furthermore, Harper revised the OPD staff. Two prominent Reaganite California generalists were eased out of the higher levels of the staff hierarchy: Deputy Assistant and Director of the Policy Development Office Edwin Gray went on to the Federal Home Loan Bank, while Deputy Director Ronald Frankum moved over to the Office of Science and Technology Policy. In addition, the experienced Roger Porter (who had served as executive secretary of President Ford's Economic Policy Board and had been executive secretary of Reagan's cabinet council on economic affairs) was promoted to deputy assistant and director of the policy office. Changes among the assistant directors helped to recruit more individuals with Washington savvy into the middle staff level.

In terms of bureaucratic competition within the EOP, two developments were noteworthy. First, Harper came to be included in Baker's legislative strategy group, thus providing him with the possibility of exercising some political advisory influence. Second, after the infamous Stockman interview in the December 1981 issue of *Atlantic Monthly* and with the cresting of budgetary affairs as the dominant focus of the administration, OMB no longer monopolized domestic policy as it once had. This provided OPD with an opportunity to develop a domestic policy advisory role. Meese remarked that now OPD's main task was "to provide additional information when it is needed and to develop policy that isn't going to come out of some other source" (Kirschten, 1982, p. 588). Similarly, Deputy Policy Assistant Porter hinted at a nascent advisory role for OPD when he described its task as being twofold: to serve as an honest broker in assuring that all views were fairly presented to the president, and to control the quality of policy analysis.

Although the foregoing bureaucratic and procedural changes seemed conducive to improving OPD's administrative performance and cultivating an advisory function, their impact was short-circuited by the spring 1983 announcement of Harper's intended resignation. In the months between announcement and actual resignation and replacement in September, Harper became a "lame duck" administrator. Without a clear sense of direction or status, the OPD lost key staff members as they moved on to other jobs and were not immediately replaced. Four of the seven council executive secretaryships fell vacant. In a number of cases, both the top and the second positions in some policy areas were vacant or in the process of turnover (Kirschten, 1983, pp. 2566–67).

Harper's successor, John A. Svahn, regarded such vacancies as both an opportunity (to build his own staff) and a challenge (to recruit able individuals so late in a term). Svahn, himself, had extensive experience as both a public administrator and as a policy management consultant. As a former social security commissioner and undersecretary of health and human services, Svahn was familiar with the policy and administrative issues involved in a major area of domestic policy. Furthermore, as a veteran of Reagan's California administration who had also served on the 1980 transition team, Svahn seemed to have an established, although not close, working relationship with the president. Although domestic issues were an important part of the 1984 presidential election, they were not its focal point. Thus OPD did not have an opportunity to provide advice and analysis for the campaign as the Carter DPS did in 1980.

Thus, as of early 1985, the role of the OPD under Svahn was unclear. Factors both supportive and restrictive to its recasting were apparent, however. It seemed highly unlikely that OPD would be cast in the role of agent. Given President Reagan's ongoing commitment to using cabinet secretaries as his primary agents, as well as the nomination of personal intimates and conservative ideologues like Edwin Meese and William Bennett to cabinet posts, it was obvious that the president already had dependable executive agents. Hence there was little need to call upon members of the domestic policy staff to act as presidential counteragents to direct and dominate cabinet officers as had been the case with the early Nixon Domestic Council.

The prospects for developing an enhanced administrative or advisory role were less conclusive. With the transfers of Edwin Meese and James Baker to the cabinet, the White House policy administration system has entered a new phase. With former Treasury Secretary Donald Regan as new White House chief of staff, a wholesale reorganization has begun. Although the precise dimensions of these changes are as yet unclear, Regan appears to have assumed some combination of the responsibilities of both Baker and Meese. Thus, he may preside over day-to-day operations as well as policy development and coordination. To assist him in his new post, Regan has already brought several members of his Treasury team into key White House administrative positions. He has also retained Svahn at OPD and designated him as one of his four key aides.

Thus, the new Regan regime has raised many unanswered questions about the role of OPD during the second term of the Reagan presidency. Apparently, the policy assistant, John Svahn, will continue to report to the president through another member of the senior staff. Therefore, whatever role the agency can play will be mediated by the ways in which Regan develops his own position as chief of Staff and how OPD fits into that evolution.

On the one hand, the prospects for developing an advisory role are contingent upon a host of potentialities. A political advisory role seems least likely since Regan himself lacks the political experience of his predecessor (Baker). A policy advisory role has better prospects for two reasons. First, Regan is expected to play an influential policy role. Thus, he may look to OPD to provide him with policy information and analysis. Second, the position of other possible bureaucratic competitors within the EOP may allow Regan and OPD to exercise a greater policy influence during Reagan's second term. For example, the influence of the CEA is at a thirty-year nadir and David Stockman left OMB in August 1985. In either case, Regan and OPD could move into the vacuum created by such conditions.

Another possibility is that OPD might be able to enhance its present administrative role. If, during the course of the current staff reorganization, OPD acquired direction over the offices of Cabinet Administration and of Planning and Evaluation, then it would have regained command over staff resources and responsibilities that it does not now exercise. Such a development would probably accord OPD a more central administrative role in domestic policy matters. In any event, the casting of OPD during the second Reagan administration will depend upon the relationships that development between Chief of Staff Regan, Policy Assistant Svahn and President Reagan; upon the capabilities of the OPD staff; upon the president's policy agenda (and its administrative requirements), and upon the influence of OPD's bureaucratic competitors.

## Summary: The Roles of a Domestic Policy Agency

At the outset, I suggested three possible roles for the EOP domestic policy office: agent, administrator, and advisor. Whatever role the domestic policy office plays in any specific administration will depend upon a number of factors. Important among these are (1) the intimacy and ease of the relationship between the president and the White House domestic policy assistant; (2)

presidential preferences and practices regarding the dependability and utility of his cabinet and other line officers; (3) the character and quality of the skills of the domestic policy assistant and of the domestic policy staff; and (4) the existence and performance of competing or overlapping agencies, particularly within the EOP.

We can now make a number of generalizations about the role and performance of this EOP agency. Clearly, the part that the domestic policy office will play in the policy process will differ according to the role into which it has been cast.

The role of administrator, as seen in the Reagan presidency, is the most limited and the least influential. The OPD performs an operational coordinating function. Since this requires few assets other than managerial competence, considerable personnel instability can be tolerated and is even likely to occur. In this role, the policy influence of the presidential assistant for policy development and of his staff at OPD is minimal.

In contrast, the role of advisor, as seen in the Carter case, has the potential for greater scope and impact. To function successfully in an advisory capacity, the assistant for domestic affairs and the domestic policy staff must be knowledgeable, preferably about both policy substance and politics. Furthermore, the head of the unit must have the confidence of, and access to, the president. In an advisory role, the presidential assistant for domestic affairs and the DPS can exercise an important, though not necessarily the dominant, influence upon the agenda-setting, formulation, and enactment stages of the domestic policy process.

Finally, the role of agent, as seen in two very different manifestations in the Nixon and Ford presidencies, presents an enigma. In the Nixon administration, John Ehrlichman and his Domestic Council staff exerted considerable control over a wide range of domestic policy issues as well as over the broad span of the policy process. Perhaps most controversially, in the role of agent the domestic policy office has the potential to become involved in the implementation stage. In doing so, however, the office incurred such political and administrative opposition that the role could not be sustained.

In the case of the Ford administration, the abortive experiment in delegating Rockefeller to be the president's chief domestic policy agent ran into other difficulties. As the vice-president, Rockefeller brought a legitimacy to the role of agent that no presidential assistant could command. Yet because of the circumstances under which both Ford and Rockefeller came to office, they did not have the opportunity to develop the personal intimacy (and with it the pattern of mutual influence and trust) necessary to support either an advisory or an agency relationship. Furthermore, the competition and opposition of other White House staff members and agencies interfered with both the organization and operation of the DC staff. Thus both the vice-president and the DC were denied the very resources they needed to perform successfully the roles they were originally assigned.

Overall, it would seem that effective performance of a domestic policy office depends upon role demands and opportunities as well as administrative and personnel resources and relationships. For example, the administrative and advisory roles can be associated with involvement early in the policy process. Optimally, a domestic policy office acting as administrator can have an important impact upon agenda-setting, while as an advisor, the office can exercise a significant influence upon policy formulation and, in some circumstances, enactment. In contrast, in the role of agent, the domestic policy office seems to seek involvement in all stages of the policy process. Ironically, attempts to secure such pervasive involvement have failed, either in the short-run (e.g., the Rockefeller Domestic Council) or in the long-term (e.g., the Nixon Domestic Council).

In a more general sense, this record suggests that there are informal constraints upon presidential usage of EOP units. Specifically, use as an agent seems to be problematic and significantly constrained by external political factors, which, in turn, make effective performance in this role particularly difficult to achieve and to maintain. In contrast, since use for administrative and advisory purposes is generally considered to be legitimate, performance effectiveness depends primarily upon factors within the presidency, that is, those factors idtified at the start of this section regarding skill, intimacy, bureaucratic competition, and presidential style.

The administrative role seems to constitute the minimal possible role for the domestic policy assistant and his staff. The requisite resources for this role include managerial skills in the policy assistant and the integration of the assistant and the staff into the White House information and paper flow network. Although it appears that a close personal relationship between the president and the policy assistant is not necessary, it does improve his prospects for effective performance.

In contrast, presidential trust is crucial, but insufficient, to successful performance in either an advisory or agency role. Although presidential trust seems to be personalized (i.e., it involves the personal loyalty of the assistant for policy affairs and, by extension, his office's staff), a domestic policy agent must also enjoy a broader political trust from other, extrapresidential political actors, such as Congress, interest groups, and members of the "permanent" bureaucracy. This combination seems to have eluded the domestic policy offices of Presidents Nixon and Ford. Thus, although Ehrlichman and the first Domestic Council had President Nixon's trust, they were not similarly regarded by other political actors. Without such political acceptance, other assets were insufficient to maintain the office's effective performance in the long run, and administrative inadequacies not only hindered effectiveness but were regarded by other political actors as further justification for distrusting the office. In the case of Vice-President Rockefeller and his Domestic Council staff, the president's trust was quickly lost (if it was ever had), and without it Rockefeller and the Domestic Council could not command adequate administrative resources nor cultivate the trust of others.

Presidential trust in an advisor derives, in part, from an assistant's expert credentials, which can be supplemented by the competence of a capable staff. In other words, a president needs to have confidence in the ability of an advisor as well as in the individual who acts as advisor. Effective performance, therefore, requires personnel who are competent in both substantive and political matters. Of course, an advisory relationship is likely to be enhanced if the president believes that the assistant (and the domestic policy staff) are personally loyal to him.

In each and every role, an incomplete or inadequate set of resources will impede the effective performance of the domestic policy assistant and the domestic policy office.

An appreciation of the different roles played by the domestic policy office and of the factors that have contributed to various role assignations facilitates comparative analysis, both among different presidencies and among different EOP units. The use of roles as an analytical concept allows one to distinguish accurately among phenomena that appear, at least superficially, similar. The variations revealed by such an analysis demonstrate many of the problems inherent in the possible institutionalization of a domestic policy office or in any presidential agency.

From this perspective, the case of the domestic policy office illustrates problems and prospects relevant for other presidential agencies. Hence the specification of roles and of the factors that determine the casting and performance of specific presidential agencies in particular roles in different presidencies enhances our understanding of the operation and impact of that discontinuous institution that is the modern presidency.

## NOTES

1. The domestic policy agency has undergone a number of changes in name. From 1970 to 1977, it was known as the Domestic Council (DC). In 1977, it became the Domestic Policy Staff (DPS), and in 1981, the Office of Policy Development (OPD). The text uses the appropriate name when discussing each administration.

2. This is based on a survey of interpretations and treatments of the law of agency by some of the leading legal authorities in the field. These works include Floyd R. Mecham, *Outlines of the Law of Agency*, 4th ed., ed. Philip Mechem, (Chicago: Callaghan & Co., 1952); Merton Ferson, *Principles of Agency* (Brooklyn: The Foundation Press Inc., 1954); Joseph L. Frascona, *Agency* (Englewood Cliffs: Prentice Hall,

1965); Warren A. Seavey, *Studies in Agency* (St. Paul, Minn.: West Publishing Co., 1949); and Francis B. Tiffany, *Handbook of the Law of Principal and Agent* (St. Paul, Minn.: West Publishing Co., 1903). Many of these works were also helpful regarding the law of service and were augmented by that of W. F. Bailey, *The Law of the Master's Liability for Injuries of a Servant* (St. Paul, Minn.: West Publishing Co., 1894).

For a broad-ranging and provocative survey of applications of agency principles and concepts in the study of American political institutions, see Barry M. Mitnick, "Agency Problems and Political Institutions," paper presented at the Midwest Political Science Association Annual Meeting, Chicago, Ill., April 1984.

3. John Ehrlichman, Interview, 10 December 1981, New York, New York. Quoted comments on the Nixon Domestic Council, unless otherwise attributed, have been derived from this interview.

4. Compiled from hearings of the Senate and House of Representatives, Subcommittee on Appropriations, *Treasury, Postal Service and General Government Appropriations*, 91st Congress, 2nd sess. through 93rd Congress, 2nd sess.

5. Using very different concepts and methodology, John Kessel has assessed the influence and importance of various EOP units during the Carter presidency. In this study, he demonstrates that domestic policy assistant Eizenstat was one of "the most important staff members" of that administration. He also discusses the "professionalism" of the DPS staff. See "The Structures of the Carter White House," *American Journal of Political Science* 27 (Summer 1983): 431–63.

6. President Reagan seemed to prefer casting presidential staff (White House Office as well as EOP generally) into the role of administrative servants. For a discussion of the role(s) of the initial Reagan EOP, see Margaret Jane Wyszomirski, "In the Service of the President: The Reagan EOP Takes Shape," paper presented at the American Political Science Association Annual Meeting, New York, N.Y., September 1981. For an examination of the status and influence of the major EOP offices during the early Reagan administration, see John H. Kessel, "The Structures of the Reagan White House," *American Journal of Political Science* 28 (May 1984):231–58.

# REFERENCES

Bonafede, Dom. 1975. Domestic Council's role broadens. *National Journal* 7 (March 22):449.
———. 1978. A new job for Watson. *National Journal* 10 (April 29):680.
———. 1979. Stuart Eizenstat—Carter's right hand man. *National Journal* 11 (June 9): 944–48.
Ehrlichman, John. 1982. *Witness to Power, The Nixon Years*. New York: Simon and Schuster.
Eizenstat, Stuart. 1977. Testimony. U.S. Congress, Senate, *Hearings of the Subcommittee on Appropriations, Treasury, Postal Service, and General Government Appropriations*, 95th Cong., 1st sess., part 1: 1033–39.
———. 1978. Testimony. U.S. Congress, Senate, *Hearings of the Subcommittee on Appropriations, Treasury, Postal Sevice, and General Government Appropriations*, 95th Cong., 2nd sess., part 3: 128–39.
Gray, Edwin. 1981. Interview with author, 10 June, Washington, D.C.
Jones, Charles O. 1977. *An Introduction to the Study of Public Policy*. 2nd ed. North Scituate, Mass.: Duxbury Press.

Kessel, John H. 1975. *The Domestic Presidency*. North Scituate, Mass.: Duxbury Press.

Kirschten, Dick, 1981. Reagan sings of cabinet government, and Anderson leads the chorus, *National Journal* 13 (May 9): 824–27.

———. 1982. Decsion making in the White House: How well does it serve the president? *National Journal* 14 (April 3): 584–89.

———. 1983. Don't look for sparks to fly from the White House Domestic Policy Office. *National Journal* 15 (December 10): 2566–67.

Laski, Harold J., 1960. The limitations of experts. In *The Intellectuals*, ed. G. C. deHuasar. Glencoe: The Free Press.

Light, Larry. 1979. White House Domestic Policy Staff plays an important role in formulating legislation. *Congressional Quarterly Weekly* 37 (October 6): 2199–204.

Light, Paul C. 1984. *Vice Presidential Power*. Baltimore: Johns Hopkins University Press.

Lyons, G. M. 1971. The president and his experts. *Annals* 394 (March): 36–45.

Moe, Ronald C. 1976. The Domestic Council in perspective. *The Bureaucrat* 5 (October): 251–72.

Nathan, Richard P. 1983. *The Administrative Presidency*. New York: Wiley.

Newland, Chester A. 1983. The Reagan presidency: Limited government and political administration. *Public Administration Review* 43 (Jan./Feb.): 1–21.

Shull, Steven A. 1979. *Presidential Policy Making: An Analysis*. Brunswick, Ohio: Kings Court Communications.

Thomas, Norman C. 1972. Presidential advice and information: Policy and program formulation. In *The Institutionalized Presidency*, ed. N. C. Thomas and H. W. Baade, pp. 114–46. Dobbs Ferry, N.Y.: Oceana Publications.

Turner, Michael. 1982. *The Vice President as Policy Maker*. Westport, Conn.: Greenwood.

Waldmann, Raymond J. 1976. The Domestic Council: Innovation in presidential government. *Public Administration Review* 36 (May/June): 260–68.

Wyszomirski, Margaret Jane. 1982. The de-institutionalization of presidential staff agencies. *Public Administration Review* 42 (Sept./Oct.): 448–58.

Paul A. Anderson

# Deciding How to Decide in Foreign Affairs: Decision-making Strategies as Solutions to Presidential Problems

Of all the organizational issues in the government, organizing the executive branch for the conduct of foreign policy has claimed more attention by scholars, policy makers, and journalists than any other single issue. Allison and Szanton (1976) cite six official studies since the Second World War with recommendations for improving the process; numerous books and articles have been written on the issue of administrative mechanisms and presidential choice (Bacchus, 1974; Clark and Legere, 1969; Destler, 1972 and 1981; George, 1980; Hammond, 1960; Hess, 1976; Jackson, 1965; Johnson, 1974; Nelson, 1981); and periodically during a president's term journalists write long articles discussing who (if anyone) is in charge of the administration's foreign policy. The amount of attention is not very surprising, for the organization of the executive branch for the conduct of foreign policy is among the most critical issues facing an administration: the president is the primary actor in foreign policy, he has wide latitude in how he may organize the White House, and his choices rarely seem optimal.

A large amount of the scholarly attention to the issue has focused on how presidents have organized and how they ought to organize the White House— the National Security Council and the Executive Office of the President. The one question that has not received close attention (but the answer to which is presumed in the other analyses) is why presidents adopt the particular organization they do. The literature on how presidents have organized the White House has assumed that presidential style and personality account for the choice of advisory systems (George, 1980; Nelson, 1981; Destler, 1981), and the literature on how presidents should organize the White House has assumed a very narrow set of decision-making objectives (George, 1980; Janis, 1982). The central point in this essay is that understanding why presidents adopt the advisory structures they do requires understanding the presidential goals and interests that an advisory system is supposed to facilitate and the structure of the task environment of foreign policy making.

It is not surprising that presidential advisory strategies are seen as simple reflections of the style and personality of the president. The broad discretionary powers granted to a president in organizing the executive branch make the choice of an advisory system a reflection of the individual holding the office, unlike the other parts of the executive branch, which are fixed by statute and supported by the jurisdictions of congressional committees. Although there is no question that presidents get to choose their advisory procedures, an exclusive emphasis on personality and personal style is misleading in two important respects. First, while personality is relatively stable, the evidence suggests advisory systems are not. During the first three years of the Nixon administration, for example, there were at least ten changes in the system of NSC committees and review groups. It is not clear, therefore, how much concepts like style and personality help in explaining changes within administrations. Second, although personality and style may be useful in understanding the general characteristics of advisory systems, they cannot easily account for the variety of ways in which presidents have sought counsel and advice. Eisenhower adopted a variety of advisory and decision-making approaches depending upon the charcteristics of the issue (Greenstein, 1982a), and during the Nixon administration six different patterns of policy making existed within the fixed Kissinger-dominated system (Kohl, 1975). At best, presidential style is useful in distinguishing one administration from another. It does not hold much promise in explaining the variety of presidential decision-making patterns.

Perhaps the greatest shortcoming of a focus on style and personality is that it ignores the institutional imperatives and political constraints on the presidency. Advisory systems are not created for the purpose of providing presidents with a means of self-expression; there is some function to the form. Because presidents are required to make decisions across a wide range of issues and to exert control over a large and complex organization, governing severely taxes the information processing capacity of a president. No single individual has the cognitive capacity to govern without some mechanism to manage and organize those information-processing and decision-making demands. Organizing is the solution to the problem of the information and decision-making demands on a president. Specialization and the division of labor allow individual expertise and specialization to be exploited; decomposing the task of governing produces smaller, more manageable subtasks; and standard operating procedures provide mechanisms for achieving coordination and control. The administrative forms a president can use to solve the administrative problem of governing are the National Security Council and the Executive Office of the President.

Although the executive branch, the Executive Office of the President, and the National Security Council are fundamentally political organizations, they are also organizations. The overwhelming tendency among political scientists is to emphasize the political aspects of the policy process at the expense of the organizational aspects. To be sure, the bureaucratic politics literature (Allison, 1971; Halperin, 1974) makes some use of organization theory, but much of that emphasis is on the political bargaining game. Even Allison's Organization Process Model, drawn directly from the works of Simon, Cyert, and March, presents a very stylized view of organization largely dominated by concerns about implementation. The fundamental presumptions of this essay are that the presidency is an organization, a political organization to be sure, but an organization nonetheless, and that behavioral theories of organization, particularly the works of Simon (1974), Cyert and March (1963), and March (1978), can provide insights into the foreign policy process.[1]

Viewing the choice of a foreign policy advisory system as a solution to the problem of managing the information-processing and decision-making demands of governing shifts emphasis away from personality and style and toward the fundamental reasons why presidents have systems of counsel and advice. Presidents have advisory and decision-making systems to help them achieve a set of goals and interests with respect to information processing, decision making, and governing. The White House is an organization that has as its primary function the task of helping presidents achieve those goals and interests. The shift in emphasis also directs attention toward viewing the president as a manager. Although it is clear that a president is not just a manager, an important part of what it is to be a president is to manage and control the executive branch. Moreover, although decision making is an important part of managing, it is clear that managing is far more than simply making decisions (Pfeffer, 1981; Kaufman, 1981): managing involves the use of language, symbols, and ritual to lead, to direct, to inspire, and to command. From this point of view, understanding presidents' solutions requires understanding the goals they are attempting to achieve and the structure of the environment in which they are attempting to achieve them.

## Presidential Goals and Interests

Much of the work on presidential goals and interests with respect to the organization of the White House for foreign policy presumes a single, overriding presidential interest in high quality information processing. Janis (1982) and George (1980), for example, both adopt the point of view that a president should be a vigilant disinterested decider, open to the advice and counsel of his staff. This perspective portrays a president as a pure decision maker–

information processor with a primary goal in seeing that the advisory system provides the basis for a well-informed choice. Thus, George (1980, p. 10) argues that a good policy-making system will accomplish five tasks:

(1) Ensure that sufficient information about the situation at hand is obtained and that it is analyzed adequately so that it provides policy makers with an incisive and valid diagnosis of the problem.

(2) Facilitate consideration of all the major values and interests affected by the policy issue at hand.

(3) Assure a search for a relatively wide range of options and a reasonably thorough evaluation of the expected consequences of each.

(4) Provide for careful consideration of the problems that may arise in implementing the options under consideration.

(5) Maintain receptivity to indications that current policies are not working out well and cultivate an ability to learn from experience

In a similar vein, Janis (1982, pp. 262–71) offers nine suggestions for improving decision making and preventing the groupthink syndrome, the first three of which are:

(1) The leader of a policy-forming group should assign the role of critical evaluator to each member, encouraging the group to give high priority to airing objections and doubts.

(2) The leaders in an organization's hierarchy, when assigning a policy-planning mission to a group, should be impartial instead of stating preferences and expectations at the outset.

(3) The organization should routinely follow the administrative practice of setting up several independent policy-planning and evaluation groups to work on the same policy question, each carrying out its deliberations under a different leader.

Although no one would encourage presidents to violate these decision-making and information-processing objectives, it is clear these objectives have real costs associated with them, costs that George and Janis recognize. Both believe, however, that a president's interest in high quality decision making and information processing can be separated from other, less central interests. In George's view, for example, presidents face trade-offs between quality decisions, timely decisions, and bureaucratic consensus. It is not clear, however, that such a clean dividing line can be drawn between quality decisions, consensus, and decision time in the complex setting of policy making. In fact,

Greenstein (1982) suggests that in policy-making settings timely decisions and political support are part of the definition of a quality decision.

Although there is no question that presidents have an interest in receiving high quality information and advice, the evidence seems to suggest that no president has consistently met all the criteria of high quality decision-making procedures. One explanation for this lack of fit between the normative ideal and reality is that presidents do not really understand how to organize the White House. An alternative explanation is that presidents have a broader range of goals and interests than those embodied in the normative ideal. From this perspective, understanding why presidents adopt the decision-making and advisory procedures they do requires understanding the broader range of presidential goals and interests. As a first approximation, presidential interests can be divided into four categories: policy interests, decision-making interests, political interests, and managerial interests.

A president brings to the office a set of policy goals and interests in the form of an agenda, a set of principles and beliefs, and a set of personal priorities (Light, 1982). A president's policy interests are a mixed and varied lot: in addition to specific proposals, there are critical issues, doctrines, and objectives, with few providing clear guides to action. These interests are not universally shared in the executive branch or the government as a whole. Other actors—including those in the White House—have points of view that differ from those of the president. Although a president can achieve some things without the cooperation of others, a president needs cooperation to achieve his interests.[2]

Decision-making interests follow from a fundamental interest in good policy. All presidents have an interest in receiving alternatives that will contribute to U.S. foreign policy objectives, in receiving the best available counsel and advice from foreign policy and defense experts, and in making well-founded choices.

A president's political interests include maintaining the support of domestic constituencies (which contribute toward reelection), maintaining the support of Congress for the administration's foreign and domestic policy agendas, exercising the traditional foreign policy leadership of the United States in world politics, and protecting and exercising the power, influence, and leadership inherent in the office of president of the United States.

The managerial interests of a president include insuring that decisions are implemented in a manner faithful to the letter and spirit of the president's intentions, maintaining coordination and control over the larger organization of the government so that lower-level actions not directly under presidential control are consistent with presidential priorities, encouraging timely response to external events and presidential directives, and maintaining some control over one of the more important presidential resources—a president's time and attention.

The range of presidential interests reflects the fact that a president is not just a decision maker: a president is also a political leader and a chief executive. Although making decisions is an important part of being a political leader or a chief executive, these other roles have important attributes that shape a president's decision-making and advisory system.

## The Environment of Policy Making

A list of goals and interests is not enough to understand a president's solution to the administrative problem of organizing a decision-making and advisory system. Goals are achieved in an environment, and understanding goal-directed behavior requires understanding the environment in which a president attempts to solve the administrative problem. As a first approximation, three elements are important in the policy-making environment: resources, opportunities, and other actors.

The presidency provides the occupant of the Oval Office with a wide variety of resources, both symbolic and real, that can be used to achieve policy goals (Hess, 1976; Neustadt, 1980; Helmer, 1981). These resources include the power and authority of the office; the administrative authority to make decisions and give orders; the ability to define the premises and presumptions that subordinates are to use in making their decisions; a "bully pulpit" from which to direct attention, define issues, and practice the art of persuasion; and domestic political power as head of a political party. But although presidents have unquestioned resources to achieve their objectives, they are not the only powerful participants in the policy process. The power of other actors, however, is far more domain-specific than that of a president, and opposition frequently resembles bureaucratic guerilla warfare waged with leaks to the press, bureaucratic maneuvers to constrain presidential options, low-level sabotage to distort implementation of presidential decisions, and attempts to mobilize domestic political interests.

Yet presidential resources are not the sole possession of a president, they are resources that other players attempt to exploit for their own ends. A president faces the problem that the resources he may use to influence the outcome of the policy process are resources that other participants can use to achieve their own policy interests. The result is that members of the larger organization compete for the limited time and attention of the president. Further demands on presidential resources are imposed by the fact that the president holds the ultimate authority in the executive branch and can give lower-level officials the power to act. The fact that governmental action does not always require presidential decision places further demands on the resources of the presidency. Finally, actors external to the executive branch, including domestic political support groups, members of Congress, and foreign governments, can place demands on the time, attention, and policy resources of a president.

Opportunities for choice are the second element of the policy-making environment. The natural flow of information and agendas in an organization produces situations calling for an organizational choice (Cohen, March, and Olsen, 1972). These choice opportunities represent the decision agenda of the organization and provide presidents (and other participants) with opportunities to achieve their policy goals and interests. Some choice opportunities arise because of regular cycles and routine actions: budgets must be made, speeches must be given, individuals must be appointed, and legislation may require regular reports to the Congress. Other choice opportunities are produced by the larger organization of the government routinely disgorging issues requiring presidential attention. Some choice opportunities arise because of the action of other actors, including the Congress and other governments. And some choice opportunities are of the president's making.

Although most of the core policy interests of the participants in the policy process can only be achieved by governmental action, all participants, including the president, face the problem that the available choice opportunities do not cleanly mesh with their frequently amorphous policy interests. Opportunities for choice in specific policy domains, what Kingdon (1984, p. 174) calls "policy windows," arrive infrequently and do not stay around very long. Moreover, those opportunities that do exist frequently come wrapped in particular substantive problems or in parochial bureaucratic conflict. Presidents rarely have the ability to define choice opportunities with their policy interests in mind. As a result, a president must attempt to achieve his substantive policy interests with frequently ill-fitting choice opportunities.

Other actors with their own goals and resources are the third element in a president's policy environment. Although a president is the single most powerful actor in the policy process, few choice opportunities provide self-executing decisions. Presidents depend upon others to implement official decisions as well as to provide information, alternatives, and advice. In the end, all presidents depend upon the support of other actors in order to achieve their policy goals.

From the perspective of administrative problem solving, the existence of other actors is more than just a political problem requiring bargaining and persuasion. Presidents depend upon others for alternatives, information, and advice, and no president can assume all participants in the policy process share his goals and interests. As a result, the counsel and advice a president receives is not innocent information but strategically presented information, biased by the goals and interests of the source. Participants in the policy process are not neutral information processors; they are individuals with training and expertise who frequently take upon themselves the obligation to see that the president acts in what the advisor sees as the national interest. While it would be a mistake to overemphasize the manipulative side of advising, it is clear that a president cannot take advice at face value and that advising and decision-making procedures reflect that fact. As Feldman and March (1981, p. 177) puts it: "Competition among contending liars turns persuasion into a contest in (mostly unreliable) information. . . . Decision makers learn not to trust overly clever people, and smart people learn not to be overly clever."

Other actors also complicate the problem of designing advisory and decision-making procedures because they can initiate governmental action without the direct participation of the president. Other actors with their own agendas, resources, and choice opportunities can produce governmental action, and a president must attempt to ensure that these independent actions are consistent with presidential interests and priorities.

These three characteristics of the environment of policy making—resources, choice opportunities, and other actors—are relatively stable from administration to administration. Although the names of some of the actors may change, the major executive branch institutions with their parochial interpretations of the national interest remain in place, and the institutions that link the White House with the larger bureaucracy (the Executive Office of the President and the Office of Management and Budget) are largely staffed with civil servants.

## Deciding How to Decide

Every president faces the problem of deciding how to organize the White House for foreign policy. The administrative problem-solving perspective suggests that how a president solves the problem will be a function of the decision-making goals and interests of the president and the structure of the environment of policy making. The fundamental proposition is that presidents adopt advisory and decision-making procedures as solutions to the problem of deciding how to decide. Understanding why presidents adopt the advisory and decision-making procedures they do requires understanding a president's goals and objectives, the structure of the task environment, and the range of available solutions, a task far more complex than characterizing a president's style or describing the structure of the National Security Council. Unfortunately we have little high-quality empirical data on how presidents have solved this problem. Most of what we know is drawn from journalistic accounts and memoirs of participants, and we can conclude from Greenstein's (1982) careful, archive-based analysis of Eisenhower's decision-making strategy that what we think we know about how presidents have decided is not particularly accurate. But the situation is improving. More political scientists are exploiting the rich archival records in presidential libraries (Anderson, 1983; Berman, 1982 and

1983; Immerman, 1982; Kumar, 1983). As more archival material becomes available, and as better techniques are developed for using archival materials in systematic research, we will be in a much better position to understand how presidents have solved the administrative problem of organizing the White House for foreign policy. But with much archival research yet to be done, it is still possible to use what we do know about presidential decision making to suggest some of the implications of the administrative problem-solving perspective for how presidents decide how to decide.

*Many Problems Beget Many Solutions*

The solution to the administrative problem depends upon the interaction between goals and the environment, and we should not expect presidents to adopt single, fixed advisory procedures. Important features of the environment depend upon the policy issue. In fact, it is more accurate to say that there are policy-making environments rather than a single environment. Issues differ with respect to the policy interests at stake, the resources available to the president, the nature of the choice opportunity, and the goals and resources of other actors. The policy interests at stake may be central or peripheral to a president; presidential resources may be high or low; the choice opportunity may be of the president's own making, a product of the bureaucracy, or the result of an external event; and other actors may support or oppose a president's goals. Different policy environments should produce different administrative solutions, and if, as Light (1982, p. 33) suggests, presidential resources decline over time, then a president's administrative solutions should change over time. It is not surprising, then, that the decision-making procedures Kennedy used for Cuban missile crisis differed from the procedures he used for the Test Ban Treaty. Or, that Eisenhower largely by-passed the National Security Council as a decision-making forum when rapid responses to the Dien Bien Phu crisis were required (Immerman, 1982). Or, that the advisory procedures Johnson used for the Vietnam issue differed dramatically from those he used in developing a strategic arms negotiating position (Berman, 1982; Rosati, 1981).

Moreover, to the extent that particular features of the environment differ between administrations—presidents, differ, for example, in their available resources and how they choose to use them—or that presidents have different beliefs about the basic nature of the policy process or make different trade-offs among policy-making goals and interests, we would expect that different presidents would adopt different decision-making procedures. Richard Nixon, for example, appeared to have been confident in his ability to understand foreign policy issues and had a great distrust of the larger bureaucracy (Destler, 1972). His primary objective was to control the policy process. Nixon adopted an advisory system designed primarily to achieve managerial interests. He seemed to feel less need to have an advisory system designed to help achieve policy, decision-making, and political interests: those he could take care of himself.

The degree to which the policy goals of a president are shared by other participants in the process can have a marked influence on presidential solutions to the administrative problem. If a president perceived that goal compatibility was high, there would be a tendency to delegate both authority and responsibility to the lower-levels of the organization and to be more open and receptive to the views of lower-level players. If a president perceived that goal compatibility was low, there would be a tendency to reserve authority and responsibility and to ask for information without revealing why the information was requested in an attempt to keep the answer free of the interests of the source.

Another way in which goal compatibility can influence advisory systems is by determining where options will be framed for presidential decision. A common State Department complaint during the Nixon administration was that Henry Kissinger controlled the framing of alternatives for presidential decisions, since he was the last person to see the president before the decision was made. The framing of alternatives is a critical point in any advisory procedure, and the State Department complaints about Kissinger's influence were undoubtedly accurate. But in an important sense the criticism misses the point: the president wanted it that way. He did not trust the State Department to frame the alternatives with his interests at heart. Other presidents have been less extreme in their distrust of the larger government, but all have been sensitive to the location of the option framing point in the policy process.

Understanding how presidents have solved the problem of deciding how to decide requires more than a catalogue of the ways in which the environment or goals can differ. The solution adopted by a president is a function of the environment, his goals, and the range of available solutions. As a first approximation, two characteristics seem helpful in distinguishing solutions to the problem of deciding how to decide: whether the policy process is open or closed, and whether the president acts as a disinterested decider or as a policy advocate. In an open policy process a variety of different views and perspectives are drawn from the larger organization while in a closed process outside participation is restricted and only those closest to a president are allowed to participate. When a president has no particular interest in the course of action adopted, when he is acting as a pure information processor, he is acting as a disinterested decider interested only in receiving the highest quality information and advice. When a president has a clear policy preference and makes that preference known to the participants, the president is acting as an advocate in the policy process.

Instances of presidential decision making illustrating the four types of solutions are readily available: the decisions leading up to the Bay of Pigs debacle took placed in a closed process with the president as a disinterested decider

(Wyden, 1979; Anderson, 1984); the decisions on Vietnam taken during 1961–1963 took place in an open process with the president as a disinterested decider (Gallucci, 1975); the decisions taken by the Johnson administration to Americanize the war in Vietnam during July 1965 took place in an open process with the president as an advocate (Berman, 1982); and as the war progressed decisions on Vietnam took place in a closed process with a president as advocate (Hoopes, 1973; Gallucci, 1975; Janis, 1982).[3]

The challenge for the administrative problem-solving perspective is to explain why presidents chose the particular decision-making solution given their goals and the structure of the policy-making environment. Although the current paucity of empirical data on presidential goals and the structure of the policy environment makes explanations of the previous cases somewhat problematic, it is possible to speculate on some of the dependencies among goals, environments, and decision-making strategies.[4]

The previous discussion identified four goals that shape a president's solution to the administrative problem: policy, decision-making, political, and managerial goals. The major aspects of the policy-making environment were presidential resources, choice opportunities, and other actors (particularly the degree to which their goals are compatible with those of the president). These factors define the context within which presidents adopt a decision-making strategy.

The various components of decision-making strategies have costs and benefits. Open processes are expensive in terms of presidential time and attention while providing benefits with respect to the legitimacy and acceptance of the resulting decision. Closed processes can conserve decision-making resources while risking acceptance by the larger bureaucracy as well as jeopardizing a president's interest in making the best possible decision. Although policy advocacy can contribute to what a president sees as his policy and political goals, advocacy can be expensive in terms of bargaining resources. A president who adopts the role of a disinterested decider can, under some circumstances, achieve decision-making interests, although he risks expending considerable time and attention in evaluating the positions of competing advocates.

Issues for which a president has strongly held policy interests should tend to produce a president-as-advocate, while those for which a president has strong decision-making interests should produce a solution in which the presidents acts as a disinterested decider. Although it might be argued that a president should always prefer a disinterested decider role to that of a policy advocate, it seems unlikely that a president with a strong interest in seeing a particular course of action adopted would fail to use the considerable persuasive resources that come with the office toward that end.

A president who perceived a low level of compatibility between his goals and the goals of other executive branch participants, Richard Nixon for example, would tend to adopt closed solutions to the administrative problem, while a president who perceived goal compatibility to be high would be expected to adopt open decision-making procedures. A president who trusts his advisors to search for courses of action consistent with his policy and political goals need not control the outcome of the decision-making process. Such a president would also be in a position to save his persuasive resources by adopting a disinterested-decider role, sure in the knowledge that he need not expend an excessive amount of his limited decision-making resources ensuring that his advisors had in fact agreed upon a course of action that helps him achieve his goals.

Although making any decision consumes valuable resources, decisions made in open policy settings—particularly when goal compatibility is low—would tend to be very expensive in terms of a president's time and attention. As a result, a president with low resources would tend to adopt closed solutions, while a president with high resources would be far more willing to adopt open decision-making procedures. Clearly, no president with low resources would adopt a disinterested-decider role in an open decision-making process under conditions of low goal compatibility and high policy interests. He might, however, adopt an open-disinterested procedure even with low resources if the issue were not central and his managerial interests were strong.

Deciding how to decide is a complex problem: there are multiple conflicting goals, the environment is complex, and any solution represents a difficult trade-off. Understanding why presidents adopt particular decision-making and advisory procedures requires understanding how particular solutions can contribute toward achieving a president's goals in a particular policy making environment. From the administrative problem-solving perspective, advisory and decision-making procedures are the product of an intendedly rational decision-making process. It would be a mistake, however, to overemphasize the decision-making rationality of the process. Policy making is continuous, and advisory procedures can develop without conscious design. But even without conscious design, decision-making and advisory procedures are shaped by presidential goals and the structure of the policy environment, and to the extent that decision-making and advisory procedures develop over time as a function of experience, explicit decision-making rationality can be replaced by adaptive rationality (March, 1978). Presidents may rarely explicitly design their advisory procedures, but they can learn.

*Decision-irrelevant Decision-making Procedures*

Although the administrative problem-solving perspective on the choice of decision-making and advisory systems views the president as a goal-directed individual attempting to achieve a set of goals in an environment, decision-making goals are not the only goals reflected in deciding how to decide. Recent research on decision making in organizations has pointed out that much of the behavior in organizations that is justified as part of decision making is actually irrelevant to making organizational decisions (Feldman and March, 1981; March and Sevon, 1984; Pfeffer, 1981). For example, Feldman and March (1981, p. 174) find that organizations typically collect large amounts of information that have no bearing on current decisions, that much of the information used to justify decisions is collected after the decision has been made, that much of the information gathered is never used for the decision for which it was requested, that regardless of the amount of available information, more information is requested, and that complaints that there is not enough information to make a decision are voiced at the same time available information is ignored. Although from a decision-making perspective these tendencies are undesirable, there appear to be good reasons for the seeming irrationality in the decision-making process, reasons that point to the fact that making decisions is not the only important function of decision-making behavior. A president is not just a high-level information processor: he is also a political leader and a manager.

Every political leader faces the twin problems of establishing legitimacy and gaining compliance. Decision-making and advisory systems can serve a president's political interests through the manipulation of symbols and rituals. Requests for briefings, studies, and analysis from the bureaucracy can act as symbols of authority by reinforcing the fact that the president is the president. Eyes-only security classifications and daily presidential intelligence briefings also have the same effect. Although there is undoubtedly some decision relevance to the information a president receives through these requests, it is not clear whether the costs of preparing, transmitting, and processing the information outweigh the incremental improvement in presidential decisions.[5]

Part of the definition of a good decision is that it be an informed decision, and choices made without the advice of the experts rarely have legitimacy in the culture of bureaucracy. Thus, the flow of information to the president plays an important role in giving legitimacy to presidential choices and gaining compliance to presidential directives. Whether the information was used or the advice heeded is generally a secondary matter, since losers who feel they have "had their day in court" are much less likely actively to oppose presidential decisions than are those who have been shut out of the process. Studies and memoranda sent to the White House have the additional effect of providing the illusion of participation to the author; and with participation comes a willingness to comply (March and Simon, 1958). Berman's (1982) analysis of Johnson's decision to expand American participation in the Vietnam conflict provides a telling glimpse of the ability of "having one's day in court" to silence dissent and coerce compliance. Both George Ball and the joint chiefs of staff were initially opposed to LBJ's desire to increase American participation without putting the United States on a war footing. Ball wanted a drastically reduced U.S. commitment and the joint chiefs were in favor of a mobilization of reserves and an increase in troop commitments by 600,000 men. LBJ allowed each to present their case (though in separate meetings). In essence, LBJ argued the JCS's case in his meeting with Ball and then turned around and argued Ball's case in his meeting with the JCS. In the end, each felt they had had their day in court and acquiesced to LBJ's desired middle alternative.

Secretary of State Dean Rusk's testimony before the Jackson subcommittee on the organization of the executive branch (quoted in Destler, 1972, p. 32) provides another example of the logic of decision-irrelevant (and to some, decision-irrational) behavior of large organizations:

> When I read a telegram coming in in the morning, it poses a very specific question, and . . . I know myself what the answer must be. But that telegram goes on its appointed course into the Bureau, and through the office and down to the desk. If it doesn't go down there, somebody feels that he is being deprived of his participation in a matter of his responsibility.
>
> Then it goes . . . back up through the Department to me a week or 10 days later, and if it isn't the answer that I know had to be the answer, then I change it. . . . But usually it is the answer that everybody would know has to be the answer.

Advisory and decision-making mechanisms can also help achieve a president's managerial interests. The most obvious managerial interest is that of coordination and control, and any plausible decision-making system will provide some mechanism for communicating presidential decisions to the bureaucracy. But in addition to the obvious communication and coordination function of presidential directives or national security decision memoranda, important coordination and control interests can be achieved on the input side of the advising process. The National Security Council system is frequently criticized because the formal meetings of the NSC are not productive forums for presidential choice. And the evidence seems to indicate that presidents have rarely used them as such. But it does not follow that, because the formal meetings are largely irrelevant to making presidential decisions, they do not fulfill important managerial functions. Decision-irrelevant decision-making meetings can provide presidents with an opportunity to direct the attention of lower-level participants, to reinforce a president's participation in the decision-making process, to communicate presidential goals, interests, and beliefs, and to interpret history and build shared images.

The attention of the president to an issue and the attendance of a president at a meeting provide powerful signals to the larger bureaucracy. Eisenhower felt that "to maintain the interest and attention of every member of the NSC, he must sit through each meeting—despite the fact he knows the presentations so well" (Greenstein, 1982, p. 133). Kennedy also used the NSC to perform the same function. According to Hilsman (1971, pp. 1–2), on one occasion Kennedy held a series of NSC meetings trying to get agreement on a policy issue. After agreement was finally reached and a handful of advisors presented a draft cable to the president for his approval, Kennedy remarked, "And now we have the inner club." Hilsman quotes McGeorge Bundy as saying that Kennedy meant that "now we had together the people who had known all along what we would do about the problem, and who had been pulling and hauling, debating and discussing for no other purpose than to keep the government together, to get all the others to come around."

Formal meetings also provide presidents with an opportunity to communicate their goals and objectives and to explain their decisions to other participants. Governments have been characterized as "organized anarchies" (Cohen, March, and Olsen, 1972; Sproull, Weiner, and Wolf, 1978), where preferences are problematic, participation is fluid, and technology is unclear. These attributes clearly fit the process of policy making in foreign affairs. Organizational action frequently lacks collective coherence because the particular cast of participants in a choice strongly influences the outcome. As a result, interpretations of history and retrospective rationality are important devices for managing organized anarchies (Cohen and March, 1974; March, 1972; Pfeffer, 1981; Weick, 1979). These symbolic acts provide direction and coherence to the organizational action by constructing and maintaining symbolic belief systems and shared interpretations of organizational action and purpose. Decision-irrelevant decision-making procedures provide presidents with a forum to engage in these symbolic acts.

Throughout the Dien Bien Phu crisis, for example, the NSC planning process slowly ground out an official options paper. Unfortunately, events were changing so rapidly that by the time the paper was ready to be considered at a formal NSC meeting, it was not immediately relevant to the choices Eisenhower faced. The central choices had already been made. But Immerman (1982) concludes that the formal consideration of the irrelevant options paper was not a waste of time. It provided an opportunity for Eisenhower to explain his decisions and to communicate his interpretation of U.S. interests in Indochina to officials who had not been part of the small informal meetings where the decisions had been made. In a similar vein, Henry Kissinger (quoted in Frei, 1983, p. 111) has remarked that during crises, "an enormous amount of time must be spent making certain that the key figures act on the basis of the same information and purpose." Decision-irrelevant decision-making meetings provide presidents with opportunities to establish common facts and goals.

The fact, then, that an advisory system serves a president's political and managerial interests as well as his decision-making interests has important implications for understanding presidential solutions to the problem of deciding how to decide. If we understand the solution to the administrative problem as being guided solely by decision-making and information-processing interests, much of the logic of the decision-irrelevant aspects of decision making is masked. Presidents are political leaders and managers as well as being decision makers, and understanding presidential solutions to the problem of decision making requires an appreciation of the multiplicity of presidential interests.

## Implications for Study, Evaluation, and Design

Why presidents adopt the advisory and decision-making procedures they do is an empirical question, and given the absence of high-quality empirical data on presidential decision making, the most useful conclusions of the administrative problem-solving perspective have to do with the direction of future research.

### Implications for Study

The implications of the administrative problem-solving perspective for the study of how presidents organize the White House for foreign policy can best be seen as extensions to two current approaches for understanding the organization of decision-making: the information-processing perspective of George (1980) and Janis (1982) and the presidential style perspective of Johnson (1975), Rockman (1983), and Cottam and Rockman (1983).

There is no fundamental difference between the information-processing and administrative problem-solving perspectives on presidential advisory systems. Both perspectives view the choice of an advisory procedure as a process directed at achieving a set of goals with respect to the policy process. The difference between the two perspectives centers on the nature of the goals that influence the choice of an advisory system. For the information-processing perspective, the objectives to be achieved have to do with high-quality information processing and decision making, and the central role of decision making as an intellectual activity in the approach results in almost identical normative advice for the president of the United States and the chief executive officer of General Motors: search widely for information, carefully examine your goals, examine a wide range of alternatives, and carefully consider the consequences of following each course of action. Where the administrative problem-solving perspective differs is in suggesting that presidents have a broader set of goals and objectives than high-quality information processing. Presidents also have legitimate political, policy, and managerial goals that shape their choice of decision-making and advisory procedures. Some presidents have given insufficient weight to high-quality information processing in their choice of advisory procedures and have adopted clearly defective decision-making procedures. But lacking a clear understanding of the goals and interests that shape the search for solutions to the administrative problem, we are left with personality defects and psychological predispositions to explain their poor choices. The administrative problem-solving perspective can contribute to a broader perspective on why presidents adopt the advisory procedures they do.

There is also no fundamental difference between explanations of presidential advisory systems based upon style and the administrative problem-solving perspective. The decision-making procedures adopted by Eisenhower differed in significant and systematic ways from the procedures adopted by Kennedy, and Kennedy's procedures differed in significant and systematic ways from Johnson's, and Johnson's procedures differed from Nixon's, and so on. That isn't the issue. The difference between the two perspectives is whether presidential decision-making style is a cause or a consequence. Style-based explanations take decision-making style as a causal factor to be used to explain why presidents made decisions in the ways that they did. The administrative problem-solving perspective views style as a consequence of the way in that particular presidents have tended to solve the administrative problem: style is the modal solution to the administrative problem. To be sure, personality, psychological predispositions, previous experience, and other individual factors influence a president's solution to the administrative problem. However, the evidence that individual presidents have adopted a wide variety of decision-making procedures suggests that relatively permanent individual factors like style and personality cannot hope to explain the diversity of presidential decision-making procedures.

Although the administrative problem-solving perspective is not fundamentally inconsistent with either style or information-processing explanations of presidential decision-making procedures, it does seek to expand the domain of analysis to reflect the variety of goals and objectives central to the solution of the problem of deciding how to decide in foreign affairs. Presidents adopt decision-making procedures in an attempt to achieve their policy, decision-making, political, and managerial goals in the complex environment of policy making.

The implications of the perspective for research on decision-making and advisory systems are simple. Understanding why advisory and decision-making procedures are adopted requires understanding presidential goals and the structure of the policy-making environment. The first imperative is to improve the quality of the empirical evidence that can be brought to bear on the issue. Memoirs and journalistic accounts are useful, but they must be supplemented with careful archival research. Understanding how presidents have decided to decide requires determining who participated in the decision, the role the president adopted in the decision process, and the goals and interests that shaped the choice of an advisory procedure. All these questions require the examination of archival records.

The second imperative is to develop techniques for systematically exploiting the archives. Although valuable insights can be gained through immersion in masses of archival data, such personal insights provide a very cumbersome and potentially unreliable empirical base. Sampling strategies, which have given students of voting behavior a powerful technology for understanding, are one potential device for collecting and summarizing archival data on decision making. Exploiting the power of sampling requires well-developed sampling units and sampling frames. For some applications it may be sufficient to select every $n$th memo, but others may require quota sampling strategies. Studying decisions will require developing strategies for identifying and sampling choice opportunities. Some questions may be appropriately answered by sampling individuals through time and then determining their decision-relevant behavior on a particular day. Although it is clear that sampling theory will not solve all of the problems inherent in systematically exploiting archives, it is imperative that research technologies be developed for exploiting archival data bases.

## Evaluation and Design

If the only legitimate presidential interest in advisory procedures was an interest in high quality information processing, evaluation and design could start with the presumption that presidents should be disinterested deciders interested only in receiving high quality information and advice. But if presidents have legitimate interests other than decision-making interests, interests, for example, in minimizing decision-making costs, holding political coalitions together, and persuading organizational subunits to accept presidential directives, then exhaustive and comprehensive search and evaluation are not the sole criteria of a high quality advisory procedure. Moreover, advisory systems designed to maximize comprehensive search and evaluation may well fall short of achieving other legitimate presidential interests. Evaluation and design, therefore, must encompass the full range of presidential interests.

The fact that advisory and decision-making procedures reflect a variety of legitimate presidential interests does not imply that "anything goes" in the design of advisory systems. Even though presidents adopt advisory systems based on a variety of goals and interests, some solutions to the design problem are better than others. Whether the solution a president adopts will be a good solution will hinge not only on the characteristics of the solution, but also on the structure of the environment. Presidents do not knowingly adopt inadequate advisory systems; they employ strategies for gathering advice and information that experience has taught them work well most of the time. And most of the time experience is right. However, sometimes the standard strategy fails to work well because the strategy is inappropriate for the particular environment, and sometimes the strategy fails to work well because the procedures were not executed properly (Anderson, 1984). A "normal failure" results when the strategy is inappropriate for the environment and a "systemic failure" results when the strategy fails to work as it should. What distinguishes normal failures from systemic failures is that in the case of normal failures inappropriate advisory procedures are executed properly and in systemic failures appropriate advisory procedures are executed improperly.

With practice and well-designed operating procedures it is possible to minimize the incidence of systemic failures in the advisory process. Unfortunately, normal failures cannot be minimized with standard administrative tinkering, for the problem is with the president's choice of a procedure, not with the procedure itself. This suggests that well-designed advisory systems cannot prevent normal failures: the problem is not that the advisory system failed, but that the solution to a president's problem of deciding how to decide was inappropriate. What the problem-solving perspective provides is a basis for understanding why presidents adopt inappropriate decision-making strategies, and once we have a better understanding of why presidents adopt inappropriate solutions to the problem of deciding how to decide, we will be in a position to provide some useful and needed advice.

## Conclusions

Deciding how to decide in foreign affairs is one of the most critical decisions every president must make. There have been two overwhelming tendencies in our approach to understanding how presidents decide to decide. The first is a tendency to treat presidential style and personality as the causes of advisory and decision-making processes. The second is a presumption that high quality information processing is the only legitimate interest served by advisory and decision-making processes. The argument in this essay is that both tendencies overstate the case. Presidential solutions to the problem of how to decide reflect a diverse set of goals and interests of the president and the structure of the policy-making environment. Advisory systems are, in Simon's (1981) term, "artificial systems" designed by man to achieve human ends. The larger implication of the argument is that to understand and improve upon the designs of presidents requires an attention to the goals, the environment, and the process of institutional design. It is only by understanding the problem from this perspective that we can fulfill the goal implicit in so much of the work on presidential decision making in foreign policy: help presidents make better decisions.

## NOTES

This is a revision of a paper delivered at the 1984 meetings of the International Studies Association. I would like to thank I. M. Destler, Henry Nau, Bert Rockman, and Donald Sylvan for their comments on some of the ideas presented here.

1. Some of the most innovative current work in organization theory is based on the proposition that organizations have an important political component (Pfeffer, 1982). That, of course, comes as no great surprise to political scientists. Perhaps reversing the perspective will have payoffs in the study of governments.

2. If everyone shared a president's goals and interests, then the only real administrative problem to be solved would be how hard a president wanted to work. If he wanted to work hard, he would open the door to the Oval Office to anyone, listen to their suggestions, and act on them. If he wanted to have an easy time of it, he would delegate almost all his authority to his subordinates, reserving for himself the symbolic chief-of-state functions, secure in the knowledge that their actions would reflect his goals and interests.

3. This four-fold classification is clearly a first approximation. A more developed classification would take the difference between crisis and routine decision settings into account as well as reflect the fact that presidential solutions shift within decision settings. During the Cuban missile crisis, for example, Kennedy shifted from a disinterested decider to an advocate (Anderson, 1984), and during the Dien Bien Phu crisis, Eisenhower used open and closed decision procedures in parallel (Immerman, 1982).

4. Naturally, all these speculations have a large *ceteris paribus* clause attached.

5. Throughout his time in office, President Kennedy received a daily intelligence checklist from the CIA summarizing current developments. During three days in February 1962, for example, the checklists totaled thirty-four pages. At that rate, JFK would have received over eleven thousand pages of current intelligence during his 1,000 days. How much of that information was really relevant is unclear; what is clear is that a memorandum for the record was produced for each of those 1,000 days indicating that he had read the checklist.

## REFERENCES

Allison, Graham T. 1971. *Essence of Decision: Explaining the Cuban Missile Crisis.* Boston: Little, Brown.

Allison, Graham T., and Peter Szanton. 1976. *Remaking Foreign Policy.* New York: Basic Books.

Anderson, Paul A. 1983. Decision making by objection and the Cuban missile crisis. *Administrative Science Quarterly* 28 (June): 201–22.

———. 1984. Normal failures in the foreign policy advisory process. *World Affairs* 146 (Fall): 148–75.

Bacchus, William I. 1974. Obstacles to reform in foreign affairs: The case of NSAM 341. *Orbis* 18 (Spring): 266–76.

Berman, Larry. 1982. *Planning a Tragedy: The Americanization of the War in Vietnam.* New York: Norton.

———. 1983. Presidential libraries: How not to be a stranger in a strange land. In *Studying the Presidency,* ed. G. C. Edwards III and S. J. Wayne, pp. 225–56. Knoxville: University of Tennessee Press.

Clark, Keith C., and Laurence J. Legere, eds. 1969. *The President and the Management of National Security.* New York: Praeger.

Cohen, Michael D., and James G. March. 1974. *Leadership and Ambiguity.* New York: McGraw-Hill.

Cohen, Michael D., James G. March, and Johan P. Olsen. 1972. A garbage can model of organizational choice. *Administrative Science Quarterly* 17: 1–26.

Cottam, Richard W., and Bert A. Rockman. 1983. In the shadow of substance: Presidents as foreign policy makers. Paper presented at the 1983 meeting of the International Studies Association.

Cyert, Richard, and James G. March. 1963. *A Behavioral Theory of the Firm*. Englewood Cliffs: Prentice-Hall.

Destler, I. M. 1972. *Presidents, Bureaucrats, and Foreign Policy*. Princeton: Princeton University Press.

———. 1981. National Security II: The rise of the assistant (1961–1981). In *The Illusion of Presidential Government*, ed. H. Heclo and L. M. Salamon, pp. 263–85. Boulder, Colo.: Westview.

Feldman, Martha S., and James G. March. 1981. Information in organizations as signal and symbol. *Administrative Science Quarterly* 26: 171–86.

Frei, Daniel. 1983. *Risks of Unintentional Nuclear War*. Totowa, N.J.: Rowman and Allanheld.

Gallucci, Robert L. 1975. *Neither Peace Nor Honor: The Politics of American Military Policy in Viet-Nam*. Baltimore: Johns Hopkins University Press.

George, Alexander L. 1980. *Presidential Decisionmaking in Foreign Policy: The Effective use of Information and Advice*. Boulder, Colo.: Westview.

Greenstein, Fred I. 1982. *The Hidden-Hand Presidency*. New York: Basic Books.

———. 1982a. Presidents, advisors, and decisionmaking: Vietnam 1954 and 1955—A perspective for comparison. Paper presented at the 1982 meeting of the American Political Science Association.

Halperin, Morton H. 1974. *Bureaucratic Politics and Foreign Policy*. Washington, D.C.: Brookings Institution.

Hammond, Paul Y. 1960. The National Security Council as a device for interdepartmental coordination: An interpretation and appraisal. *American Political Science Review* 54 (December): 899–910.

Helmer, John. 1981. The presidential office: Velvet fist in an iron glove. In *The Illusion of Presidential Government*, ed. H. Heclo and L. M. Salamon, pp. 45–81. Boulder, Colo.: Westview.

Hess, Stephen. 1976. *Organizing the Presidency*. Washington, D.C.: Brookings Institution.

Hilsman, Roger. 1971. *The Politics of Policy Making in Defense and Foreign Affairs*. New York: Harper and Row.

Hoopes, Townsend, 1973. *The Limits of Intervention*. New York: McKay.

Immerman, Richard H. 1982. The anatomy of the decision not to fight: Multiple advocacy or presidential choice? Paper presented at the 1982 meeting of the American Political Science Association.

Jackson, Henry M., ed. 1965. *The National Security Council: Jackson Subcommittee Papers on Policy Making at the Presidential Level*. New York: Praeger.

Janis, Irving L. 1982. *Groupthink*. 2d ed. Boston: Houghton Mifflin.

Johnson, Richard T. 1974. *Managing the White House: An Intimate Study of the Presidency*. New York: Harper and Row.

———. 1975. Presidential style. In *Perspectives on the Presidency*, ed. A. Wildavsky, pp. 262–300. Boston: Little, Brown.

Kaufman, Herbert. 1981. *The Administrative Behavior of Federal Bureau Chiefs*. Washington, D.C.: Brookings Institution.

Kingdon, John W. 1984. *Agendas, Alternatives, and Public Policies*. Boston: Little, Brown.

Kohl, Wilfred L. 1975. The Nixon-Kissinger foreign policy system and U.S.-European relations: Patterns of policy making. *World Politics* 28 (October): 1–43.

Kumar, Martha Joynt. 1983. Presidential libraries: Gold mine, booy trap, or both? In *Studying the Presidency*, ed. G. C. Edwards III and S. J. Wayne, pp. 199–224. Knoxville: University of Tennessee Press.

Light, Paul C. 1982. *The President's Agenda: Domestic Policy Choice from Kennedy to Carter, with Notes on Ronald Reagan*. Baltimore: Johns Hopkins University Press.

March, James G. 1972. Model bias in social action. *Review of Educational Research* 42: 413–29.

———. 1978. Bounded rationality, ambiguity, and the engineering of choice. *The Bell Journal of Economics* 9: 587–610.

March, James G., and Guje Sevon. 1984. Gossip, information, and decision-making. In *Advances in Information Processing in Organizations*, ed. L. S. Sproull and P. D. Larkey, vol. 1, pp.95–108. Greenwich, Conn.: JAI Press.

March, James G., and Herbert A. Simon. 1958. *Organizations*. New York: Wiley.

Nelson, Anna Kasten. 1981. National Security I: Inventing a process (1945–1960). In *The Illusion of Presidential Government*, ed. H. Heclo and L. Salamon, pp. 229–62. Boulder, Colo.: Westview.

Neustadt, Richard E. 1980. *Presidential Power: The Politics of Leadership from FDR to Carter*. New York: Wiley.

Pfeffer, Jeffrey, 1981. Management as symbolic action: The creation and maintenance of organizational paradigms. In *Research in Organizational Behavior*, ed. L. L. Cummings and B. M. Staw, vol. 3, pp. 1–52. Greenwich, Conn.: JAI Press.

———. 1982. *Power in Organizations*. Marshfield, Mass.: Pitman.

Rockman, Bert A. 1983. Presidential and executive studies: The one, the few, and the many. Paper presented at the annual meeting of the American Political Science Association, September.

Rosati, Jerel A. 1981. Developing a systematic decision-making framework: Bureaucratic politics in perspective. *World Politics* 43 (January): 234–52.

Simon, Herbert A. 1974. How big is a chunk? *Science* 183: 482–88.

———. 1981. *The Sciences of the Artificial*. 2d ed. Cambridge, Mass.: MIT University Press.

Sproull, Lee, Stephen Weiner, and David Wolf. 1978. *Organizing an Anarchy: Belief, Bureaucracy, and Politics in the National Institute of Education*. Chicago: University of Chicago Press.

Weick, Karl E. 1979. *The Social Psychology of Organizing*. Reading, Mass.: Addison-Wesley.

Wyden, Peter. 1979. *Bay of Pigs: The Untold Story*. New York: Simon and Schuster.

James E. Anderson

# Presidential Management of Wage-Price Policies: The Johnson and Carter Experiences

Until well into the twentieth century most people assumed that government could do little to control fluctuations in the business cycle, which was supposedly governed by natural economic laws. Change in thought and action occurred, however, as a consequence of such factors as the experience with the Great Depression, the advent of Keynesian economics, the development of better tools of economic analysis, and the fiscal aspects of World War II. The national government is now expected to act to stabilize the economy, and the president is held responsible for developing appropriate policies to achieve this goal. Presidential administrations are evaluated to an important degree on how well, or whether, they succeed at this task.

In his role as economic manager, however, the president has more responsibility than authority. Authority over fiscal policy is shared with Congress, and monetary policy is under the control of the formally independent Federal Reserve Board. International economic policies and mandatory wage and price controls require congressional legislation. To act successfully as economic manager, the president requires the consent and cooperation of many others—in Congress, in the departments and agencies, in his own executive office, and in society. Persuasion and bargaining are more important than command in the macroeconomic policy arena.

Voluntary wage and price guidelines or guideposts, which are the subject of this essay, are the only instrument of macroeconomic policy that can be instituted by the president alone. This creates an incentive for their use. Three Democratic presidents—John F. Kennedy, Lyndon B. Johnson, and Jimmy Carter—have used them in seeking to stabilize the economy. Because the Kennedy administration experience with voluntary wage and price guidelines was quite limited, my focus is on the Johnson and Carter administrations.

A policy decision by an administration to employ wage-price guidelines

173

creates a number of management problems. First, there is a need to develop reasonably clear substantive standards to inform affected parties concerning acceptable wage and price behavior and to guide the administration's intervention in wage-price matters. Second, some sort of administrative structures or arrangements are needed to handle implementation of the wage and price standards. Should these be formal or informal, regularized or ad hoc in nature? Who in the administration should be involved and in what manner? Third, unless the administration wants to rely only on general pronouncements and exhortations, what sorts of pressures, techniques, or "levers" are to be used in gaining consent and compliance from businesses and unions? How these management problems are resolved will have important consequences for guidelines policy as an operational reality.

This discussion of wage-price guidelines in the Johnson and Carter administrations will be structured around these management problems.[1] This will provide a comparative view of the management styles of the two administrations. No attempt will be made to evaluate the impact of their wage-price policies.

## Substantive Policy Standards

The wage-price guideposts used by the Johnson administration were inherited from the Kennedy administration. They received the explicit approval of President Johnson in his 1964 *Economic Report* (President Kennedy had never endorsed the guideposts as his own). Generally, guidepost policy was viewed as a supplement to monetary and fiscal policies, as a way of dealing with cost-push inflationary pressures (or "administered" prices and wages), especially when the economy was operating at less than full employment.

In 1964 and 1965 the administration focused its efforts primarily on wage and price increases in major industries. Notable victories for the guideposts were won in the steel, aluminum, and copper industries, but the automobile industry in 1964 proved resistant to administration pressures. Late in 1965, as inflationary pressures in the economy intensified because of increased Vietnam spending, guidepost activity began to pick up, and the first eight months of 1966 constituted a period of intense guidepost activity. Although guidepost activity continued for the remainder of 1966 throughout 1967, it was characterized by lessened intensity and publicity.

Developed within the Council of Economic Advisors (CEA) and first set forth in their 1962 annual report, the theory underlying the guideposts was that inflationary pressures in the economy would be mitigated if discretionary wage and price decisions were brought generally into accord with what would happen in competitive markets. The CEA outlined the guideposts in these terms:

The general guide for non-inflationary wage behavior is that the rate of increase in wage rates (including fringe benefits) be equal to the trend rate of *overall* productivity increase. General acceptance of this guide would maintain stability of labor cost per unit of output for the economy as a whole—though not of course for individual industries.

The general guide for non-inflationary price behavior calls for price reduction if the industry's rate of productivity increase exceeds the over-all rate—for this would mean declining labor costs; it calls for an appropriate increase in price if the opposite relationship prevails; and it calls for stable prices if the two rate of productivity increase are equal.[2]

Some modifications and exceptions were also provided. Thus, wage increases could exceed the general guidepost rate if necessary for an industry to attract an adequate supply of labor.

A table in the 1964 annual report of the CEA led to the development of the famous 3.2 percent wage guideline. At a press conference preceding the release of the report, discussion turned to which of the figures in the table was the correct one for wage increases. As CEA chairman Gardner Ackley recalls: "Finally, someone from the press said, 'well, the figure really ought to be 3.2 percent.' And I don't think Walter Heller said 'no'; so that's how 3.2 got its [designation]."[3] Thus 3.2 percent, which was the average or trend rate of productivity for the previous five years, became the standard for noninflationary increases.

The 3.2 standard was continued in use during 1965 and 1966. No numerical figure for wage increases was contained in the CEA's 1967 annual report. Rather, following a general discussion of the need for wage restraint, the council concluded: "If restraint cannot mean an average wage advance only equal to the rise in productivity, it surely must mean wage advances which are substantially less than the productivity trend plus the recent rise in consumer prices."[4] Although this led the press to conclude that the guideposts had been abandoned, the administration continued its efforts to hold down price increases, especially in the first half of 1967. The guidepost policy was never formally abandoned by the Johnson administration. Throughout, guidepost policy was viewed as a supplement to monetary and fiscal policies.

In October 1978, President Jimmy Carter announced a new anti-inflationary program, directed at the growing inflationary pressures in the economy. The program included reduction in the growth of federal spending, a commitment to reduce the cost of economic regulatory programs, voluntary wage and price standards, and a tax-based incomes program.

The idea for a program of voluntary wage and price standards apparently originated in the Department of Labor (DOL).[5] In July 1978, some of Secretary Ray Marshall's top assistants urged upon him the need to advocate a voluntary program of wage and price restraint. They were concerned because 1979 would be a major collective bargaining year with several large unions—the teamsters, the auto, electrical, and rubber workers, and others—scheduled to negotiate new contracts. High settlements in these cases would intensify inflationary pressures and compound the administration's economic problems. Persuaded by their arguments, Marshall sent the president a memorandum that set off a policy planning episode within the administration, which to then had been characterized by drift in the macroeconomic policy area. As one account explains:

> The gush of enthusiasm reflected the depth of the Administration's frustration and the source of the proposal itself. That Marshall, the internal advocate for organized labor, which was considered hostile to any wage-price program, had embraced the concept was regarded as an amazing stroke of good fortune. "There were a lot of people who like guidelines or standards," said one official, "but who thought they could never get it passed. When the Secretary of Labor came in, everyone went nuts." "Everyone" included the three main economic agencies: Treasury, the Council of Economic Advisers and the Council on Wage and Price Stability.[6]

Marshall's memorandum had discussed the variety of retaliatory techniques that could be taken to secure compliance with wage and price standards by either companies or entire sectors of the economy. Thus, if steel prices increased too fast, the government could relax import restrictions that protected the companies against foreign competition. Again, if the teamsters union reached an excessive wage settlement, the government could ease regulation of the trucking industry and make it easier for nonunion firms to get started.

However, the deputies group of the Economic Policy Group (EPG), which did much of the policy development work on the basic standards, found that such techniques were not so useful or powerful as they appeared.[7] Most tariffs and import quotas could not be changed without congressional approval, while many officials wanted to deregulate the trucking industry as a matter of general policy. The deputies group did identify procurement policy as a tool to back up the guidelines, although there was some doubt as to the legality of its use. Generally, there was reluctance within the administration to adopt anything that harkened of mandatory controls. As finally approved by the president, the wage-price program provided only for publicity and the denial of government contracts as enforcement instruments.

The EPG deputies group also hammered out the basic form of the wage and price standards. The DOL people wanted a high number for wages, whereas the CEA, Office of Management and Budget (OMB), and Council on Wage and Price Stability (CWPS) wanted a low number. A 7 percent figure for annual wage increases was finally agreed on and approved by EPG and the president. There was no basic disagreement among the deputies group on the price standards. The subsequent task of drafting detailed regulations incorporating and elaborating the wage and price standards was handled by a few top-level people in CWPS.

Several factors contributed to shaping the content of the Carter wage-price standards. First, there was agreement that a voluntary program intended to break the wage-price spiral needed to impose comparable restrictions on pay and prices, because the program would depend for success "on support from the widest possible range of individuals and organizations." Second, coverage of the standards should be sufficiently broad that widespread compliance would reduce inflation substantially. However, coverage should not be so broad that compliance would be impractical or cause economic inefficiency, as by extending to highly competitive markets. Third, the standards should attempt to balance effectiveness with economic efficiency and simplicity with equity.[8] The standards were formally published in the Federal Register.

The price standard set an *aggregate* price increase *goal* of 5.75 percent for the first year of the program. There was, however, no single, simple numerical limitation on prices. Rather, companies were expected to keep *average* price increases 0.5 percent lower than their average in the 1976–1977 base period, up to a limit of 9.5 percent. Price increases justified by uncontrollable increases in costs (as for raw materials) could exceed the standard so long as profit margins did not exceed those of the base period. Modified standards were developed for industries in which the basic price standard was inappropriate because of highly volatile raw material costs (as in petroleum refining), institutional idiosyncrasies (as in insurance), and difficulties in making required computations (as in wholesale and retail trade). These modified standards generally set limits for gross margins, fee increases, or dividend payments. Some prices were exempt from the standards, such as oil and gas prices (which were regulated by the government) and farm commodities like meat and grain (whose prices were set by supply and demand). Other commodities whose prices were heavily influenced by market forces could be exempted on a case-by-case basis. Interest rates and professional fees were also exempt.

The pay standard was simpler and did not differ much from a single numerical limit on the rate of wage increases. It provided that *average* increases in wages (including the cost of private fringe benefits but excluding social security and other government-imposed costs) were not to exceed 7 percent. Allowances for cost-of-living increases and other exceptions permitted considerable variation in the effective pay standard since these could be added to the 7 percent figure. Workers earning less than four dollars an hour were excluded from coverage, as were wage contracts signed before 24 October 1978. In the second year of the program, the wage standard was modified to a range of 7.5 to

9.5 percent. As this brief summary indicates, the Carter price and wage standards were much more complex than the Johnson guideposts.

Changes were made in the Carter standards from time to time in the course of their implementation. Three tendencies in the evolution of the standards are especially worth noting. First, issued as formal standards, they became more formal in applications. Companies with special problems, for example, had to negotiate formal exceptions; once granted, these became the basis for future interpretations of the standards.[9] Second, and related to this, the standards soon became more detailed and complex. As the CWPS notes in its report:

> Once an exception was created for a specific type of situation, or modifications were made to account for institutional characteristics, or operational realities of certain industries, there was necessarily increased complexity. This complexity was further compounded by attempts to respond to the requests from those subject to the standards for greater and greater specificity concerning precisely what situations were or were not covered by an exception or modification.[10]

A third tendency was for the standards to become less voluntary. CWPS officials viewed compliance as a requirement, not as a matter of choice by the affected parties.

## Administering Wage-Price Policies: Organization

The administrative structures used between 1964 and 1968 to implement the guideposts were informal, fluid, and ad hoc in nature. If one setup did not prove satisfactory, it would be abandoned and another would be devised to take its place. The problem of organization was never fully resolved. Nonetheless, there were two constant elements in this administrative fluidity. One was the Council of Economic Advisers, which played the central, integrating role in activity throughout the Johnson administration. Although this operational role was not consonant with its regular staff and advisory duties, it fell to the CEA by default. No other agency was available or, more accurately, was suitable and willing to handle the tasks. Second, after mid-1965 Joseph Califano was the central White House official involved in guidepost activity, acting variously as catalyst, coordinator, and wielder of influence.

The use of informal, fluid, ad hoc administrative arrangements fitted Johnson's preference that the guidepost program should be a "low visibility program." LBJ also preferred to keep himself out of public view, especially after the 1966 airline machinists strike when he had announced a wage settlement that was subsequently rejected by the union membership. The strike was then settled substantially in excess of the guidepost figure. On the other hand, he was deeply involved in guidepost activity, monitoring what was being done, suggesting levers, making operating decisions, and making telephone calls and other appeals to involved parties. The guideposts in a very real sense were the president's program.

The essential quality of the Johnson administration's structural arrangements can be illustrated by reference to 1966, when the White House decided to intensify guidepost enforcement because of increasing inflationary pressures. An interagency technical committee, consisting of representatives from the CEA and the departments of labor, commerce, agriculture, and interior, was organized to improve the reporting system for proposed wage and price changes. The committee was also to help provide the data needed for particular guideposts actions. A special three-member price staff was assembled by Ackley to work on price matters.[11] One of the members of this staff (Saul Nelson, who had worked with Ackley on price controls during the Korean War) headed an Interagency Staff Price Committee, which included representatives from the labor, agriculture, commerce, and defense departments. Its task was to provide more action-oriented groups with needed information.

The CEA also organized its staff internally to deal with pricing matters. Various staff members were assigned first- and second-line responsibilities for such areas as oil, steel, copper, aluminum, textiles, stockpiles, defense procurement, sulphur, food, and manpower shortages. Their duties included following the field closely day-by-day through trade journals and other sources, developing and maintaining statistical records, keeping up agency contacts, following government actions, devising new actions with respect to their industries, and preparing for crisis.[12] John Douglas, an assistant attorney general with the justice department's civil rights division, was brought in to strengthen the CEA's legal and operational capacities.

Information flowed in to this new setup from various agencies: the Bureau of Labor Statistics, Bureau of Mines, Business and Defense Services Administration, General Services Administration, and Department of Agriculture. The Nelson price committee met on Thursday afternoons to review and anticipate developing price problems and to consider appropriate actions. It used information from the various agencies and followed an agenda prepared by the CEA. Ackley and Califano, and others as needed, met on Friday mornings "to discuss developments in the price situation."[13] "Weekly Price Reports" were sent by the CEA to the president to keep him informed of price and wage developments and of actions considered, proposed, or taken to deal with them. On the council itself, James Duesenberry was assigned responsibility for guidepost matters, although Ackley also took an active role.

With this new administrative setup in place, the administration engaged in a high level of guidepost activity during the first half of 1966. By midyear, however, administrative problems had reappeared. The Nelson interagency committee ceased to meet. It had not been very successful because it lacked sufficient strength (because of the lower level and status of its administrative apparatus) to secure needed action from other agencies. Bureaucratic resistance and inertia were perennial problems that had to be overcome.

To help invigorate the price-fighting campaign, Califano recruited John E. Robson, a former Harvard Law School classmate. The early warning reports on prices now went to Robson, who, with the assistance of Duesenberry, reviewed them to see what might be done to fend off or reduce proposed increases. Robson's time was spent seeking information, identifying levers, proposing actions, attending the weekly price meeting, working on stockpile releases, and the like. He was assisted in his endeavors by an ad hoc "Price Policy" committee, which included representatives from the departments of commerce, labor, treasury, defense, and the Bureau of the Budget. (Califano and Ackley, of course, continued to be deeply involved in the guidepost program.) In mid-October Robson informed Califano that he had been involved in seventeen "principal price actions" in such areas as eggs, copper, shoes, textiles, oil, furniture, farm machinery, and defense procurement.[14]

Responsibility for administering the Carter wage-price standards was formally assigned to the CWPS, a staff agency established by legislation in 1974, and now located in the Executive Office of the President. With a staff of a few dozen people, its primary responsibility had been to monitor and report on potentially inflationary economic activities in the public and private sectors. (The statute creating CWPS specifically prohibited the government from imposing mandatory price and wage controls.)

The membership of the council consisted of the secretaries of treasury, labor, commerce, housing and urban development, and state, the director of OMB, and the assistant to the president for domestic affairs. (This duplicated the membership of EPG.) Alfred E. Kahn, a well-known economist and former chairman of the Civil Aeronautics Board, was appointed by President Carter in October 1978 to chair the council and to serve as his "chief inflation fighter." The staff of CWPS was under the control of a director. During the period of the wage-price standards, this position was held first by Barry Bosworth and then by R. Robert Russell, both economists.

At the time it was assigned administration of the wage-price standards program, CWPS had only 39 staff members and no direct experience with such a program. Several tasks confronted the agency in getting the program underway. These included:

> (1) drafting the standards, (2) explaining to company and union representatives and the general public the structure of the program and the policies and rationales underlying the various provisions of the standards, (3) setting up procedures for responding to questions, (4) deciding how to

handle requests for exceptions, and (5) developing strategies for monitoring compliance, methods for measuring whether there was noncompliance, and ways of persuading noncompliers to return to compliance.[15]

To handle these tasks, the size of the staff was increased to 129 in the winter of 1978–1979 and to 233 in the spring of 1979. In the process CWPS was transformed from a small staff agency into a somewhat bureaucratized operating agency with standards, procedures, forms, and hierarchial structure.

The expansion of the CWPS staff occurred during the time when wage and price policies were being developed, refined, and modified on an almost daily basis. This made it difficult for existing staff adequately to inform new employees concerning the actual content of policies. Consequently, different employees had different impressions about various provisions of the standard, and these differences sometimes led to conflicting advice to the public. Some who were aware of this situation continued asking the same question about the standards until they found a staff member with the answer they wanted. This allowed them later to contend that they had relied in good faith on the council's advice.[16]

The director of CWPS handled the day-to-day administration of the standards program. Chairman Kahn preferred to remain aloof because of his ambivalence about the program. He did exercise approval over all major decisions, handle appeals, and take some of the political "heat" that the standards generated. However, he was more interested in securing action to alleviate the inflationary impact of the government's economic regulatory and other programs. Kahn did not have the influence on administration policies that he felt he should have and at one point offered to resign.

In the fall of 1979, following the "National Accord" negotiated by the Carter administration and the AFL-CIO, the structure for standards administration was enlarged to include pay advisory and price committees. The Price Committee, which was composed of five public members, appeared to have little impact on price policy. The Pay Advisory Committee was another matter. Chaired by Harvard economist John Dunlop, it was a tripartite committee, composed of five representatives each from organized labor, the business community, and the public. Tension, conflict, and continual struggle over the pay standard characterized the PAC-CWPS relationship.

Two other matters of a structural sort should be briefly noted All major changes in the pay and price standards required approval by the EPG (recall the EPG-CWPS overlap). Second, the administration's weekly "inflation breakfast" was an important means by which President Carter was kept informed on wage-price matters. Usually present at these sessions with the president were the core members of EPG, Kahn and Bosworth or Russell. Presidential decisions on the standards and other inflation-related issues were sometimes made at these meetings.

## Administering Wage-Price Policies: Techniques and Tactics

Guidepost activity during the Johnson administration extended over a four-year period, with enforcement varying in intensity from time to time. Price increases received much more attention than wage increases. Although the guideposts were depicted as voluntary by Johnson administration officials and lacked the sanction of law, a variety of techniques and levers were used to give them some backbone. These techniques and levers can be grouped into three categories: intangibles, tangibles, and governmental symbolism.[17]

Intangible techniques involved publicity, discussions, conferences, and appeals by public officials to persuade private parties to act as the administration preferred—to hold down or delay price increases, for instance. Various appeals were made by President Johnson over the telephone, through correspondence, or in direct meetings. Thus in 1966 he appealed to a group of 150 businessmen attending a White House dinner to delay capital investment because this sector of the economy showed signs of overheating. Many of them subsequently informed the White House that they were acting to restrain investments. Appeals to businesses from CEA and other officials—whether in the form of speeches, letters, telegrams, telephone calls, small meetings, or conferences—focused more directly and fully upon the economic conditions surrounding wage or price increases. Although the secretaries of commerce, labor, interior, agriculture, treasury, and defense, and other officials were sometimes involved, the greatest burden fell on the CEA.

Thus the CEA in 1966 was involved in "perhaps 50 product lines" where price increases were imminent or announced. Letters or telegrams were sent to all the principal producers of a product. Telephone calls were used if the matter was really urgent. Those who had raised prices were asked to reconsider, and those who had not were requested to hold off if at all possible. In all cases invitations were extended to discuss the matter with the CEA. In the meetings that frequently followed, which were usually not publicly reported, the companies indicated why they thought a price increase was appropriate. The CEA presented whatever relevant information it had, explained the public interest in price stability, and urged the companies to consider this in their decisions. In its 1967 annual report the CEA concluded: "The outcome of these activities cannot be fully known. In a number of cases, it is clear that price increases which were announced or contemplated have been rescinded, reduced in amount or coverage, or delayed. Some companies have indicated that their subsequent price decisions were affected even where their decision in the immediate case was not changed."[18]

Tangible techniques or levers were fashioned from other government policies and programs and were intended to bring more direct and recognizable governmental or economic pressure to bear on those affected. Levers varied in availability, number, and usefulness from situation to situation. They included the actual or proposed manipulation of such matters as strategic stockpile sales, import controls, export controls, procurement policies, antitrust action, regulatory programs, Taft-Hartley Act emergency strike procedures, grants-in-aid for highway construction, sales of surplus agricultural commodities.

To illustrate, in July 1966 the administration engaged in a successful effort to induce American Metal Climax (Amax) to rescind a 5 percent increase in the price of molybdenum. Ackley reported that the government had several "potential influences on Amax":

(a) The government has been helpful in connection with, among others:
—Zambian copper shipments;
—getting approval of the Puerto Rican government on a potential copper development (still pending);
—Amax's new facility using Bonneville power;
—Amax's direct investment to develop the Mt. Newman iron ore operation in Australia.

(b) Amax has a strong interest in maintaining the high import duty on molybdenum (30¢ a pound), which in the past has prevented molybdenum exported at lower prices from reentering the domestic market, and which will in the future be a strong protection from Canadian imports. Bills to repeal the duty have been introduced by Congressmen representing steel producers.

(c) The steel industry has urged that the export controls be imposed on molybdenum in order to maintain adequate supplies in this county. Amax strongly opposed this action.

(d) The stockpile is a potential lever.[19]

A Department of Justice memorandum also reported that Amax was "the subject of a current preliminary antitrust investigation."[20] (There is no evidence that the administration ever used antitrust action to secure compliance with the guideposts.) Such levers could be used to convey the impression that it was in the self-interest of those involved to accede to the administration's request. They could also be used to create a sense of obligation ("you owe us one") on the part of private parties.

Governmental symbolism involved action taken to demonstrate that the government itself was acting in conformity with the guideposts and thus to influence others by good example. The best illustration of this involved the annual legislation to increase the pay of federal employees. Each year a memorandum was prepared by the CEA stating that the pay increase was within the limits of the wage guidepost. Thus, in 1966, after the use of some creative arithmetic, CEA member Arthur Okum concluded that the annual rate of increase was precisely 3.2 percent. "The government," he wrote, "will once again be setting a good example for private wage settlements in giving full recognition to the importance of non-inflationary conduct."[21] Interestingly, a handwritten note on the CEA's file copy states, "Written at Joe Califano's order." That the Johnson administration might engage in a bit of chicanery will surprise very few people. To be effective, symbolism need not be fully pure in origin.

In contrast to the extensive search for and use of levers by the Johnson administration, the only sanctions used by the Carter administration to secure compliance with its wage-price standards were publicity and the denial of government contracts. In actuality, no company was ever denied a contract because of its violation of the wage-price standards. (A few dozen were listed as violators.) Companies out of compliance could still receive contracts if they were the lowest bidder or if the contracting agency found it in the national interest to waive the compliance requirement. In late June 1979 the Department of Defense took such action in the case of the Amerada Hess oil company. This created skepticism as to the potential effectiveness of the contract sanction.

In some instances CWPS permitted companies to take "corrective action" to avoid a finding of noncompliance against themselves. This might involve a price rollback or a price freeze that continued until a company had "paid back" to the marketplace the revenues gained by exceeding the standards. The CWPS believed that compliance with standards, and not a long list of noncompliers, was needed to reduce inflation. As Robert Russell, then deputy director, stated: "We've found that fear of public disclosure as a noncomplier is much more of an effective lever than is any threat to withhold government purchases. The Sears case is a good example of that.[22] However, CWPS also realized that if the publicity sanction was used too frequently it would lose its effectiveness.

The "Sears case" referred by to Russell occurred in the spring of 1979 and involved intervention by President Carter. He recounted the incident in a speech to a labor organization:

> I made a telephone call to the president of Sears Roebuck one afternoon because they were out of compliance, and I said, "Tomorrow morning I'm calling a press conference to let the American people know about this problem." And he said, "Mr. President, would you just give me a couple of hours before?" And I waited and he called back in a responsible way

and said, "We're reducing all the prices in our catalog. We're refunding overcharges, and in our open store we're taking action also to comply with the price guidelines."[23]

He went on to say that Warner-Lambert, Fabergé, and others had done the same. Presidential involvement of this sort was limited, however. In June 1979, the *New York Times* editorially criticized the Carter administration for its failure to use the White House as a "bully pulpit" to win compliance for the guidelines and convince the public of their importance.[24]

Because of the lack of formal sanctions and the unwillingness to use many informal levers to gain compliance, the effectiveness of the Carter wage-price standards depended substantially upon public support and voluntary compliance from business and labor. Initially, the business community seemed favorably disposed toward the standards, since they were preferable to mandatory standards. In the early days of the program, a letter from the president was sent to the heads of the Fortune 500 companies requesting a statement of support for the program. Over 450 responded positively. In late March 1980, Kahn and Secretary of the Treasury William Miller again wrote to the heads of these companies requesting a commitment to compliance. This time only about 60 percent bothered to respond; some made very qualified responses, others explained why they would not make such a commitment.

What accounts for this shift in sentiment? In part, the program had not lived up to what was expected of it (for a time it was described by administration officials as the "centerpiece" of their anti-inflation program). Second, business questioned the fairness of the program because of some CWPS decisions involving the pay standard, citing, for example, a wage agreement between the teamster's union and Trucking Management, Inc., in April 1979. Several quite favorable interpretations of the terms of the contract were needed to bring it into compliance with the pay standard. Because this happened at a time when some tough actions on the price standards were taken, it created the impression in the business community that the pay and price standards were not being impartially applied.

What then of the attitude of organized labor? Ranging from cool to hostile during development of the Carter wage-price program, it did not much improve after the program went into operation. Carter administration officials were agreed that labor's support was needed to make the standards effective. Labor leaders in turn insisted that they could support the program only if they had a major role in writing or revising the pay standard. This led to the previously mentioned national accord and the creation of the Pay Advisory Committee.

Tension quickly developed between the CWPS and the PAC, which was dominated by its chairman John Dunlop, a former secretary of labor. Dunlop was responsive to labor's viewpoint. Conflict was especially sharp over the form the pay standard should take for the second year of the program. At the first meeting of the pay committee Kahn advised the group that it could advise on but not decide how the pay standard might be revised. But, he said, the White House would give "very, very serious consideration to its recommendations".[25] Dunlop was strongly opposed to a single numerical pay standard, as were labor leaders. He advised the administration that if a numerical range were not used as the new pay standard, labor support might collapse. In early 1980 the PAC recommended that a 7.5 to 9.5 percent range be used as the new pay standard. Most of the EPG came to favor this range, and it was approved by the White House. Since no real effort was made to hold workers to the lower end of the range, it became a 9.5 percent standard for any union strong enough to get that much. When conflicts involving the pay standard occurred between CWPS and PAC, they were usually settled in favor of the latter by EPG.

In February 1980, the same month as the new pay standard was adopted, the inflation rate hit 18 percent on an annual basis. One consequence was a flurry of activity in the upper reaches of the Carter administration which produced yet another anti-inflationary program. Featured this time were selective credit controls, a balanced budget for fiscal year 1981, a gasoline conservation fee (i.e., a higher tax on gasoline), continued monetary restraint, continued efforts to reduce the costs of economic regulation, and an increase in the scope and intensity of efforts to enforce the wage-price standards. The last item is what is of interest here. In his 14 March address on economic policy, the president elaborated on it:

> I am sharply expanding the price and wage monitoring activities of the Council on Wage and Price Stability. Its current staff . . . will be more than tripled. The Council will establish teams of experts to track wage and price developments in each major industry. The Council will meet with leaders from specific industries to secure their cooperation. When necessary we will ask large firms for pre-notification of significant price increases that seem out of line with the standards. I mean to apply those standards with vigor and toughness to both business and labor.

Soon after the speech, the administration announced that there would be no general loosening of the price standard, as CWPS had recommended. This was seen as inequitable, given the new pay standard, by many businesses.[26]

The intensified implementation effort never really got very far off the ground because Congress refused to appropriate the funds needed to increase the CWPS staff. Most of the activities projected in the president's speech were not undertaken.

For a time, though, the president did become more actively involved in the standards program. A few meetings with industry groups—hotels and motels, food processing, machinery, chemicals, retail food and drug chains, agricultural production—were held in the spring of 1980. Organized and run by Alfred Kahn, they included an appearance by the president and participation by other administration officials. The discussion focused generally on pricing problems, the need for industry support, and what government could do to help reduce costs. They were not really "jawboning" sessions, with the partial exception of the hotel and motel industry meeting when the president strongly criticized the industry for lack of restraint in its setting of room rates. The president also made a few public statements criticizing companies, such as the Mobil Oil Corporation, for being out of compliance with standards. Soon after, Mobil agreed to take corrective action agreeable to CWPS. Finally, the president sent agency heads a memorandum reaffirming his support for the contract sanction, "instructing them not to delegate the authority to waive the certification requirements or grant a contract to a non-complier, and asking them to consult with the Chairman of the Council before granting a waiver."[27] Not much was accomplished by this burst of presidential activity, and it came to an end in the summer of 1980.

By early fall 1980 it was clear that the wage-price program was in deep trouble. The alteration of the pay part of the program to meet labor's objections won limited tolerance at best. Business was unhappy over what it saw as inequitable treatment under the program. When CWPS sought comments on the form the program should take in its third year, almost all the comments it received recommended abandonment of the program. It is doubtful that the wage-price program would have been continued in a second Carter administration. This doubt was resolved by Ronald Reagan's defeat of Carter.

## Concluding Comments

The preceding discussion, which involves two cases of presidential action, does not permit the development of really strong generalizations about presidential management. It does, however, provide a basis for developing some useful insights, comparisons, and propositions.

Presidential power, Neustadt states, is the power to persuade, which in his view includes the power to bargain. An extralegal program, such as voluntary wage and price guideposts (or standards) depends substantially for its effectiveness upon the ability and willingness of the president to persuade and bargain, and to do some things that do not fit neatly into these categories, such as the use of informal sanctions or levers. It is my notion that Lyndon Johnson had a much better understanding of the power inherent in the presidency than did Jimmy Carter. He was, moreover, willing to draw on the power of the office and invested a good bit of time, energy, and prestige in his (this possessive pronoun is used deliberately) guidepost program. Pragmatic and activist in style, he was willing to make personal and group appeals, twist arms, give guidance, and take other actions to secure compliance.

Jimmy Carter, in contrast, for most of the time stood somewhat aloof from his administration's standards program. Coming into office opposed to mandatory wage and price controls, he continued this opposition throughout his term. He accepted the use of voluntary standards because at the time it appeared as the least of evils, given his need for some sort of anti-inflationary policy. He was not, however, much inclined to engage in jawboning or arm-twisting. A Johnson administration official recalled telling a Carter wage-price official some stories about Johnson's arm-twisting activities. The response was that were such tales told to Carter, "he would throw up."[28] There was also a fear within the White House that Carter would suffer a loss of prestige from being too closely involved with the program.

The experience of both administrations indicates that it is easier to secure political support for a voluntary wage-price program from business than from organized labor. Businesses are more sensitive to public opinion and more susceptible to levers wielded by an administration. Labor's basic ideology holds that pay standards are really inconsistent with free collective bargaining because they limit the exercise of labor's power and may be used by businesses as a bargaining ploy to hold down wage increases. Given that labor has been a major source of electoral support for Democratic administrations, they are reluctant to push labor too hard.

Gardner Ackley, who was always concerned about the lack of public and group support for the Johnson guideposts, later attributed this lack to the manner in which the guideposts had been developed.

> To a considerable extent, the Kennedy-Johnson "guideposts" were simply dreamed up by economists and then promulgated. I have long considered the absence of any real participation by the interest groups in the origination and modification of the guideposts—and, as a consequence, the absence of any sense of responsibility on their part for the success or failure of the effort—to have been the greatest weakness of the guidepost system.[29]

Carter administration officials consulted with labor and business groups in both the development and revision of their program. Moreover, labor was brought formally into the administration of the program through the Pay Advisory Committee. All of this was to little avail. Support is not inherent in the technique of participation, waiting only to be unleashed by its use. In this instance, labor remained fundamentally opposed to meaningful wage standards. Consequently, the Carter administration's use of a "corporatist inclusion" tactic failed to win labor support.

Indeed, the actions of the Carter administration to win labor support had the effect of politicizing the standards program. Labor support, of course, was also desired for the 1980 presidential election, and it became hard to separate electioneering from programmatic concerns. Whatever the motive, the quest for labor support led to the national accord, the creation of PAC, the liberalization of the pay standard, and the non-use of sanctions against pay standard violators. These in turn led to morale problems within the CWPS, a decline in business support, and a reduction in the impact of the program.

The Johnson administration also encountered substantial criticism of its wage guidepost from organized labor. After a couple of notable failures to hold wage settlements to the guidepost figure in 1966, administration officials spent little time either in applying the guideposts to labor agreements or seeking formal labor support for the guideposts. Less visible than the Carter administration's efforts to obtain labor's support, this inaction created fewer political problems for Johnson.

The application of the Johnson guideposts was largely characterized by haphazard case-to-case activity. John Robson described it as an "ad hoc, reactive, fire-fighting sort of operation." There were no systematic procedures or standards for determining when action would be taken.[30] Nor was there any effective way to determine in most instances whether a price increase was in accord with the guideposts. As one close observer commented:

> It has become apparent that the cost data readily available to the Administration is not sufficient to make a tight guidepost case in controversial price situations. The hard fact is that the CEA is not in a position to make defensible independent cost and productivity calculations for most industries. The Administration's position on prices is, therefore, not likely to be based on whether or not a price increase is "warranted," but rather on efforts to have price changes reexamined in the light of their indirect or "ripple" effects on customers, suppliers, and the economy.[31]

The Carter administration's wage-price standards operation was much more systematic and substantively informed. It utilized more elaborate standards, regularized reporting of price and wage data, computerized data analysis, and systematic monitoring of prices and wages. It was, in all, a much more formal program. Moreover, its greater regularity and visibility contributed to greater fairness and consistency in its implementation. The Johnson program was sometimes criticized for a lack of fairness and due process. Thus, a Johnson administration official later said that in the Amax case they were looking for someone to "knock off" to demonstrate the effectiveness of the guideposts.

If wage and price programs are ranged along a continuum, with mandatory controls at one pole and fully voluntary standards supported by only general announcement and exhortation at the other, the Johnson program would be located closer to the mandatory pole than would the Carter program. Although less formal in nature, the use of various tangible and intangible levers gave the Johnson program a more coercive quality. The Carter program had many of the attributes of a mandatory program—elaborate standards, reports, monitoring, procedures—but a reluctance to use the limited sanctions available and a shortage of other actions to secure compliance locates it closer to the purely voluntary pole.

In conclusion, the experience of the two administrations demonstrates the importance of presidential involvement and support for the effectiveness of a voluntary wage-price program. The Carter program was better structured, more systematic, and more inclusive of affected groups. The Johnson program, in comparison, was characterized by stronger presidential support and much involvement by top-level administration officials. The yield was a marginally more effective program. Whether this was a wise use of presidential and top-level time and energy is an arguable question. So is the question of how best to administer a presidential program to influence wages and prices.

## NOTES

1. The discussion of the Johnson administration guidepost policy draws substantially upon James E. Anderson and Jared R. Hazleton, *Managing Macroeconomic Policy: The Johnson Presidency* (Austin: University of Texas Press, 1985). In addition to cited sources, the discussion of the Carter standards policy benefits from interviews with Carter administration officials.

2. *Annual Report of the Council of Economic Advisors, 1962*(Washington, D.C.: U.S. Government Printing Office, 1962), p. 189.

3. Gardner Ackley, Oral History Interview, pp. 29–30, LBJ Library.

4. *Annual Report of the Council of Economic Advisors, 1967* (Washington: D.C.: U.S. Government Printing Office, 1967), p. 129.

5. Robert J. Samuelson, "Economic Policy—Is the Administration in Control?" *National Journal* 10 (2 December 1978), pp. 1932–38.

6. Ibid., p. 1935.

7. The Economic Policy Group, which was the primary unit for economic policy development in the Carter administration, included the secretaries of treasury, labor, commerce, housing and urban development, and state, the director of OMB, and the director of the Domestic Policy Staff.

8. Council on Wage and Price Stability, *Evaluation of the Pay and Price Standards Program* (16 January 1981), pp. 1 and 2. Hereafter cited as CWPS, *Evaluation*.

9. W. Kip Viscusi, "The Political Economy of Wage-Price Regulation: The Case of the Carter Pay-Price Standards," in *What Role for Government?* ed. Richard J. Zeckhauser and Derek Leebaert (Durham, N.C.: Duke University Press, 1983), p. 158.

10. CWPS, *Evaluation*, p. 2.

11. Memo, Gardner Ackley for Joe Califano, 5 January 1966, WHCF, FG11-3, LBJ Library.

12. Memo, Otto Eckstein for Gardner Ackley, 31 January 1966, CEA microfilm #55, LBJ Library.

13. Memo, Joe Califano for the President, 11 February 1966, WHCF, BE5-2, LBJ Library.

14. Memo, John E. Robson for Joseph A. Califano, 12 October 1966, Califano Papers, Pricing Folder, LBJ Library.

15. CWPS, *Evaluation*, p. 35.

16. Ibid.

17. This categorization borrows from Alan Altshuler, "The Politics of Managing a Full Employment Economy," paper presented at the 63d Annual Meeting of the American Political Science Association, Chicago, 5–9 September 1967, pp. 16–19.

18. *Annual Report of the Council of Economic Advisors, 1967*, pp. 125–26.

19. Memo, Gardner Ackley for Mr. Joseph A. Califano, 11 July 1966, WHCF, CM/Molybdenum, LBJ Library.

20. "Re: Molybdenum—American Metal Climax," 11 July 1966, WHCF CM/Molybdenum, LBJ Library.

21. Memo, Arthur Okun for the President, 25 May 1966, CEA microfilm #69, LBJ Library.

22. Quoted in Maxwell Glen, "Carter's Wage-Price Policy No Longer a Do-It-Yourself Scheme," *National Journal* 11 (2 June 1979), p. 910.

23. *Public Papers of the Presidents: Jimmy Carter, 1980–81* (Washington, D.C.: U.S. Government Printing Office, 1981), I, p. 581.

24. *New York Times*, 5 June 1979, p. A20.

25. *New York Times*, 18 October 1979, p. D1.

26. This viewpoint was shared by the General Accounting Office. See its *The Voluntary Pay and Price Standards Have Had No Discernible Effect on Inflation* (Washington, D.C.: U.S. Government Printing Office, 1980), pp. 92–93.

27. CWPS, *Evaluation*, p. 6.

28. Interview with author, 29 June 1979.

29. Testimony before Joint Economic Committee, *Hearings on the President's New Economic Program*, 92nd Cong., 2d sess., 1971, pp. 245–46.

30. Interview with author, 14 August 1979.

31. Myron L. Joseph, "Wage-Price Guideposts in the U.S.A.," *British Journal of Industrial Relations* 5 (November 1967), pp. 318–19.

William F. West and Joseph Cooper

# The Rise of Administrative Clearance

Three broad trends characterized executive-legislative relations at the federal level during the first half of the twentieth century. Though not perfectly regular in their pace or momentum, these trends were nonetheless persistent over time and powerful in their ultimate results. The first was decentralization of power in both the formal and party structures of the House and Senate. The second was growth in the role, power, and prestige of the presidency. The third was expansion in the volume and scope of bureaucratic authority and discretion.

Two of these trends have clearly continued to have substantial impacts in the second half of the twentieth century. Fragmentation in the Congress has increased as levels of party voting have grown weaker and subcommittee government has become institutionalized.[1] At the same time, increases in administration activity accelerated in direct proportion to the growth of federal programs and outlays in the years from 1965 to 1980.[2] In contrast, after the mid-1960s the presidency suddenly became an object of attack and skepticism. Vietnam and Watergate turned former admirers of the office into critics who questioned its supposed assumption of "imperial" power and supported the reassertion of congressional prerogatives.[3] Furthermore, even stalwart friends of the presidency began to see weaknesses that had not formerly been noticed and to fear that the office was not strong enough to carry the burdens the system placed upon it.[4]

Yet up to the 1960s all three trends were highly interrelated. Their root cause was the growth in the volume and scope of federal responsibilities, both at home and abroad. Such expansion strained congressional integrative capacity and increased bureaucratic power. By so doing it also encouraged expansion of the institutionalized presidency as a means of adapting to congressional weakness and bureaucratic strengths without giving up forms of governmental action that large portions of the public thought essential.[5]

Given their common linkage to the fundamental dynamic of governmental growth, one might expect any disruptions of the interrelated trends toward congressional decentralization, an administrative state, and presidential expansion to be temporary. Indeed, there is strong evidence to suggest that this is true. Congressional resurgence in the 1970s was brief and did little to counter the trend toward decentralization. Likewise, the salience of Watergate and Vietnam has diminished in the 1980s, and President Reagan's handling of his office has reawakened expectations regarding its potential. Thus, a number of observers detect a renewed emphasis on strengthening the president's administrative capabilities.[6]

This essay focuses on an important recent extension of the power of the presidency. Its purpose is to analyze and assess the system of review over administrative rulemaking established by President Reagan through Executive Order 12291 at the very start of his administration. Given the scope of rulemaking by executive agencies, this order was significant on its face. It gave the Office of Management and Budget (OMB) power to review and delay all rules proposed by executive agencies. In addition, it required that review and justification proceed in terms of cost-benefit analysis. However, these actions assume even greater significance if placed in institutional and historical perspective. Our analyses of E.O. 12291 therefore is framed in terms of the trends identified above and the character of executive-legislative politics in the 1980s. It deals first with the origins of E.O. 12291 in the 1970s; second, it analyzes the organization and operation of review under E.O. 12291; third, it examines the character and impact of review under E.O. 12291; and finally, it assesses the implications of E.O. 12291 for the institutionalized presidency, bureaucratic politics in the 1980s, and the role of Congress

## Strengthening Executive Control

Faced with a growing and increasingly complex and interrelated bureaucracy, every president since Richard Nixon has required some or all agencies to conduct analyses of their proposed regulations and has empowered an executive agent to review those analyses. Reagan's E.O. 12291 is a descendant of similar but less ambitious predecessors in this regard. Partly in response to the limitations of earlier orders, it has established the most rigorous analytical requirements and the most comprehensive and powerful executive review mechanism to date.

### Developments Under Nixon, Ford, and Carter

President Nixon's OMB instituted Quality of Life reviews in 1971, essentially as an attempt to reconcile environmental regulations with other administration objectives. Although the program technically applied to all environmental regulations, as implemented it affected only rulemaking by the Environmental Protection Agency. Under its provisions, the EPA was required to circulate proposed regulations among other agencies and to respond to their comments. In the event that an agency felt that the EPA had failed adequately to address its objections, it could call for a meeting, presided over by the OMB for the purpose of resolving disputed issues. The role of OMB in these meetings was strictly advisory, with the EPA retaining final rulemaking authority. However, the process did serve as a means of identifying controversial issues and of making executive preferences known.[7]

The breadth of rulemaking oversight was expanded in 1974 under the Ford administration. Executive Order 11821, as amended by E. O. 11949, required agencies to prepare Inflation Impact Statements (IIS) for all "major" regulations. A major regulation was later defined to be a rule having a yearly impact in excess of $100 million. As supervised by OMB, an IIS was to include an analysis of a rule's benefits and costs, as well as an assessment of the benefits and costs of alternative approaches. Cost criteria developed by OMB pursuant to the order included adverse effects of regulations on productivity, competition, and the availability of goods and services.[8]

In addition to OMB, the Council on Wage and Price Stability (COWPS) (an Executive Office agency created by Congress earlier in 1974) was given substantial responsibilities under the Ford program: it was allowed to review agency proposals and their supporting IISs, to prepare its own analyses, and to participate in subsequent rulemaking proceedings. COWPS studies and recommendations were to be included as a part of agency rulemaking records. As under Quality of Life reviews, however, OMB and COWPS input under E.O. 11821 was ultimately limited to the presentation of reasoned arguments and the exertion of informal pressures.[9]

Efforts by the Carter administration to control and rationalize regulatory administration paralleled but went beyond earlier developments. Among other things, his E.O. 12044, issued in March 1978, required that agencies articulate their rulemaking agenda in semiannual "regulatory calendars," that they reevaluate old rules, and that they conduct "regulatory analyses" of proposed rules having an economic impact of $100 million or more per year. As subsequently directed by OMB in conjunction with COWPS and the Council of Economic Advisors, agency analyses were required to give detailed attention to the direct and indirect "burdens" and "gains" likely to result from proposed actions and to include a comparative evaluation of other regulatory alternatives.[10]

Carter also created a Regulatory Council, composed of representatives from thirty-six executive and independent agencies, and a Regulatory Analysis Review Group (RARG), composed of representatives from seventeen executives agencies and presided over by the chairman of the Council of Economic

Advisors. The Regulatory Council's primary mission was to screen proposed rules in order to ensure that federal agency policies did not contradict or duplicate one another. RARG's responsibility was to scrutinize the regulatory analyses accompanying fifteen to twenty especially significant proposed rules each year. Working with studies conducted by COWPS staff, RARG would produce reports on regulatory analyses to be filed with agencies' rulemaking records. Once more, however, outside review of administrative actions was advisory under the Carter order.

## Reagan's E.O. 12291

The Nixon, Ford, and Carter programs enhanced executive awareness of and influence over administrative rulemaking, yet each of these efforts had important limitations. Most obviously, executive influence was hortative in each case. Although recommendations from the Executive Office and the White House were not to be taken lightly, they were still only recommendations that agencies could ignore in favor of their own analysis and sense of mission. Also, the scope of review under each mechanism was from comprehensive. This was especially true of Nixon's Quality of Life reviews, which pertained only to environmental rules, and of Carter's RARG reviews, which were limited in number to between fifteen and twenty per year. Finally, compliance with the analytical requirements that provided the basis for review under the Ford and Carter orders was sporadic and varied from agency to agency. This was due partly to the fact that agencies themselves were responsible for deciding whether a proposed rule exceeded the $100 million threshold—hardly a cut-and-dried determination. In addition, some agencies contended that cost-benefit considerations conflicted with their enabling mandates. Where analyses were conducted, they varied greatly in their quality and methodology.[11]

The Reagan administration's efforts to gain control over regulatory rulemaking reflect a keen awareness of the limitations of earlier oversight devices. Executive Order 12291, issued in February 1981, requires that agencies justify major rules on the basis of "regulatory impact analyses" (RIA), a rigorous and comprehensive cost-benefit analysis that requires a detailed appraisal of the incidence and magnitude of a rule's negative and positive effects, as well as a similar examination of alternative courses of action. As subsequently specified by OMB, it must quantify projected costs and benefits "where possible."[12] RIAs must accompany both proposed and final regulations, and they must also be conducted for major rules already in effect. A major rule is defined as one having an economic impact of $100 million per year, or one that otherwise creates important economic problems, such as significant price increases. Executive Order 12291 requires a less rigorous analysis for nonmajor regulations. The order's vagueness regarding the nature of these latter studies may be intended to permit administrative flexibility in choosing levels of analytical effort appropriate in light of the specific nature and importance of proposed rules.

The Reagan program also provides substantial opportunities for the executive to review and to delay, alter, or block agency regulations. For major rules, RIAs must be submitted to OMB sixty days prior to the publication of notice of proposed rulemaking in the Federal Register, and again thirty days prior to the publication of a final regulation. Nonmajor rules must be submitted ten days prior to notice and to final publication. In both cases, OMB is empowered to scrutinize agency rules and the analyses accompanying them. It may stay the publication of notice of proposed rulemaking or the promulgation of a final rule by requiring agencies to respond to its criticisms of their analyses, and it may ultimately recommend disapproval of regulations felt to lack adequate justification.

Supervisory authority over OMB's activities under E.O. 12291 was originally vested in the Task Force on Regulatory Relief, created by Reagan in January 1981. Chaired by Vice-President Bush, this group included the OMB director, the treasury secretary, the attorney general, the commerce secretary, the labor secretary, and other presidential advisors. Disputes between OMB and proposing agencies concerning the desirability of proposed regulations were to be brought before the Task Force for resolution. The Task Force was disbanded in August 1983, claiming to have completed its primary mission of identifying and eliminating burdensome regulations already in existence. Since then, the formal mechanism for resolving disagreement between OMB and an agency on the merits of a rule has remained very vague. However, it probably involves review by one of several cabinet councils (depending on the substance of the regulation in question). As a practical matter, the escalation of conflict to such a high level has been rare.

Although Reagan's approach to regulatory oversight parallels those of earlier administrations, E.O. 12291 is more powerful and ambitious than its predecessors in a number of respects. Analytical provisions under the Ford and Carter orders were less precise and rigorous than those imposed by the Reagan administration, permitting considerable latitude with regard to the quality and approach of agency studies. RIA requirements are also more difficult to evade than those imposed by earlier orders. This is largely because OMB has been given final discretion to designate major rules and thus force submission of analyses for review. Furthermore, agencies are required to provide formal explanations of any legal reasons that prevent them from complying with the order's analytical requirements.

In general, the executive also enjoys stronger obstructive powers under E.O. 12291 than under previous programs. OMB possesses formal authority to require that agencies address its objections and may thus delay the development of both major and nonmajor regulations at two stages in the rulemaking process—before notice and before final publication. The ability to force reconsideration of a rule before notice is considered by the order's architects to be especially significant since an agency's "sunk costs" are not likely to be as great at that stage of the process.[13] Whether OMB, a cabinet council, or even the president have final legal authority to block a rulemaking initiative is a matter of dispute not addressed directly in the executive order, and in practice agency heads have issued regulations over OMB objections in a few instances. The president does, however, possess the power to remove recalcitrant agency heads, and those who framed the Reagan order felt that this possibility would help ensure executive control. Yet they also felt that such extreme action would seldom be necessary given the loyalty of top political appointees to the basic policy initiatives of the president and the severe costs involved in any prolonged and intense conflict with OMB.

## The Review Process Under E.O. 12291

Despite a good deal of literature on E.O. 12291, relatively little has been written about the conduct of regulatory review. This is due in part to the fact that review tends to be loosely structured and varies from case to case. Partly because of this, perhaps, and partly to protect its ability to serve presidential policy goals, OMB has also been reluctant fully to disclose the processes used in reviewing proposed regulations and in resolving conflicts with agencies. Notwithstanding these difficulties, however, it is possible to identify the actors involved in regulatory review and to outline its general contours.

### The OIRA

Responsibility for reviewing proposed rules under E.O. 12291 rests with the Office of Information and Regulatory Affairs, an organization within OMB created by the Paperwork Reduction Act of 1980. As table 1 indicates, OIRA is composed of five divisions. Three divisions—the Regulatory Policy Branch, the Reports Management Branch, and the Information Policy Branch—are staffed by "desk officers," most of whom have law degrees or graduate training in fields such as public policy, business, or public administration. Every agency whose regulations are reviewed under E.O. 12291 is placed under one of these three divisions. In turn, each desk officer is assigned responsibility for an agency, part of an agency, or a few small agencies. The two other divisions within OIRA are staffed primarily by economists and statisticians. They also possess between them the authority to review all executive branch rules, dividing responsibility according to economic versus social regulation. All five divisions are supervised by the deputy administrator of OIRA. His attention to day-to-day activities leaves the administrator free to take a broader perspective concerning the office's functions.

**TABLE 1**
Office of Information and Regulatory Affairs

Administrator

Deputy Administrator

| Regulatory Policy Branch | Reports Management Branch | Information Policy Branch | Economic Regulations and Statistics | Social Regulations and Statistics |
|---|---|---|---|---|
| Branch Chief | Branch Chief | Branch Chief | Branch Chief | Branch Chief |
| 13 Desk Officers | 12 Desk Officers | 10 Desk Officers | 7 Analysts | 7 Analysts |
| 4 Support | 8 Support | 3 Support | 2 Support | 2 Support |
| Major Regulatory Agencies: DOE, DOI, DOT, USDA, ACUS, ACHP, EPA, PCC, NRC, CEQ, TVA, NSF, FTC, CAB, FMC, ICC, CPSCM, FERC | Major Paperwork Agencies: ED, HHS, DOL, HUD, VA, RRB, ACTION, Bank Supervisory Agencies | Major ADP Agencies: FEMA, SBA, NCUA, FCC, NASA, State, AID, ITC, GSA, OPM, DOC, DOD, DOJ, SEC, CFTC | | |

*Source:* Office of Information and Regulatory Affairs.

Every regulation received by OMB for review is initially sent to an OIRA desk officer and an OIRA economist, as well as to an official from the budgeting side of OMB responsible for the agency in question. Economists are few in number, however, and their role is to give rigorous attention to rules on a very selective basis. Desk officers therefore serve as the key reviewers within OIRA for the great majority of regulations. Upon receipt of a proposed or final rule, the appropriate desk officer examines the agency's supporting analysis and prepares a "regulatory docket worksheet." This document is essentially a brief summary and assessment of the agency's analysis that is distributed for approval to the relevant OIRA economist, to the budget official involved in the review, and to the desk officer's branch chief.

In some respects, OIRA operates in effect as a loosely structured matrix organization in its reviewing capacity. The formal process of distributing worksheets to various actors for their approval obviously brings different perspectives and training to bear in the evaluation of each regulation. In addition, desk officers often draw informally on various sources of expertise as they review agency analyses and prepare their recommendations. Where appropriate, for example, they may consult with economists and statisticians from other divisions. They may also consult with other desk officers whose particular training or experience is pertinent to the technical, policy, or economic issues posed by the regulation at hand.[14]

## The Dynamics of Review and Conflict Resolution

Within the context of these general procedures, review often involves a good deal of communication and negotiation between OMB and the agencies proposing regulations. This process may actually begin well before proposals are initially submitted to the OIRA for review. At least some desk officers make it a practice to convey review criteria to the agencies under their purview and to monitor significant rules as they are being formulated. During this stage, desk officers may express reservations about the soundness of agency proposals or may emphasize the need to collect more rigorous supporting data. Likewise, agency staff may contact their OIRA counterparts to ensure that they are proceeding on safe ground. Such early communications, which are typically of an informal, off-the-record nature, can serve the interests of both parties by reducing sunk costs in troublesome regulations and thus limiting future conflict and delay.[15]

After proposed and final rules are formally submitted for review, differences between the OMB and agencies may again be resolved through communication and accommodation. Agencies may upgrade their analyses or may modify or even drop regulations in response to questions and criticisms raised by desk officers or others involved in the review process. The interaction between agencies and OMB is typically informal at this stage as well. Referring both to these and to earlier "pre-submittal" communications, for example, the OMB reported to the General Accounting Office (GAO) that "such communications are generally through telephone conversations or meetings at the staff level. We find that the exchange of the kind of technical information needed in producing and reviewing regulatory impact analyses is generally more efficiently and productively carried out informally by staff rather than through formal, written memoranda."[16]

In all agencies, a separate office, typically the general counsel's office or a policy office, acts as a conduit for communications between the OMB and rulemaking staff after and sometimes before regulations have been submitted for review. One purpose for this arrangement is to ensure accountability. Another may be to facilitate negotiation. The Office of Policy Analysis fulfills this role at EPA, for example, in theory at least because it is sensitive both to the president's broad economic objectives and to the perspectives and statutory mandates of EPA's various program offices such as noise abatement and toxic wastes.[17]

In the event that rulemakers are unwilling to yield to reviewers' objections, conflict is resolved through a process of escalation to higher and higher levels within OMB and the agency. As discussed earlier, disputes may be taken to one of several cabinet councils should the director of OMB and the agency head be unable to resolve their differences, and ultimately the White House may serve as the final arbiter. In practice, however, there are important limitations on the ability and willingness of the White House to intervene that lower-level actors are undoubtedly aware of and respect. One is that it simply lacks the resources to settle a large number of disputes, and another is that it is often reluctant to bear the political costs of taking stands on controversial regulatory issues. As a result, almost all disputes are settled in some way at the agency-OMB level.

It is true, of course, that regulatory statutes typically vest rulemaking authority not in the president, but in agency heads. Therefore, cabinet secretaries or administrators can legally issue rules against OMB's objections and in the absence of approval from higher authority. More than anything, perhaps, this prerogative is significant as a bargaining lever in negotiations with OMB. Decisions to exploit this device are likely influenced by several factors, including the intensity of OMB opposition, pressures from groups favoring and opposing the regulation, the commitment of agency personnel to the policy in question, and the White House's level of interest and its probable reaction. Statutory mandates and congressional prodding can serve as especially powerful inducements for agency heads to resist OMB's opposition. Some statutes declare deadlines for issuing rules, for instance, and proponents of regulation may use (or threaten to use) these to secure court orders forcing agencies to act. Some statutes also require agencies to further particular objectives, apparently to the exclusion of other considerations, thus precluding a comprehensive assessment of social costs and benefits.[18]

As a practical matter, however, one should emphasize that agency intransigence in the review process is rare and that it is characterized by a good deal of circumspection where it does occur. One reason for this is simply that most of Reagan's appointees share the administration's basic perspectives on regulation. Another is that agency heads serve at the pleasure of the president and are understandably reluctant to oppose OMB if they feel that it is promoting his policy objectives. Most important, perhaps, is the fact that OMB, itself, has substantial budgetary, legislative, and other powers that can be used to punish recalcitrant agencies. Although the degree to which it might use these powers to enforce regulatory review remains ambiguous, desk officers and budget examiners do, as a general practice, "work together in a closely coordinated partnership" according to one OIRA official.[19] Even more significant is the observation that many agency officials perceive that OMB is willing to use its other prerogatives in support of E.O. 12291.[20] Thus in the words of James Miller, a former OIRA administrator and an architect of the Reagan order, "When you're the toughest kid on the block, most kids won't pick a fight with you."[21]

## The Character of Review Under E.O. 12291

Our knowledge of the precise nature of oversight under E.O. 12291 is even more limited than our knowledge of the review process. Much oversight under the Reagan order is conducted informally and off the record, and even Congress has had difficulty in eliciting information concerning its criteria, purpose, and extent. Again, however, one can at least characterize review in general terms. Although close scrutiny of agency proposals has been far from comprehensive, E.O. 12291 has provided a systematic means for delaying, blocking, and altering those regulations most troublesome to the president and groups in the electorate closely allied with him.

### The Criteria for Review

There has been a good deal of controversy concerning the criteria used in regulatory review under E.O. 12291. Supporters of the program maintain that decisions are based on the objective appraisal of agency analyses, while critics contend that review is frequently political, reflecting the values of the administration and of the groups it favors. In truth, both objective and political criteria are undoubtedly present in the review process to some degree, although the mix between the two is difficult to discern.

The orientation of desk officers and economists is obviously crucial in determining the nature of regulatory review, since it is they who examine regulations most closely, identifying issues for their superiors to consider. The great majority of these people undoubtedly perceive themselves as objective policy analysts. They are not political appointees, and many of them have done similar kinds of work for OMB or other agencies under previous administrations. Many of these officials would probably take offense at any accusation that their review is based on political considerations as impugning their professional integrity. Among other things, they would likely point to the dispassionate, "academic" tone of their reports and to OIRA's policy proscribing communications between themselves and outside interests as evidence of their objectivity.[22]

Yet political considerations do come to bear, even in the initial stages of the review process. If the dominant ethic among desk officers is to promote economic efficiency as objectively as possible, it is also their job, as agents of the president, to consider the political ramifications of agency policies. As an OIRA official put it: "All bureaucrats make political judgments. That's what it's like to be a yuppie in the federal government. . . . Analysis is dispassionate to the extent that it is sterile, but it is political. We would like to believe that cost-benefit analysis is a science, but it isn't."[23]

The president's general policy goals thus inevitably influence review under E.O. 12291. Although it is obviously impossible for political officials in OMB and the White House to consider all the regulations that are submitted for review, it is likely that they will be alerted to those rules that are most significant in terms of the administration's objectives. One reason for this is that OMB and the White House usually receive communications from affected interests concerning important and controversial regulations well before they are formally submitted to OIRA. In addition, it is logical to assume that desk officers are motivated to please their political superiors and that they take special care to identify issues that are sensitive to the administration as a result. In fact, some of the administration's regulatory goals have been communicated to the "front line" through memoranda that, as one OIRA official put it, have established a system of "bells and whistles" for reviewers to respond to.[24] The General Accounting Office recognized the importance of presidential objectives in the review process when it stated that "our review of OMB oversight under E.O. 12291 leaves doubt about whether OMB's role is basically procedural. While one can imagine a purely procedural form of oversight, the location of OMB in the Executive Office of the President is likely to facilitate substantive oversight to make regulations conform to the President's general policy orientation."[25]

Review under E.O. 12291 may also be influenced by group pressures, especially in the case of interests that are close allies of the president. In this regard, critics of the program contend that OMB has served as an appeals board for business interests subject to unwanted regulations. Many OIRA officials deny that review is affected by such considerations, citing the ban on communications between agency staff and affected interests to bolster their argument. However, this ban only applies after notice of proposed rulemaking appears in the Federal Register. Moreover, desk officers have ignored this policy in some instances, apparently with the blessings of their superiors.[26] In addition, OIRA staff frequently rely on a variety of indirect means to monitor the reactions of affected interests to rules that are being formulated. These include trade publications, newspapers, and the letters OMB receives and places on file. Sometimes, in fact, desk officers include clippings from such sources with the "decision packages" sent to their superiors for review. Beyond this, direct communications between affected interests and *political* appointees in OIRA, OMB, and the White House are not proscribed, and have sometimes been encouraged.[27] Indeed, a prominent industry attorney and former high-ranking EPA official stated that "anybody representing a client who didn't [seek to influence OMB review] would be damn negligent."[28] In some instances OMB has even gone so far as to solicit the views of industries affected by regulations it has received for review.

Political influence under E.O. 12291 has been documented in a number of studies. In his interviews with participants in the process and his examination of several EPA rules, for example, Erik Olson finds ample evidence that OMB has acted at the behest of the White House, industry representatives, and other agencies in its reviewing capacity. He suggests that "where OMB has budgetary, policy, philosophical, or political problems with a rule, it merely uses regulatory analysis as a key tool in holding up or changing the EPA action."[29] George Eads and Michael Fix come to similar conclusions. After examining OMB review of actions by OSHA, EPA, the National Highway Traffic Safety Administration, and other agencies, they conclude that, although oversight was based on objective policy analysis in some instances, in others "OMB's involvement in regulation was *clearly* political—and nothing else."[30]

Of course, anecdotal evidence does not necessarily present a balanced picture of review under E.O. 12291, and in fact it may tend to reflect sensational or anomalous cases. If OMB review is motivated in some general or overall sense by presidential policy goals, the extent to which its intervention in particular cases is controlled by political considerations is difficult to determine. The impressions of participants in the process are understandably biased by the roles they play. Thus, OIRA officials are inclined to report that they base their decisions on sound economic criteria. On the other hand, agency staffers often spend years developing and justifying regulations, and are understandably unwilling to concede that OMB criticisms are founded on objective considerations.

Any systematic investigation of reviewing decisions is made difficult by a lack of data. Again, communications between OMB and agencies are usually informal and off the record. Even where OMB does object to regulations in writing, it frequently justifies its objections with unspecific allusions to previous informal discussions with agency staff. Finally, the review mechanism itself can well serve to conceal the true basis for OMB decisions since unstated assumptions regarding the assessment of benefits and costs inevitably affect the character of analysis.

Nonetheless, it remains true that, where effects are quantified, numerous opportunities exist to implement political preferences through scientific analysis.[31] Not only does an emphasis on quantification give advantage to more tangible values, this advantage may be extended by the way values are given priority, either consciously or unconsciously. Thus, cost-benefit analysis provides an ideal mechanism for interjecting presidential policy preferences into the review process presented and legitimated as objective analytical considerations. Reacting adversely to this possibility, the GAO report noted that "while regulatory analysis has the potential for bringing objective data, facts, and analysis into regulatory decisionmaking, it is a fragile tool readily subject to misuse."[32]

*The Impact of E.O. 12291*

Aside from the criteria used by OMB, it is also important to consider the extensiveness of regulatory review under E.O. 12291. Indeed, this is especially important given the rationale for presidential oversight generally and the avowed objectives of the Reagan administration in particular. In the first instance, advocates of strong, centralized executive control argue that it can promote comprehensive planning in the public interest by ensuring that the diverse parts of the federal bureaucracy are in harmony with presidential policy. In the second instance, supporters of E.O. 12291 in the administration and elsewhere endorse it as an effective mechanism for blocking ill-conceived regulations that they and the White House allege had become a major problem by the time Reagan took office.

OMB has judged most regulations to be consistent with the terms of E.O. 12291. As shown in table 2, 87.3 percent, 84.1 percent, and 82.3 percent of the rules submitted for review were promulgated without change (but not without delay in many instances) in 1981, 1982, and 1983, respectively. Only a small fraction of regulations—a yearly average of 3.2 percent—were withdrawn or returned for reconsideration. The great majority of rules that have not been consistent with the executive order have been promulgated after "minor change." OMB does not include a definition of minor change with its data, but GAO notes that these "typically involved clarifications in the preamble to the *Federal Register* notice rather than substantive changes to the rule."[33] OMB's statistics do not include a "major change" category.

One should not necessarily infer from these data that review under E.O.

12291 has limited effects, however. Case studies such as those alluded to earlier indicate that OMB on important occasions does secure significant modifications in rules, and these, too, must be reported in the minor change category.[34] In addition, although the percentages of rules returned for reconsideration or withdrawn are quite small, the absolute numbers of rules that fall into these categories hardly seem insignificant. In 1983, for example, thirty-two regulations were returned for reconsideration and thirty-nine were withdrawn. Included were rules that would have established policy in a wide variety of important areas.[35]

An even more important point is that the figures in table 2 may represent only a small fraction of the policy influence exerted by OMB and the White House in the regulatory review process. For this reason, in fact, GAO asserts that such data are of little value in assessing the effects of E.O. 12291.[36] As mentioned, informal contacts between OMB and agencies are common before proposed and final regulations are submitted for review, and these may result in the modification of proposals or the termination of rulemaking efforts altogether. Even in the absence of such communications, the threat of review can serve as a powerful influence on the formulation of regulations. A high-ranking EPA official commented, for instance, that agency staffs are always conscious of OMB's and the administration's priorities and their probable reactions as they prepare and seek to justify rules.

What, then, can one say about the effects and the effectiveness of OMB review inder E.O. 12291? It undoubtedly falls far short of comprehensiveness,

TABLE 2
OMB Actions on Rules, 1981–1983

| Action Taken | 1981 | 1982 | 1983 |
|---|---|---|---|
| Consistent | 2447 | 2214 | 2044 |
| | (87.13)[a] | (84.1) | (82.3) |
| Consistent with minor change | 136 | 271 | 316 |
| | (4.9) | (10.3) | (12.7) |
| Returned for reconsideration | 45 | 55 | 32 |
| | (1.6) | (2.1) | (1.3) |
| Withdrawn | 50 | 32 | 40 |
| | (1.8) | (1.2) | (1.6) |
| Sent improperly or exempt | 88 | 24 | 0 |
| | (3.1) | (0.9) | (0.0) |
| Emergency, statutory, or judicial deadline | 39 | 37 | 50 |
| | (1.4) | (1.4) | (2.0) |
| Total | 2803 | 2633 | 2482 |

Source: Office of Management and Budget, Third Annual Report on the Administration of President Reagan's Executive Order 12291 on Federal Regulation, 13 July 1984.
a. The figures in parentheses are percentages. They may not add to 100 due to rounding.

given the small size of OIRA's staff (about seventy-five) and the large number of regulations that are submitted (roughly twenty-five hundred per year). As the GAO report notes, "OMB has not had sufficient staff . . . to give most rules more than brief attention."[37] It follows, therefore, that the program has not ensured coherence among the regulatory approaches of different agencies at the federal level. Indeed, it appears as if OMB has made little effort to identify conflicting regulations. Again to quote the GAO report: "OMB does not appear to exercise its powers under E.O. 12291 to reduce conflicts among regulations or to ensure consistent application of the regulatory analysis process. . . . OMB officials told us that they make no systematic effort to uncover potential conflicts among proposed regulations, or between proposed rules and existing rules, and that they are addressing the issue in only an ad hoc way."[38]

If E.O. 12291 has not ensured comprehensive oversight, however, it has proved to be an effective tool in those areas where reviewers have taken an interest. Again, though agency heads retain formal or legal discretion to promulgate rules, they have seldom been willing to do so over the protests of OMB or the White House for the reasons discussed earlier. Given the character of analysis review as an "ad hoc control mechanism," an assessment of its impact must obviously go back to the criteria used in determining which rules to scrutinize most closely. Rules that are controversial, that are incompatible with the president's objectives, or that otherwise offend key interests generally come to the attention of OMB in one way or another, and there can be little doubt that such considerations serve as important cues in the review process. In short, then, analysis review has been selected and ad hoc, but it has been utilized and utilized effectively where policy issues and/or political controversy have become salient concerns of the Reagan administration.

The Reagan order has also helped further the administration's goal of reducing the level of federal regulation. Aside from the identification and elimination of inefficient regulations already in existence by the vice-president's task force, E.O. 12291 has apparently had a chilling effect on the issuance of new rules. Thus, OMB reports that the number of proposed and final rules published in the Federal Register dropped from 43,247 in the forty months preceding E.O. 12291 to 33,364 in the forty months following the order—a decline of 22.9 percent.[39] This reduction has resulted in part from the appointment of conservative political executives and from cutbacks in agency budgets and staff. But it is also partly attributable to E.O. 12291. As table 2 shows, a relatively small though significant number of regulations have been withdrawn or returned for reconsideration pursuant to OMB review. Probably a much more telling observation is the decline in proposed rules—something that has undoubtedly been precipitated in part by real or anticipated OMB resistence.

## Conclusion

The establishment of an executive clearance procedure for administrative rules has significant implications for the American political system. It suggests, in combination with some other developments, that a new and more powerful form of administrative presidency is emerging to complement a well-established legislative presidency. In addition, it provides support for the belief that the fundamental character of administrative politics is undergoing significant change. Finally, it testifies to the continuing, perhaps even more difficult, problems Congress faces in attempting to maintain its traditional institutional prerogatives and powers.

### An Administrative Presidency

It is commonplace to speak of an institutionalized presidency. The tale of the growth since 1933 in the number, size, internal complexity, and functions of executive staff units is a familiar one.[40] What is perhaps less understood and certainly less noted is that the expansion in these resources has had a greater impact in securing the president's role as leader of the legislative process than as leader of the administrative process.

The fact that the president's legislative capabilities expanded so greatly without a corresponding growth in his administrative capabilities is not difficult to understand. In the decades following Roosevelt's election in 1933, increased coordination and control of the legislative process was critical to a president interested in providing policy leadership to the nation. Moreover, though Congress cooperated willingly in creating an institutionalized presidency to compensate for its declining capacity to provide either integrated leadership in the lawmaking process or comprehensive oversight in the administrative process, its role and power in the latter area were easier to defend in the face of more energetic presidential leadership. Whereas in the lawmaking process Congress often had to choose obstruction as its main line of defense, in the administrative process it could continue to participate actively by relying on its committees to exploit the leverage its formal powers conferred.

However, the 1980s are not the 1950s. Over time, the administrative process has steadily gained in importance as a locus for policy making vis-à-vis the lawmaking process, and delegations of discretionary authority have continued and cumulated. Moreover, the growth in the relative importance of the administrative process in policy making has accelerated since Johnson's landslide election in 1964 both as a result of the fulfillment of an old policy agenda and the emergence of a host of new policy concerns.

These trends have characterized all areas of the administrative process, but they have been especially pronounced in regulatory areas. For example, Congress enacted 182 regulatory statutes and created 24 new regulatory agencies between 1966 and 1981 as compared with 58 statutes and 8 new agencies between 1946 and 1965. Similarly, the number of pages in the Code of Federal Regulations has increased from 22,876 in 1960 to 35,281 in 1965 to 54,482 in 1970 to 71,307 in 1975 to 104,938 in 1982. In contrast, the number of pages of public bills enacted into law increased only from 2236 in the 80th Congress (1947–1948) to 3582 in the 96th Congress (1979–1980).[41]

As a result, since the mid-1960s deficiencies in the president's ability to coordinate and control the implementation of policy have increased in salience relative to deficiencies in his ability to coordinate and control the initiation of policy. This has been especially so with regard to presidents not intent on providing a new, comprehensive, and expansive policy agenda to the nation. But all chief executives, from President Nixon on, have recognized a heightened imperative for enhancing their power in the administrative process.

This restructuring of concern has, in turn, led to a variety of institutional developments designed to improve the president's ability to manage the executive branch. In the area of personnel, the creation of a senior executive service was motivated in large part by the desire to alter the incentives of top civil servants in ways that would make them more responsive to presidential policy objectives and less guarded and parochial in their behavior. Developments with respect to political executives have been equally, if not more, important. The recruitment of political executives has become increasingly systematic and institutionalized within the White House.[42] In addition, recent presidents have also attempted to gain more control over the bureaucracy through the use of their spending and reorganization prerogatives, as well as through the use of cabinet councils and techniques such as program budgeting and management by objectives.[43]

Under President Reagan, several of these sources of leverage have been used in a highly sophisticated manner and with more telling effect. This is particularly true of the appointment of political executives, the exploitation of the powers of the Office of Personnel Management, and the use of cabinet councils.[44] Regulatory review, in the form established by E.O. 12291, both accords with the trend toward an administrative presidency and constitutes a forceful extension of it. As discussed above, such review has its precedents in the 1970s and emerged out of experience with several different review mechanisms or devices. However, these earlier devices involved far less stringent forms of review. At best, they only enabled the president to influence the general contours of administrative policy. In contrast, E.O. 12291 has enabled OMB and the White House to screen and to shape the substance of individual regulations. In a real sense, it has given the president, through OMB, an administrative capability analogous to his long-established capability to clear agency proposals for legislation. As indicated earlier, executive control of administrative rulemaking under E.O. 12291 has not been comprehensive by any means. However, it has been effective as a tool for furthering presidential policy goals in those instances in which OMB has desired to exercise control. Moreover, the scope and impact of such review can be increased simply by deciding to do so and providing the necessary additional staff.

## A New Politics of Administration

If it is true that the emergence of an administrative presidency is tied to the cumulative effects of change in the operating conditions and institutional strains of government in twentieth-century America, then it also follows that these new patterns of presidential influence should be linked to significant alterations in the character of administrative politics generally. The establishment of a clearance mechanism for administrative rules as a key component of a strengthened administrative presidency testifies in several ways that the character of administrative politics has in fact changed substantially.

First, the advent of E.O. 12291 fits and substantiates the thesis that the complexity of politics in late twentieth-century America has severely attenuated the rule and power of "subgovernments" or "iron triangles." For example, Hugh Heclo argues that although subgovernments have not disappeared, their influence has given way to much larger and more contentious "issue networks." The fundamental reason for this, according to Heclo, is that the tremendous explosion of government has created a more complex, interdependent, and conflictual system of policies and expectations. Heclo believes that the "clouds of issue networks that have accompanied expanding national policies" have not actually replaced subgovernments, but have come "to overlay the once stable reference points with new forces that complicate calculations, decrease predictability, and impose strains on those charged with governmental leadership."[45] Similarly, Lawrence Dodd and Richard Schott argue that the overlaps and conflicts among formerly well-bounded governmental subsystems increased significantly as subcommittee government replaced committee government in the 1970s.[46] And they too identify growth in the complexity of policy issues and demands as a prime cause.

Now in a context in which disaggregated policy making no longer simply relieves tension, but begins to produce it as well, it is not surprising that pressure for more centralization would emerge and express itself primarily through the institutionalized presidency. Certainly, Congress could not be the source of enhanced policy coordination. Given its endemic weaknesses with respect to integration, Congress is always far more apt to be the prisoner of complexity than its master.[47] Nor is it surprising that the focus of the effort for increased coordination would be administrative rules, since they provide perhaps the primary governing mechanism of an administrative state. The establishment of clearance for administrative rules thus clearly reflects basic change in the parameters and underlying conditions of administrative politics in the United States.

Second, E.O. 12291 is more than a reflection of change; it is an engine of change as well. This is true in part simply because the clearance mechanism provides agents of the president with substantially augmented ability to identify and resolve conflicts among subgovernmental goals and other recognized interests. However, it is also true because the clearance process institutionalizes a new mode of oversight—cost-benefit or analysis review. This mode relies on highly tangible criteria and introduces new terms of discourse, based ostensibly on objective analysis. As such, it is well suited to serve as a coordinating instrument in an era in which "issue networks" have begun to overlay and submerge "subgovernments." As Heclo emphasizes, debate within issue networks has become the province of technocratic specialists who typically express their arguments as objective answers to policy questions. Cost-benefit analysis thus provides a useful and highly acceptable medium for registering and comparing those arguments. Nonetheless, the technique is not neutral in its impact on administrative politics. It alters the rules of the game, the strategies of the players, and the determinants of success. Moreover, since the assumptions that inform analysis are ultimately subject to hierarchical influence, reliance on the technique provides new grounds for implementing executive direction and legitimizing executive intervention.

In sum, then, the Reagan order can be viewed both as a response to a new system of bureaucratic policy making, the political needs of which have reinforced traditional academic appeals for a strong administrative presidency, and as an ingredient in this new system of bureaucratic policy making that is capable of even greater expansion and impact.

*Congress and the Future of Executive Review*

The establishment of a clearance procedure for administrative rules has significant implications for Congress as well. Over the past half century Congress has been able neither to resist the expansion in the volume and scope of federal responsibilities nor to prevent this expansion from creating an administrative state in which bureaucrats are vested with great authority and great discretion. Congress, nonetheless, has sought to adapt both to the exigencies of modern government and to its disadvantages as a legislative body in an era of increasing substantive and political complexity. It thus has adopted a variety of strategies to maintain its influence in administrative policy making.

One approach Congress has taken has been to strengthen its traditional oversight mechanisms and apply them more rigorously. House and Senate committee systems have been restructured several times in the past half century; congressional staff has been upgraded and substantially augmented; annual authorization has become commonplace; and the use of appropriations riders has multiplied.[48] This strategy, however, has declined in effectiveness as the volume, interdependence, and contentiousness of administrative politics has increased. After all, the structures and resources of a collegial body of less than six hundred members have only highly finite plasticity. The ad hoc and after-the-fact qualities of congressional oversight have simply become more pronounced and more limiting as increases in substantive and political complexity strain its institutional capabilities.

A second congressional strategy has been to develop a new and powerful oversight technique—the legislative veto. And indeed, just as our analysis would predict, the number of vetoes exploded in the 1970s, both with regard to rulemaking and other important types of administrative action. In 1983, however, the Supreme Court outlawed one-house, two-house, and committee forms of the veto, leaving Congress with only the joint resolution and waiting period forms of the device. These are either less powerful or more time-consuming than the forms the Court has disallowed, and there is little doubt that Congress's ability to exploit the veto mechanism has been substantially impaired and perhaps even permanently destroyed.[49]

Under these circumstances, E.O. 12291 assumes much greater importance for Congress's long-run ability to maintain its role and influence in the administrative process. The third strategy Congress has adopted is the traditional one of delegating discretionary authority directly to agency heads. The expectation, of course, is that agency heads will be easier to hold to account and more responsive to congressional committees. Central clearance of rules through OMB, however, can cancel out these effects. It can be used to superimpose presidential authority no matter what type of relationship Congress has formally prescribed and informally sought to encourage. The precipitous decline in congressional enthusiasm since the Court's ruling against the veto for legislation that would formally authorize executive review can largely be explained in these terms.

In closing, it is not our intent to suggest that the president has seized control of the administrative process or that Congress is on the verge of disappearing as a force in administrative politics. Reagan's regulatory review program is quite new. It has operated with limited resources and has not sought to institute detailed and intense review in all areas of its formal jurisdiction. Moreover, this initiative remains subject to modification, if not injury, at the hands of the federal courts both on grounds of infringing authority delegated to agency heads and of operating through *ex parte* contacts that violate standards of fairness and accountability in the administrative process mandated by Congress and the courts. Thus, our conclusions about the significance of E.O. 12291 relate as much to trends and future potential as to current realities.

Nonetheless, as we argued earlier, the forces supporting a powerful presidency are deeply rooted in twentieth-century America. The institutional dynamics of American democracy in this century revolve around the presidency. Increases in complexity and bureaucratic power are countered by an expanding presidency, despite the costs and dangers involved. Those dynamics may be disrupted by events, such as Watergate, and slowed by declines in the rate of growth of federal responsibilities. But they reassert themselves and continue over time to dominate short-term situations and events. Hence, it is not likely that the Reagan review program will disappear as the antiregulatory mood of the early 1980s dissipates. Indeed, the reach of regulatory review was expanded significantly in January 1985 when agencies were required to submit yearly rulemaking agenda to OMB for approval.[50] Thus, barring injury from the courts, the greater probability is that executive oversight will grow in size and impact over time as part of a more highly institutionalized presidency.

## NOTES

1. Roger Davidson, "Subcommittee Government: New Channels for Policy Making" and Barbara Sinclair, "Coping with Uncertainty: Building Coalitions in the House and Senate," in *The New Congress*, ed. Thomas Mann and Norman Ornstein, (Washington, D.C.: AEI, 1981), pp. 99–134 and 178–223.

2. For the growth of federal spending see U.S. Department of Commerce, Bureau of the Census, *Statistical Abstract of the United States, 1984*, 104th ed. (Washington, D.C., 1983). As an illustration of the growth of bureaucratic activity, the Code of Federal Regulations has grown from 28,876 pages in 1960; to 35,281 in 1965; to 54,482 in 1970; to 71,307 in 1975; to 104,938 in 1982.

3. See, for example, Fred Greenstein, "Change and Continuity in the Modern Presidency," in *The New American Political System*, ed. Anthony King (Washington, D.C.: AEI, 1975), pp. 45–87.

4. See James Sundquist, *The Decline and Resurgence of Congress* (Washington, D.C.: Brookings Institution, 1981), pp. 460–85; and National Academy for Public Administration, "A Presidency for the 1980's," in *The Illusion of Presidential Government*, ed. H. Heclo and L. Salamon (Boulder, Colo.: Westview, 1981), pp. 297–347.

5. See Joseph Cooper, "Strengthening the Congress: An Organizationa Analysis," *Harvard Journal on Legislation* 12 (1975), 338–44; and Sundquist, *Decline and Resurgence*, pp. 15–199.

6. See, for example, Richard Nathan, *The Administrative Presidency*, (New York: John Wiley, 1983).

7. See Michael S. Baram, "Cost-Benefit Analysis: An Inadequate Basis for Health, Safety, and Environmental Regulatory Decisionmaking," *Ecology Law Quarterly* 9 (1980). Also see Paul R. Verkuil, "Jawboning Administrative Agencies: Ex Parte Contacts by the White House," *Columbia Law Review* 80 (1980).

8. Ibid.

9. Ibid.

10. Ibid.

11. Ibid.

12. "Interim Regulatory Impact Analysis Guidance," Executive Office of the President, Office of Management and Budget, 12 June 1981.

13. "Deregulation HQ," interview with Murray L. Weidenbaum and James C. Miller, *Regulation*, March/April 1981.

14. Author's conservations with OIRA officials, June 1984.

15. Ibid.

16. "Improved Quality, Adequate Resources, and Consistent Oversight Needed If Regulatory Analysis Is to Help Control Costs of Regulations," by the Comptroller General, Report to the Chairman, Committee on Governmental Affairs U.S. Senate (Washington, D.C.: GAO/PAD-83-6, 2 November 1981) p. 62 (hereafter cited as "GAO Report").

17. Author's conversations with EPA and OIRA officials, June 1984.

18. Author's conversations with EPA, OSHA, OIRA, and other officials, June 1984. Indeed, agencies may issue rules against their *own* better judgment under such circumstances.

19. Conversation with OIRA official, December 1984.

20. Author's interviews with EPA officials, June 1984.

21. "Deregulation HQ," p. 21.

22. Author's interviews with OIRA officials, June 1984.

23. Ibid.

24. Ibid.

25. GAO Report, p. 55.

26. Erik D. Olson, "The Quiet Shift of Power: Office of Management and Budget Supervision of Environmental Protection Agency Rulemaking Under Executive Order 12291," unpublished manuscript, March 1984, p. 55, note 351, p. 70.

27. Ibid., p. 55.

28. Felicity Barringer, "Feud Tests OMB as Regulatory Watchdog," *Washington Post*, 26 November 1982, p. A–15. Quoted from George C. Eads and Michael Fix, *Relief or Reform: Reagan's Regulatory Dilemma* (Washington, D.C.: The Urban Institute Press, 1984), p. 138.

29. Olson, "The Quiet Shift," p. 45.

30. Eads and Fix, *Relief or Reform*, p. 137.

31. See, for example, Glen D. Nager, "Bureaucrats and the Cost-Benefit Chameleon," *Regulation*, September/October 1982.

32. GAO Report, p. 48.

33. GAO Report, p. 49.

34. Olson, "The Quiet Shift"; Eads and Fix, *Relief or Reform*. Also see Howard Ball, *Controlling Regulatory Sprawl: Presidential Strategies from Nixon to Reagan.* (Westport, Conn.: Greenwood Press, 1984), chap. 5.

35. "Executive Order 12291 on Federal Regulation: Progress During 1983," Executive Office of the President, Office of Management and Budget, July 1984, pp. 24–34.

36. GAO Report, pp. 52–56.

37. Ibid., p. 53.

38. Ibid., p. 51.

39. "Executive Order 12291," p. 45.

40. See, for example, Sundquist, *Decline and Resurgence*, pp. 15–199.

41. For information on the growth of regulatory statutes and agencies see Ronald J. Penoyer, *Director of Federal Regulatory Agencies* (St. Louis; Center for the Study of

American Business, 1981), pp. 89–122. For information on the number of pages of public bills see Norman Ornstein et al., *Vital Statistics on Congress, 1982* (Washington, D.C.: AEI, 1982), p. 137.

42. G. Calvin MacKenzie, "The Paradox of Presidential Personnel Management," in *The Illusion of Presidential Government*, H. Heclo and L. Salamon, eds. (Boulder, Colo.: Westview, 1981), p. 130.

43. See Robert E. DiClerico, *The American President* (Englewood Cliffs, N.J.: Prentice-Hall, 1979), pp. 130–46; and John Helmer, "The Presidential Office: Velvet Fist in an Iron Glove, in *The Illusion of Presidential Government*, H. Heclo and L. Salamon, eds. (Boulder, Colo.: Westview, 1981), pp. 45–83.

44. Nathan, *The Administrative Presidency*, pp. 69–97; Hugh Heclo, "One Executive Branch or Many?" in *Both Ends of the Avenue*, Anthony King, ed. (Washington, D.C.: AEI, 1983), pp. 26–58; Lester M. Salamon and Alan J. Abramson, "Governance: The Politics of Retrenchment," in *The Reagan Record*, ed. L. Palmer and I. V. Sawhill (Cambridge, Mass.: Ballinger, 1984), pp. 31–68.

45. Hugh Heclo, "Issue Networks and the Executive Establishment," in *The New American Political System*, ed. Anthony King (Washington, D.C.: American Enterprise Institute, 1979).

46. Lawrence Dodd and Richard Schott, *Congress and the Administrative State* (New York: Wiley, 1979), pp. 106–212.

47. Joseph Cooper, "Organization and Innovation in the House of Representatives," in *The House at Work*, ed. J. Cooper and G. C. MacKenzie (Austin: University of Texas Press, 1981), pp. 319–40.

48. See Arthur Maass, *Congress and the Common Good* (New York: Basic Books, 1983), pp. 107–41.

49. See Robert Gilmour and Barbara Craig, "After the Congressional Veto," *Journal of Policy Analysis and Management* 3 (1984), 373–92; and Joseph Cooper, "The Legislative Veto in the 1980s," in *Congress Reconsidered*, ed. L. Dodd and B. Oppenheimer (Washington, D.C.: Congressional Quarterly Press, forthcoming).

50. This requirement could give OMB power over administrative rulemaking analogous to its power to screen and alter agency budget requests. Relatedly, it could give OMB a comprehensive check on rulemaking initiatives in their nascent stages, before agencies have developed substantial organizational commitments to the policies in question. Of course, the impact of this new tool will be determined by the energy and resources devoted to its use. Again, however, it appears to be significant as an extension of the trends discussed in this essay. See David Burnham, "Reagan Authorizes a Wider Role for Budget Office on New Rules," *New York Times*, 5 January 1985, p. 16.

Steven A. Shull

# Epilogue

Public policy and the presidency are inherently interrelated. Until recently, however, the scholarly relationship has been relatively casual, and "public policy" and "the presidency" have come to represent distinctive subfields of research. The purpose of this volume is to sharpen the linkages that exist across the artificiality of the "subfields." There are, as I shall stress shortly, good reasons to incorporate a policy focus into presidential studies.

The policy approach provides a number of advantages to presidency scholars. It helps remind us of the necessary interaction among institutions, processes, and policies. Additionally, a policy perspective facilitates comparison, generalization, and concern for practical and theoretical relevance. The policy focus helps research to move from idiosyncratic studies of *presidents* to a broader understanding of *the presidency*.

Using a policy approach to study the presidency places the office in the broader context of structural and environmental factors and can help us understand the entire political system and the president's role in it. The president cannot act in isolation, and his influence depends to a great extent on whom he is interacting with. Despite the slow and incremental nature of policy change, presidents can influence the policy agenda. Institutional factors and actors, then, are important in presidential policy making.

A policy approach also helps us recognize that the roles of various institutional actors overlap and that presidential power contains both relative and absolute components: relative in the sense of opportunities, absolute in the sense of constraints. Government, even the executive branch, is not monolithic, and thus, skill in interacting is essential to the president who seeks to pursue policy goals. A president who is knowledgeable of the structural and environmental constraints and opportunities has a greater chance of success. Clearly then, negotiating these structural and environmental factors is essential

215

to a president's success as a policy maker. The essays in this volume cover most of the important actors and arenas of interaction facing the president.

A second major policy component useful in studying the presidency is policy process. The roles of presidents and other governmental and nongovernmental actors are of varying importance throughout the policy process. Thus, the relationship of any actor to the president in policy making depends upon the stage of the policy process. While these stages lack a uniformly accepted conceptual designation, there is a general recognition that visible presidential influence wanes as the policy process unfolds from agenda setting to implementation and evaluation. Perhaps that is one reason why we know more about the presidency in the early stages of policy making than in its later ones. Ironically, each of the editors of this volume previously has addressed this problem.

Although the lines separating policy stages are blurred, they remind us of the fluid, sometimes random nature of the policy process and of the potential for presidential influence in it. Examining process reminds us that change, however small, is a continuous feature of policy making. There are numerous decision points to be utilized throughout the American policy process that may alter outputs and outcomes. We can conclude that policy process is a very broad and diffuse concept, but it is central to understanding the role of the president as a policy maker. Several of the essays contribute to this understanding through analysis of inputs at the early stages and analysis of later outputs and outcomes.

The third contribution of the policy approach is the emphasis on policy content. While this may seem to some scholars to be removed from conceptual development, typologies here have revealed that the substantive policy sector is a very important variable for analyzing policy processes and determining the relative success and role of the president in shaping outcomes.

The primary utility of these three policy components is their interrelationship, not their separate usage. Policy *process* usually is thought of as the dependent variable, influenced by *actors* and policy *content*. Stated differently, the president interacts with other institutions in the process of policy making. The influence of the president and other actors varies at different stages but also depends upon the content (substance) of the policy issues being considered. All three components are interdependent and provide various constraints as well as possibilities for presidential leadership. Policy content, thus far, probably has provided at least as much theoretical closure to presidential studies as has policy process.

The theoretical virtues of comparability are also facilitated by presidency-policy research. The three elements of the policy approach all seek to move from the discrete to more general understandings. Many types of comparisons are possible, for example, across targets of influence and persuasion, policy stages, and policy sectors. None of our essays is limited to a single president: virtually all draw at least minimal comparisons across presidencies and even within the same one. Thus, the presidency scholar need not study chief executives cross-nationally, as desirable as that might be, to incorporate a truly comparative research design.

In addition to comparability, which most of our contributors aim for in a variety of ways, the policy perspective leads to empirical research that posits presidents as part of an interdependent system. Thus, we assert our view that the policy approach helps us to understand better the president's role in the context of the entire political system and leads to serious efforts at integration of micro-research and theorizing at the system level.

Future presidency-policy research needs to examine more closely the interrelationship of policy concepts. Is the process of policy making influenced most heavily by institutions, or is the content area of policy a more powerful predictor of outputs and outcomes? Within policy content, how can we derive better and more explanatory substantive and analytical typologies? Are environmental constraints more significant limitations on presidents than structural ones? How does the structure and environment for presidential policy making in the United States compare to conditions in Europe and elsewhere?

While we are convinced of the utility of a policy approach to studying the presidency, we are also aware of its limitations. It is often touted as having direct relevance to decision makers but we are not yet ready to grant such immediate applicability. We believe presidents and others can learn something from studies using policy concepts, but we also think that any future prescriptive power is dependent upon the strength of the underlying theory. First, we must tighten conceptualization, propositions, and even variables; at this point we are more concerned with theory-building, at least at the middle-range, than with practical utility through prescriptive recommendations.

To the degree that a policy perspective assists in associating and interpreting disparate information in a more theoretically integrating context, it is a useful perspective. While recognizing that we hold many pieces of the presidential policy puzzle, unifying schemes in which to fit these pieces are elusive. The study of policy actors, processes, and content forces us, however, to think about how these pieces fit together. We do not claim to have arrived at an overall theory of presidential policy making but believe that some links have been added. So, ironically, we end this book realizing that our work is only beginning.

# Notes on Contributors

JAMES E. ANDERSON is a professor of political science at the University of Houston. He has written several articles on public policy and policy making and is currently doing research and writing on the Lyndon Johnson administration. He is coauthor of two popular policy texts: *Public Policy in the Eighties* and *Public Policy and Politics in America*.

PAUL A. ANDERSON is assisstant professor of political science at Carnegie-Mellon University. He received his Ph.D. in political science from Ohio State University and his research interests are in foreign policy, decision making and organizational theory. His articles have appeared in *American Journal of Political Science, Behavioral Science, Administrative Science Quarterly,* and *Philosophy of Social Science.*

RYAN J. BARILLEAUX is an assistant professor of political science at the University of Texas at El Paso. A former aide to Senator J. Bennett Johnston, he received his doctorate in government from the University of Texas at Austin in 1983. His work on the presidency and American public policy has appeared in *Presidential Studies Quarterly* and *American Political Science Review.*

JOHN P. BURKE is currently assistant professor of political science, University of Vermont. He received his doctorate at Princeton University, where he was also affiliated with the Presidency Studies Program.

JOSEPH COOPER is Dean of Social Sciences and Lena Gohlman Fox Professor of Political Science at Rice University. He is the Program Chair for the 1985 American Political Science Association meetings. His scholarly research has focused on congressional structures and processes as well as on aspects of legislative-executive relations.

GEORGE C. EDWARDS III, professor of political science, Texas A&M University, is the author of *The Policy Predicament* (with Ira Sharkansky), *Presidential Influence in Congress, Implementing Public Policy, The Public Presidency, Presidential Leadership* (with Stephen Wayne), numerous articles, and several edited volumes on the presidency and policy making.

LORRAINE M. MCDONNELL is a political scientist at the Rand Corporation and a visiting lecturer at the University of California, Santa Barbara. Her research has focused

221

primarily on education policy and its implementation through the intergovernmental system, and on presidential advisory networks. She is a coauthor of a forthcoming study of the presidency and macroeconomic policy.

CHARLES W. OSTROM, JR. is an associate professor at Michigan State University. He is a co-author with Dennis M. Simon and Brian L. Job, of *The Politics of Presidential Decision Making*.

BENJAMIN I. PAGE holds the Erwin Chair in Government at the University of Texas and is a research associate at the National Opinion Research Center, where he is studying relationships among public opinion, political decision makers, and the mass media. He is author or co-author of *The American Presidency, Who Gets What from Government, Choices and Echoes in Presidential Elections, The Politics of Representation*, and numerous articles.

RICHARD ROSE, a Truman Democrat from Missouri, has been writing about politics and public policy in America and Europe for more than a quarter of a century. He is professor and director of the Centre for the Study of Public Policy, University of Strathclyde, Glasgow, Scotland. His books, as author or co-author, include: *Presidents and Prime Ministers, Managing Presidential Objectives, Can Governments Go Bankrupt?, Understanding Big Government, Do Parties Make a Difference?, Electoral Behavior*, and *Politics in England*.

ROBERT Y. SHAPIRO is assistant professor of political science at Columbia University and a Research Associate at the National Opinion Research Center. His interests are American politics, the policy-making process, public opinion, and quantitative methods. He has published recent articles in the *American Political Science Review, Public Opinion Quarterly*, and *Political Methodology*.

STEVEN A. SHULL, professor of political science at the University of New Orleans, is the author of *Interrelated Concepts in Policy Research, Presidential Policy Making*, and *Domestic Policy Formation: Presidential-Congressional Partnership?* His most recent articles have appeared in *American Politics Quarterly, Social Science Quarterly*, and *Western Political Quarterly*.

LEE SIGELMAN is professor of political science at the University of Kentucky. He has done extensive research in various subfields of American politics, including the presidency, public opinion, and the relationship between public opinion and the presidency. He is editor of *American Politics Quarterly*.

DENNIS M. SIMON is an assistant professor of political science at the University of Minnesota. His current research includes a study of presidential vetoes and *The Politics of Presidential Decision Making* (with Charles W. Ostrom, Jr. and Brian L. Job).

NORMAN C. THOMAS is Charles Phelps Taft Professor of Political Science and head of the Department of Political Science at the University of Cincinnati. He is co-author of *Presidential Politics* and has written widely on the presidency and national policy-making processes.

DAN THOMAS is associate professor of political science, Wartburg College, Waverly, Iowa, where he teaches courses in world politics and political behavior. His research interests are primarily in the area of political psychology. He has published articles in *Presidential Studies Quarterly, Political Behavior, Psychological Reports, Policy*

Studies Journal, Journal of Social Psychology, Experimental Study of Politics, and elsewhere.

M. STEPHEN WEATHERFORD, an associate professor at the University of California at Santa Barbara, has concentrated most of his recent research on questions of political economy. His articles have examined the effect of national economic conditions on political mobilization and voting patterns. He is currently working on a study of the presidency and macroeconomic policy.

WILLIAM F. WEST is an assistant professor of political science at Texas A&M University. He has written *Administrative Rulemaking: Politics and Processes*, as well as articles in a number of journals.

MARGARET JANE WYSZOMIRSKI is director of the Graduate Public Policy Program at Georgetown University. Her work on presidential staff and staff agencies has been published in journals such as *Public Administration Review* and is forthcoming in book form as *Presidential Personnel: Roosevelt to Reagan* and *White House Government: The Politics and Structures of the Modern Presidency* (with Kevin V. Mulcahy).

# Index

# Pitt Series in Policy and Institutional Studies

Bert A. Rockman, Editor